University Success

ORAL COMMUNICATION

INTERMEDIATE TO HIGH-INTERMEDIATE

Tim McLaughlin
Christina Cavage
Series Editor: Robyn Brinks Lockwood
Authentic Content Contributors: Tim McLaughlin,
Gareth Powell, and Pia Rigby

University Success Oral Communication, Intermediate to High-Intermediate Level

Copyright © 2018 by Pearson Education, Inc.

Pearson Education, 221 River Street, Hoboken, NJ 07030

Staff credits: The people who made up the *University Success* team, representing content development, design, manufacturing, marketing, multimedia, project management, publishing, rights management, and testing, are Pietro Alongi, Stephanie Bullard, Kimberly Casey, Tracey Cataldo, Sara Davila, Dave Dickey, Gina DiLillo, Warren Fischbach, Nancy Flaggman, Lucy Hart, Sarah Henrich, Gosia Jaros-White, Niki Lee, Amy McCormick, Jennifer Raspiller, Robert Ruvo, Katarzyna Skiba, Kristina Skof, Katarzyna Starzynska-Kosciuszko, Joanna Szyszynska, John Thompson, Paula Van Ells, Joseph Vella, Rebecca Wicker, and Natalia Zaremba.

Project coordination: Robyn Brinks Lockwood

Project supervision: Debbie Sistino

Contributing editors: Lida Baker, Eleanor Barnes, Andrea Bryant, Barbara Lyons, Leigh Stolle, and Sarah Wales-McGrath

Cover image: Oleksandr Prykhodko / Alamy Stock Photo

Video research: Constance Rylance

Video production: Kristine Stolakis, assisted by Melissa Langer

Text composition: EMC Design Ltd

Library of Congress Cataloging-in-Publication Data

A catalog record for the print edition is available from the Library of Congress.

Printed in the United States of America
ISBN-10: 0-13-465271-1
ISBN-13: 978-0-13-465271-9

1 18

Contents

PART 1: FUNDAMENTAL ORAL COMMUNICATION SKILLS

PART 2: CRITICAL THINKING SKILLS

PART 3: EXTENDED LECTURES

Welcome to *University Success*

INTRODUCTION

University Success is a new academic skills series designed to equip intermediate- to transition-level English learners with the reading, writing, and oral communication skills necessary to succeed in courses in an English-speaking university setting. The blended instructional model provides students with an inspiring collection of extensive authentic content, expertly developed in cooperation with five subject matter experts, all "thought leaders" in their fields. By utilizing both online and in-class instructional materials, *University Success* models the type of "real life" learning expected of students studying for a degree. *University Success* recognizes the unique linguistic needs of English language learners and carefully scaffolds skill development to help students successfully work with challenging and engaging authentic content.

SERIES ORGANIZATION: *THREE STRANDS*

This three-strand series, **Reading**, **Writing**, and **Oral Communication**, includes five distinct content areas: the Human Experience, Money and Commerce, the Science of Nature, Arts and Letters, and Structural Science, all popular fields of study among English language learners. The three strands are fully aligned across content areas and skills, allowing teachers to utilize material from different strands to support learning. Teachers can delve deeply into skill development in a single area, or provide additional support materials from other areas for richer development across the four skills.

THE *UNIVERSITY SUCCESS* APPROACH:
AN AUTHENTIC EXPERIENCE

This blended program combines the utility of an interactive student book, online learner lab, and print course to create a flexible approach that adjusts to the needs of teachers and learners. Its skill-based and step-by-step instruction enables students to master essential skills and become confident in their ability to perform successfully in academic degree courses taught in English. Students at this level need to engage with content that provides them with the same challenges native speakers face in a university setting. Many English language learners are not prepared for the quantity of reading and writing required in college-level courses, nor are they properly prepared to listen to full-length lectures that have not been scaffolded for them. These learners, away from the safety of an ESL classroom, must keep up with the rigors of a class led by a professor who may be unaware of the challenges a second-language learner faces. Strategies for academic success, delivered via online videos, help increase students' confidence and ability to cope with the challenges of academic student and college culture. *University Success* steps up to the podium to represent academic content realistically with the appropriate skill development and scaffolding essential for English language learners to be successful.

PUTTING STUDENTS ON THE PATH TO *UNIVERSITY SUCCESS*

Intensive skill development and extended application—tied to specific learning outcomes—provide the scaffolding English language learners need to become confident and successful in a university setting.

Global Scale of English	10	20	30	40	50	60	70	80	90

CEFR	<A1	A1	A2 +	B1 +	B2 +	C1	C2

INTERMEDIATE TO HIGH-INTERMEDIATE LEVEL B1–B1+ | 43–58	ADVANCED LEVEL B2–B2+ | 59–75	TRANSITION LEVEL B2+–C1 | 68–80
Authentic content with careful integration of essential skills, the Intermediate to High-Intermediate level familiarizes students with real-world academic contexts.	Challenging, authentic content with level-appropriate skills, the Advanced level prepares students to exit the ESL safety net.	A deep dive for transition-level students, the Transition level mirrors the academic rigor of college courses.
INTENSIVE SKILL PRACTICE	**INTENSIVE SKILL PRACTICE**	**INTENSIVE SKILL PRACTICE**
Intensive skill practice tied to learning objectives informed by the Global Scale of English	Intensive skill practice tied to learning objectives informed by the Global Scale of English	Intensive skill practice tied to learning objectives informed by the Global Scale of English
AUTHENTIC CONTENT	**AUTHENTIC CONTENT**	**AUTHENTIC CONTENT**
■ Readings: 200–2,000 words ■ Lectures: 15–20 minutes ■ Multiple exposures and chunking	■ Readings: 200–3,000 words ■ Lectures: 20 minutes	Readings and lectures of significant length: ■ 200–3,500-word readings ■ 25-minute lectures
EXPLICIT VOCABULARY INSTRUCTION	**EXPLICIT VOCABULARY INSTRUCTION**	**CONTENT AND FLUENCY VOCABULARY APPROACH**
■ Pre- and post-reading and listening vocabulary tasks ■ Glossing of receptive vocabulary ■ Recycling throughout each part and online	■ Pre- and post-reading and listening vocabulary tasks ■ Glossing of receptive vocabulary ■ Recycling throughout each part and online	■ No direct vocabulary instruction ■ Online vocabulary practice for remediation
SCAFFOLDED APPROACH	**MODERATELY SCAFFOLDED**	
Multiple guided exercises focus on comprehension, application, and clarification of productive skills.	Guided exercises focus on comprehension, application, and clarification of productive skills.	
VOCABULARY STRATEGIES	**VOCABULARY STRATEGIES**	
Vocabulary strategy sections focus on form, use, and meaning.	Vocabulary strategy sections focus on form, use, and meaning to help students process complex content.	
GRAPHIC ORGANIZERS		
Extensive integration of graphic organizers throughout to support note-taking and help students process complex content.		

Key Features

UNIQUE PART STRUCTURE

University Success employs a unique three-part structure, providing maximum flexibility and multiple opportunities to customize the content. The series is "horizontally" aligned to teach across a specific content area and "vertically" aligned to allow a teacher to gradually build skills.

Each part is a self-contained module allowing teachers to customize a non-linear program that will best address the needs of students. Parts are aligned around science, technology, engineering, arts, and mathematics (STEAM) content relevant to mainstream academic areas of study.

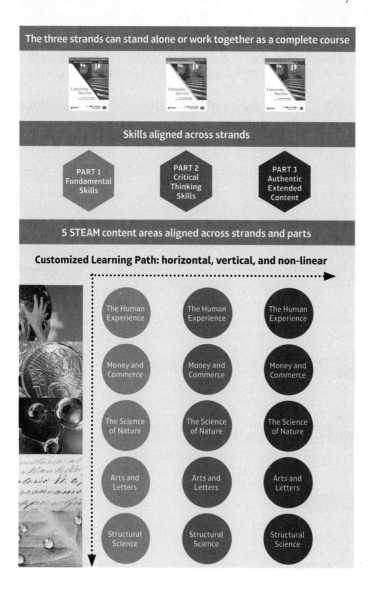

THE THREE PARTS AT A GLANCE

Parts 1 and 2 focus on the fundamental oral communication skills and critical thinking skills most relevant for students preparing for university degrees. In Parts 1 and 2, students work with comprehensive skills that include:

• Being an active participant in class
• Developing and clarifying ideas
• Reaching conclusions and summarizing
• Identifying relationships between ideas
• Giving presentations

Part 3 introduces students to extended practice with skills. Content created by top university professors provides students with a challenging experience that replicates the authentic experience of studying in a mainstream university class.

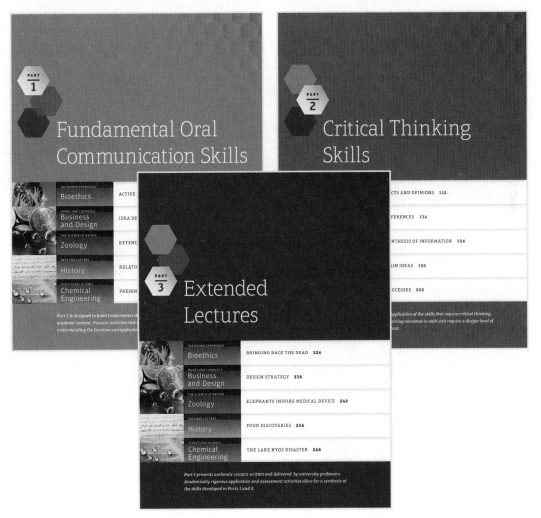

Student Book

MyEnglishLab

Our everyday experiences are based on how we interact with nature

CHEMICAL ENGINEERING

Presentations

UNIT PROFILE

In this unit, you will learn about lake ecology. Ecology is how plants, animals, and people are connected to each other and to their environment. You will also learn about a situation in deep water called hydrostatic pressure.

You will prepare and give an individual presentation on a process related to lake ecology.

OUTCOMES
· Identify parts of a presentation
· Plan for a presentation
· Make predictions
· Explain order with linking words
· Choose the right level of formality

For more about CHEMICAL ENGINEERING, see ● ●.
See also ⌊ R ⌋ and ⌊ Ⓥ ⌋ CHEMICAL ENGINEERING ● ● ●.
90   CHEMICAL ENGINEERING   PART 1

A **unit profile** outlines the content.

Outcomes aligned with the Global Scale of English (GSE) are clearly stated to ensure student awareness of skills.

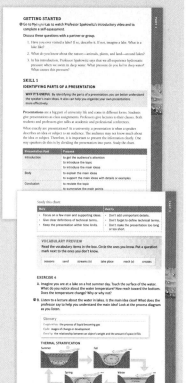

GETTING STARTED

Go to MyEnglishLab to watch Professor Spakowitz's introductory video and to complete a self-assessment.

Discuss these questions with a partner or group.

1. Have you ever visited a lake? If so, describe it. If not, imagine a lake. What is a lake like?
2. What do you know about the nature—animals, plants, and land—around lakes?
3. In his introduction, Professor Spakowitz says that we all experience hydrostatic pressure when we swim in deep water. What pressure do you feel in deep water? What causes this pressure?

SKILL 1
IDENTIFYING PARTS OF A PRESENTATION

WHY IT'S USEFUL By identifying the parts of a presentation, you can better understand the speaker's main ideas. It also can help you organize your own presentations more effectively.

Presentations are a big part of university life and come in different forms. Students give presentations in class assignments. Professors give lectures to their classes. Both students and professors give talks at academic and professional conferences.

What exactly are presentations? At a university, a presentation is when a speaker describes an idea or subject to an audience. The audience may not know much about the idea or subject. Therefore, it is important to present the information clearly. One way speakers do this is by dividing the presentation into parts. Study the chart.

Presentation Part	Purpose
Introduction	to get the audience's attention
	to introduce the topic
	to introduce the main ideas
Body	to explain the main ideas
	to support the main ideas with details or examples
Conclusion	to restate the topic
	to summarize the main points

Study this chart.

Do's	Don'ts
· Focus on a few main and supporting ideas.	· Don't add unimportant details.
· Give clear definitions of technical terms.	· Don't forget to define technical terms.
· Keep the presentation within time limits.	· Don't make the presentation too long or too short.

VOCABULARY PREVIEW

Read the vocabulary items in the box. Circle the ones you know. Put a question mark next to the ones you don't know.

seasons   sand   streams (n)   take place   reach (v)   creates

EXERCISE 4

A. Imagine you are at a lake on a hot summer day. Touch the surface of the water. What do you notice about the water temperature? Now reach toward the bottom. Does the temperature change? Why or why not?

B. Listen to a lecture about the water in lakes. Is the main idea clear? What does the professor say to help you understand the main idea? Look at the process diagram as you listen.

Glossary
Evaporation: the process of liquid becoming gas
Cycle: stages of change or development
Density: the relationship between an object's weight and the amount of space it fills

THERMAL STRATIFICATION
Summer   Fall

Spring   Winter

Presentations   91

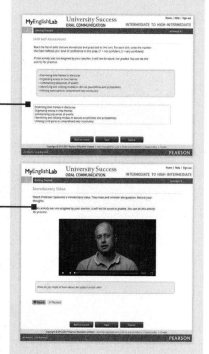

Self-assessments provide opportunities for students to identify skill areas for improvement and provide teachers with information that can inform lesson planning.

Professors provide a **preview** and a **summary** of the content.

Why It's Useful sections highlight the need for developing skills and support transfer of skills to mainstream class content.

A **detailed presentation** demonstrates the skills' value in academic study.

A **variety of listening types**, including lectures, academic discussions, and expert panel discussions, represent "real-life" university experiences.

Visuals on the page support information in the listenings.

Student Book

MyEnglishLab

Vocabulary previews and **vocabulary checks** before and after each listening.

Additional **listenings online** encourage the application of skills.

Vocabulary exercises accompany each new online listening and are designed to assess learner understanding of content-related vocabulary.

Integrated skills provide practice with high-level authentic academic content in reading and writing in addition to listening and speaking.

Additional **MEL exercises** are designed to have learners apply the information presented.

Language skill study provides support for pragmatic and grammatical skills.

Vocabulary strategies offer valuable means for recognizing and retaining vocabulary, such as guessing meaning from context, analyzing word families, and identifying collocations.

Student Book

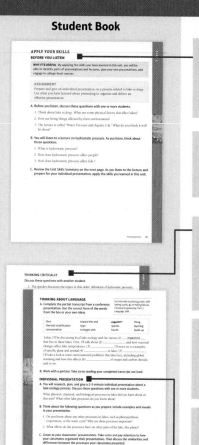

MyEnglishLab

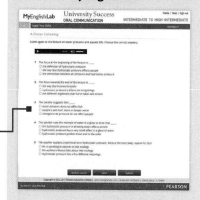

Parts 1 and 2 end with an extended **Apply Your Skills** section that functions as a diagnostic or formative assessment.

A closer listening gives students the opportunity to hear the lecture again and answer critical thinking questions.

Critical thinking activities ask learners to engage at a deep level with the content, using information from the lecture to address specific real-world applications.

Visually thinking sections provide an opportunity for students to analyze and create charts, graphs, and other visuals.

Each unit concludes with a **student research and presentation** task—a talk, panel discussion, or class debate—related to the unit theme.

Student Book

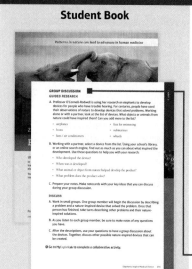

MyEnglishLab

Students view an **authentic lecture** presented by a professor working in a specific STEAM field. The lectures are presented in sections, to allow for clarifications and comprehension checks. After the lecture, students complete a **script analysis** activity.

Students use critical thinking skills to consider a **situation** related to the lecture and record their thoughts.

As a **final project**, students prepare and participate in a presentation or discussion.

STRATEGIES FOR ACADEMIC SUCCESS AND SOFT SKILLS

Strategies for academic success and soft skills, delivered via online videos, help increase students' confidence and ability to cope with the challenges of academic study and college culture. Study skills include how to talk to professors during office hours and time management techniques.

TEACHER SUPPORT

Each of the three strands is supported with:

- Comprehensive **downloadable teaching notes** in MyEnglishLab that detail key points for all of the specialized, academic content in addition to tips and suggestions for how to teach skills and strategies.
- **An easy-to-use online learning management system** offering a flexible gradebook and tools for monitoring student progress
- Essential tools, such as **audio and video scripts** and **word lists**, to help in lesson planning and follow-up.

ASSESSMENT

University Success provides a package of assessments that can be used as precourse diagnostics, midcourse assessments, and final summative assessments. The flexible nature of these assessments allows teachers to choose which assessments will be most appropriate at various stages of the program. These assessments are embedded in the student book and are available online in MyEnglishLab.

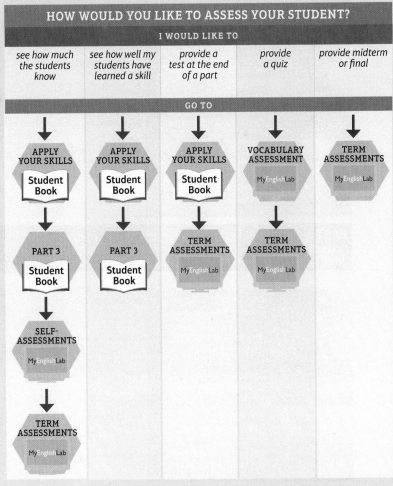

Scope and Sequence

PART 1 Fundamental Oral Communication Skills is designed to build fundamental skills step-by-step through exploration of rigorous, academic content.

		Fundamental Skills
	BIOETHICS **Active Participation**	Listening actively to follow a lecture or discussion Taking turns in a discussion
	BUSINESS AND DESIGN **Idea Development**	Demonstrating an understanding of ideas in a discussion Rephrasing to clarify information
	ZOOLOGY **Extended Discourse**	Formulating probing questions Describing conclusions
	HISTORY **Relationships Between Ideas**	Comparing similar ideas Contrasting different ideas
	CHEMICAL ENGINEERING **Presentations**	Identifying parts of a presentation or lecture Planning for a presentation

PART 2 Critical Thinking Skills moves from skill building to application of the skills that require critical thinking.

		Critical Thinking Skills
	BIOETHICS **Facts and Opinions**	Identifying and expressing facts Identifying and expressing opinions
	BUSINESS AND DESIGN **Inferences**	Making inferences Giving oral summaries to relate ideas
	ZOOLOGY **Synthesis of Information**	Taking notes on research lectures Relating source information to an audience
	HISTORY **Main Ideas**	Identifying main ideas Paraphrasing to relate main ideas
	CHEMICAL ENGINEERING **Processes**	Interpreting and listing steps in a process Utilizing visual aids in a presentation

PART 3 Extended Lectures presents authentic content written and delivered by university professors. Academically rigorous application and assessment activities allow for a synthesis of the skills developed in Parts 1 and 2.

		Lecture
	BIOETHICS **Bringing Back the Dead**	Bringing Back the Dead
	BUSINESS AND DESIGN **Design Strategy**	Design Strategy
	ZOOLOGY **Elephants Inspire Medical Device**	A Study of Elephants and Sound Communication
	HISTORY **Four Discoveries**	Four Discoveries That Changed History
	CHEMICAL ENGINEERING **The Lake Nyos Disaster**	The Lake Nyos Disaster

Integrated Skills	Language Skills	Vocabulary Strategy	Apply Your Skills
Taking organized notes	Identifying subject relative clauses	Creating a vocabulary journal	Prepare and participate in a panel discussion about conservation and de-extinction, exploring the causes of extinction, conservation efforts, and ideas for the future
Answering specific questions about a text	Using tag questions to invite agreement	Using a dictionary to improve vocabulary	Prepare and participate in a brainstorming discussion about a new idea for an app, using your knowledge of design thinking
Summarizing listenings	Connecting ideas with *so* and *therefore*	Guessing meanings of unknown words	Prepare and deliver an individual presentation about an elephant behavior or body part, explaining what the behavior means and why it is interesting
Understanding relationships between Ideas	Utilizing the simple past passive	Creating flashcards to study vocabulary	Prepare and deliver a pair presentation that compares and contrasts two historical sites, and discusses what is significant about them
Making predictions	Explaining order with linking words	Choosing the right level of formality	Prepare and deliver an individual presentation about a process related to lake ecology and the effects that that process has on other parts of the lake

Integrated Skills	Language Skills	Vocabulary Strategy	Apply Your Skills
Identifying bias	Expressing conditions with *if*	Examining abbreviations	Prepare and participate in a class debate about whether or not scientists should use germline gene editing to treat diseases
Answering Inference Questions	Expressing present possibility with modal verbs	Using synonyms to understand new vocabulary	Prepare and participate in a panel discussion about various business strategies, including what role that strategy plays in a company's success
Synthesizing information from multiple sources	Using complement clauses after *about*	Recognizing collocations to expand vocabulary	Prepare and deliver an individual presentation on a particular animal's means of communication and how it was discovered
Rephrasing to simplify ideas	Constructing the present perfect passive	Utilizing a dictionary to understand grammatical behavior	Prepare and deliver an individual presentation about an historical site, document, or artifact from your home culture and include a visual
Explaining a scientific process	Showing sequence with time adverbs	Developing vocabulary by understanding word families	Prepare and participate in a pair presentation on a weather condition, including how global warming may affect the process that creates it.

Research / Assignment

Research, prepare, and deliver an individual presentation on a particular animal that could and should be considered for de-extinction

Research, prepare, and participate in a group presentation about a particular product or service and its strengths and weaknesses

Research, prepare, and participate in a group discussion about the inspiration for the development of a particular device

Research, prepare, and participate in a panel discussion about an important discovery

Research, prepare, and participate in a pair presentation about the sequence of events that led to a particular natural disaster

A Note from Robyn Brinks Lockwood

Series Editor for *University Success Oral Communication*

When I talk to EAP students, they often tell me that they thought they were prepared for study at the university level. They studied English for years and had used a wide variety of textbooks preparing for academic study. Yet, when they actually start classes at the university, they are quickly overwhelmed by the lectures and discussions. Lectures are far longer than any they practiced with and far more authentic than the scripted lectures offered in most ESL textbooks. Discussions include native speakers rather than just their peers in the second-language classroom. Some professors are not sympathetic to the fact that they are studying this in their second language. The *University Success* series is different. It offers authentic content; that is, there are lectures that are 15–20 minutes long and a variety of genres, such as presentations, student discussions and presentations, and debates.

The Transition and Advanced Levels in the series offer little or no scaffolding to propel students into a successful university experience. The Intermediate to High-Intermediate Level wants to help students get to those levels. Lectures are still authentic, but they are more scaffolded. Multiple exercises are guided and focus on prediction, comprehension, application, and clarification to build student confidence. Students have the opportunity to then apply these skills to a 15- to 20-minute lecture that includes multiple exposures and chunking. Vocabulary strategies, rather than the simple list of academic words, are offered. Students will learn to understand abbreviations and analyze meaning using word parts. By doing so, they can actually learn more words than simply those in the book. Additionally, this level offers graphic organizers that support note-taking and processing of complex content.

The goal of this level of *University Success Oral Communication* is to offer instruction in listening and speaking skills and provide ample opportunity for students to actually apply the skills beyond scripted lectures and speaking activities. Once they finish this level, they can easily move into the higher levels, where they will succeed with less scaffolding and continue crossing the bridge to academic study.

PART 1 – FUNDAMENTAL SKILLS

The first five units of this level of *University Success Oral Communication* offer fundamental skills that students learn intensively and systematically. Content centers around five of the major disciplines students encounter during their first two years of academic study and common areas international students choose to pursue as majors: social science, business, natural science, humanities, and engineering. Students may be familiar with the skills, but they have not had adequate opportunities to practice with authentic college-level material. The lecturers and professors who provided content for this book are all from Stanford University. They introduce themselves and their fields via short vignettes that help students prepare for the material. The listening passages in this section are shorter, so students can focus on applying the skill before tackling a lecture in Part 3.

PART 2—CRITICAL THINKING SKILLS

The next five units continue the exploration of the topics from Part 1. The listening passages are longer but, as in Part 1, they are supported by explicit vocabulary instruction such as vocabulary previews, glossing of content vocabulary, extensive recycling, and vocabulary strategies.

PART 3—EXTENDED LECTURES

Part 3 includes university lectures given by the same Stanford University lecturers and professors students "met" in Parts 1 and 2. Skills practice and vocabulary instruction are applied to the lectures, which are 15–20 minutes in length. These lectures are exactly what students need because they will encounter this type and length of content in mainstream classes. Part 3 of *University Success* does something no other ESL series does to prepare students—it offers content from professors at a world-renowned university and gives students the chance to practice with materials that will help them advance both in this series and into true academic studies.

SUBJECT MATTER EXPERTS

 Henry T. (Hank) Greely is the Deane F. and Kate Edelman Johnson Professor of Law and Professor by courtesy of Genetics at Stanford University. He directs Stanford's Center for Law and the Biosciences and its Program on Neuroscience in Society. The author of *The End of Sex*, he serves as president of the International Neuroethics Society; on the Committee on Science, Technology, and Law of the National Academy of Sciences; and on the NIH Multi-Council Working Group on the BRAIN Initiative.

 Juli Sherry is the Design Lead at Worldview Stanford, where she develops hybrid courses and learning experiences for professionals. She facilitates sessions on Design Thinking, creating visualizations and experiences to communicate complex ideas and expose students to potential futures including drones, food substitutes, and wearable technologies. As a business strategist, designer, and entrepreneur, she develops strategic brands for small businesses and startups to help drive her clients' businesses into the future.

 Caitlin O'Connell-Rodwell is an adjunct professor at Stanford University School of Medicine. She has studied elephants for the last 25 years, authored seven popular books and dozens of scientific papers and magazine articles about elephants, and was the focus of the award-winning Smithsonian documentary *Elephant King*. She taught creative science writing for Stanford and *The New York Times*, and has won numerous awards for her writing. She currently blogs for National Geographic from her field site in Namibia.

 Award-winning archaeologist and author **Patrick Hunt** has taught at Stanford University for 25 years. He directed the Stanford Alpine Archaeology Project from 1994 to 2012 and continues to conduct research in the region. Hunt is a National Geographic Expeditions Expert and a National Lecturer for the Archaeological Institute of America as well as an elected Fellow of the Royal Geographical Society. In addition to publishing over 100 articles, he is the author of 20 published books including the bestseller *Ten Discoveries That Rewrote History* and most recently, *Hannibal*.

 Andrew Spakowitz is a professor in the Department of Chemical Engineering at Stanford University, where he established a theoretical and computational lab that develops physical models to understand and control critical biological processes and cutting-edge materials applications. In 2009, he was awarded the NSF CAREER Award in 2009 for work in modeling DNA in living cells. In addition to his research and teaching programs, Professor Spakowitz established an outreach program that developed a comprehensive science lab curriculum for high school students who are being treated for cancer or other illnesses.

SERIES EDITORS

 Robyn Brinks Lockwood teaches courses in spoken and written English at Stanford University in the English for Foreign Students graduate program and is the program education coordinator of the American Language and Culture undergraduate summer program. She is an active member of the international TESOL organization, serves as Chairperson of the Publishing Professional Council, and is a past chair of the Materials Writers Interest Section. She is a frequent presenter at TESOL regional and international conferences. Robyn has edited and written numerous textbooks, online courses, and ancillary components for ESL courses and TOEFL preparation.

 Maggie Sokolik holds a BA in Anthropology from Reed College, and an MA in Romance Linguistics and PhD. in Applied Linguistics from UCLA. She is the author of over 20 ESL and composition textbooks. She has taught at MIT, Harvard, Texas A&M, and currently UC Berkeley, where she is Director of College Writing Programs. She has developed and taught several popular MOOC courses in English language writing and literature. She is the founding editor of *TESL-EJ*, a peer-reviewed journal for ESL / EFL professionals, one of the first online journals. Maggie travels frequently to speak about grammar, writing, and instructor education. She lives in the San Francisco Bay area, where she and her husband play bluegrass music.

 Lawrence J. Zwier is an Associate Director of the English Language Center, Michigan State University. He holds a bachelor's degree in English Literature from Aquinas College, Grand Rapids, MI, and an MA in TESL from the University of Minnesota. He has taught ESL / EFL at universities in Saudi Arabia, Malaysia, Japan, Singapore, and the US. He is the author of numerous ELT textbooks, mostly about reading and vocabulary, and also writes nonfiction books about history and geography for middle school and high school students. He is married with two children and lives in Okemos, Michigan.

Acknowledgments

Working as part of the *University Success* team to create an exciting and innovative new series has been a privilege and a pleasure. First and foremost, I'd like to thank the staff at Pearson, especially Sara Davila and Amy McCormick for giving me the opportunity to take part. Thank you to Debbie Sistino for getting me on board and up to speed at the start. Even bigger thanks to Leigh Stolle and Lise Minovitz for the many comments, suggestions, revisions, and additions that turned raw first drafts into refined final pages—this book would not have been completed without you both. Thanks also to Pia Rigby and Gareth Powell for supplying high-quality content under the tightest of deadlines. I'd be in no position to develop educational materials without the support of the teachers in my life, past and present. Special thanks to Rodrigo Bergamasco Bottura and Nancy Boblett, whose professional guidance (and friendship) continues to make me a more thoughtful educator. And a final thank you to my friends and family for pushing me forward, most of all my dad, who has always encouraged me to take on new challenges and reach far beyond my comfort zone.—*Tim McLaughlin*

My continued gratitude to the entire Pearson team for their dedication, support and guidance. A special thank you to Debbie Sistino for always being willing to listen, and putting students' needs first. An even bigger thank you to Eleanor Barnes, my tireless editor, who is able to effortlessly clarify my ideas and words. My gratitude to Robyn Brinks Lockwood for her vision. Teachers create for students. The students I have been fortunate enough to work with the last 27 years have shaped my vision of ELT materials, so thank you. Thank you for making me want to do it better day in and day out. Lastly, thank you to my friends and family. Your support and love means the world.—*Christina Cavage*

Reviewers

We would like to thank the following reviewers for their many helpful comments and suggestions:

Jamila Barton, North Seattle Community College, Seattle, WA; **Joan Chamberlin**, Iowa State University, Ames IA; **Lyam Christopher**, Palm Beach State College, Boynton Beach, FL; **Robin Corcos**, University of California, Santa Barbara, Goleta, CA; **Tanya Davis**, University of California, San Diego, CA; **Brendan DeCoster**, University of Oregon, Eugene, OR; **Thomas Dougherty**, University of St. Mary of the Lake, Mundelein, IL; **Bina Dugan**, Bergen County Community College, Hackensack, NJ; **Priscilla Faucette**, University of Hawaii at Manoa, Honolulu, HI; **Lisa Fischer**, St. Louis University, St. Louis, MO; **Kathleen Flynn**, Glendale Community College, Glendale, CA; **Mary Gawienowski**, William Rainey Harper College, Palatine, IL; **Sally Gearhart**, Santa Rosa Junior College, Santa Rosa, CA; **Carl Guerriere**, Capital Community College, Hartford, CT; **Vera Guillen**, Eastfield College, Mesquite, TX; **Angela Hakim**, St. Louis University, St. Louis, MO; **Pamela Hartmann**, Evans Community Adult School, Los Angeles Unified School District, Los Angeles, CA; **Shelly Hedstrom**, Palm Beach State University, Lake Worth, FL; **Sherie Henderson**, University of Oregon, Eugene, OR; **Lisse Hildebrandt**, English Language Program, Virginia Commonwealth University, Richmond, VA; **Barbara Inerfeld**, Rutgers University, Piscataway, NJ; **Zaimah Khan**, Northern Virginia Community College, Loudon Campus, Sterling, VA; **Tricia Kinman**, St. Louis University, St. Louis, MO; **Kathleen Klaiber**, Genesee Community College, Batavia, NY; **Kevin Lamkins**, Capital Community College, Hartford, CT; **Mayetta Lee**, Palm Beach State College, Lake Worth, FL; **Kirsten Lillegard**, English Language Institute, Divine Word College, Epworth, IA; **Craig Machado**, Norwalk Community College, Norwalk, CT; **Cheryl Madrid**, Spring International Language Center, Denver, CO; **Ann Meechai**, St. Louis University, St. Louis, MO; **Melissa Mendelson**, Department of Linguistics, University of Utah, Salt Lake City, UT; **Tamara Milbourn**, University of Colorado, Boulder, CO; **Debbie Ockey**, Fresno City College, Fresno, CA; **Diana Pascoe-Chavez**, St. Louis University, St. Louis, MO; **Kathleen Reynolds**, William Rainey Harper College, Palatine, IL; **Linda Roth**, Vanderbilt University ELC, Greensboro, NC; **Minati Roychoudhuri**, Capital Community College, Hartford, CT; **Bruce Rubin**, California State University, Fullerton, CA; **Margo Sampson**, Syracuse University, Syracuse, NY; **Sarah Saxer**, Howard Community College, Ellicott City, MD; **Anne-Marie Schlender**, Austin Community College, Austin, TX; **Susan Shields**, Santa Barbara Community College, Santa Barbara, CA; **Barbara Smith-Palinkas**, Hillsborough Community College, Dale Mabry Campus, Tampa, FL; **Sara Stapleton**, North Seattle Community College, Seattle, WA; **Lisa Stelle**, Northern Virginia Community College Loudon, Sterling, VA; **Jamie Tanzman**, Northern Kentucky University, Highland Heights, KY; **Jeffrey Welliver**, Soka University of America, Aliso Viejo, CA; **Mark Wolfersberger**, Brigham Young University, Hawaii, Laie, HI; **May Youn**, California State University, Fullerton, CA

Fundamental Oral Communication Skills

Part 1 is designed to build fundamental skills step by step through exploration of rigorous, academic content. Practice activities tied to specific learning outcomes in each unit focus on understanding the function and application of the skills.

How advances in biosciences raise legal, social, and ethical concerns

BIOETHICS

Active Participation

UNIT PROFILE

In this unit, you will learn about bioethics, threats to wildlife, and causes of extinction (when a whole species dies off). You will also learn about efforts to save different animal and plant species.

You will prepare and participate in a panel discussion on wildlife conservation.

OUTCOMES

- Listen actively to follow a lecture or discussion
- Take turns in a discussion
- Take organized notes
- Identify subject relative clauses
- Create a vocabulary journal

For more about **BIOETHICS**, see ❷❸. See also ⃞R⃞ and ⃞W⃞ **BIOETHICS** ❶❷❸.

GETTING STARTED

⊙ Go to MyEnglishLab to watch Professor Greely's introductory video and to complete a self-assessment.

Discuss these questions with a partner or group.

1. An endangered species is a group of animals in danger of becoming extinct. What do you know about endangered species? Have you ever seen any?

2. Should people be concerned about endangered species? Why or why not?

3. In his introduction, Professor Greely says that people are causing mass extinctions. Do you agree with this? How are people killing off animals?

SKILL 1

LISTENING ACTIVELY TO FOLLOW A LECTURE OR DISCUSSION

WHY IT'S USEFUL By being an active listener, you can learn more from classroom lectures and be more engaged in discussions in and outside of class.

What kind of person **listens actively**? It is someone who is deeply interested in his or her learning, a person who is prepared to listen to lectures, take part in class discussions, and participate in group projects.

Active listeners pay attention to the way others speak. They notice the vocal variety, or changes in sound, in a speaker's voice. For example, good listeners notice these three common features of speech:

- volume
- speaking rate (speed)
- intonation

To **stress key points or ideas**, speakers often do any one or all of the following:

- increase the volume of their voice
- decrease their speaking speed
- raise their intonation

When someone speaks more loudly, more slowly, and with higher intonation, you can hear the idea better. (Speakers deliver less important information more quietly, more quickly, and with lower intonation.)

Study the chart.

Stressing Information	Example
Increased volume	**PLANT** and **ANIMAL** species are becoming **EXTINCT FASTER** than ever before.
Decreased speed	Threats to wildlife include / disease / global warming / and pollution.
Raised intonation	Large amounts of water pollution are killing off animals and plants in our oceans.

Noticing stressed words and phrases helps active listeners to understand information that the speaker thinks is important.

TIP

- Stay focused. You can only understand the stressed words if you understand the context— the surrounding information.
- When the speaker says something slowly, pay extra attention. It's a good idea to note down this information.

VOCABULARY PREVIEW

Read the vocabulary items in the box. Circle the ones you know. Put a question mark next to the ones you don't know.

categories	populations	follows	policy	researchers	prevent

Glossary

Conservation: the protection of natural things such as animals, plants, forests, etc.

Threatened: in danger

Vulnerable: easy to hurt

EXERCISE 1

A. Think of a kind of animal that existed in the past but is no longer here. What happened?

B. Listen to excerpts from a lecture about categories in conservation. Underline the words and phrases that the professor stresses.

A Siberian tiger and a loggerhead sea turtle

1. The report was from the IUCN, which is the International Union for Conservation of Nature.

2. We'll talk about four of those risk categories today: low-risk, vulnerable, endangered, and extinct.

3. In my opinion, we have very little time left to prevent a mass extinction. That is, the end of—the death of—many plant and animal species.

4. We'll look at the Siberian tiger—a species that once lived all over Northeast Asia but is now down to only about 250 adults.

C. Why do you think the professor stresses these words and phrases in each excerpt? Discuss your ideas with a partner.

EXERCISE 2

A. Now listen to the whole lecture. Then read the statements. Circle *T* (True) or *F* (False). Correct the false statements.

T / F   1. Animal populations have fallen by 74 percent since 1970.

T / F   2. The IUCN focuses on the health of animal species.

T / F   3. IUCN reports are used by policymakers for conservation efforts.

T / F   4. The loggerhead sea turtle is not endangered anymore.

B. Check (✓) the topics that the professor plans to talk about in the lecture.

☐ the IUCN categorization system

☐ how the IUCN system is used for conservation policy

☐ the problems faced by the Siberian tiger

☐ conservation efforts to protect the loggerhead sea turtle

EXERCISE 3

A. Work with a partner. Take turns reading the excerpts in Exercise 1, Part B. Change your volume, speed, and intonation to stress keywords.

B. Was it easy for you to stress keywords and phrases by changing volume, speed, and intonation? What other ways can you think of to stress keywords and phrases?

VOCABULARY CHECK

A. Review the vocabulary items in the Vocabulary Preview. Write their definitions and add examples. Use a dictionary if necessary.

B. Read each sentence. Write the vocabulary item from the box that is the best synonym for the underlined word or phrase. Use the correct form.

category	follow	policy	population	prevent	researcher

1. The government needs to change its <u>plan</u> on environmental conservation. The current plan is based on old ideas. ....

2. How can we <u>stop</u> the climate in the world from getting warmer?

   ....

3. The <u>number of people</u> in this city is about 2,500,000. ....

4. It is helpful to put similar things into <u>groups</u> so you can understand them better. ....

5. By <u>tracking</u> animal populations that are going extinct, we can hopefully use that information to save other species. ....

6. <u>People who do scientific studies</u> usually know their subjects very, very well. ....

🔊 **Go to MyEnglishLab to complete vocabulary and skill practices, and to join in collaborative activities.**

SKILL 2

TAKING TURNS IN A DISCUSSION

WHY IT'S USEFUL By taking turns, you can have more engaging discussions in academic settings. By understanding basic turn-taking strategies, you can enter discussions politely and also let others speak.

It is helpful to know how discussions work and what you can do to participate in them better. Understanding **turn-taking in a discussion** is key to this. People use turn-taking to keep discussions organized, by having only one person speak at a time. Following are a few key points about turn-taking.

Noticing the End of a Turn

How do you know when someone is about to stop speaking? Ask native speakers and they will tell you that they "just know." Language experts will say that speakers often signal that they are about to finish speaking by decreasing their volume, decreasing their speed, or using falling intonation.

Signaling the End of a Turn	Example
Decreased volume	Yeah, and because of the smaller population, fewer fossils were created. So, there were fewer fossils to discover. ...
Decreased speed	And after that, the population began to decline. But / it didn't disappear / altogether.
Falling intonation	Scientists thought this species had gone extinct millions of years ago—66 million years to be exact. And there are many stories similar to this one.

CULTURE NOTE

You may really like to share your opinions, especially in academic settings. However, if you talk too much, people might think that you are interested only in your own opinions and not the opinions of others. If you talk too little, they may think you are completely uninterested in the discussion. Find the right balance between speaking and letting others speak even when you have a lot to say.

Taking Your Turn

When it is your turn to talk, start by acknowledging the speaker. In other words, show the speaker that you heard what he or she said. Then start sharing your thoughts.

Here are some expressions for acknowledging the speaker and starting to share your thoughts:

	Expression	Example
Acknowledging the previous speaker	That's a good point about … I see what you're saying about …	**That's a good point about** conservation policy. **I see what you're saying about** protecting national parks.
Sharing your thoughts	I'd like to say … One idea is … Here's my idea: …	**I'd like to say** that policymakers need to consider the IUCN report. **One idea is** to protect the habitats of endangered species. **Here's my idea:** We provide a few examples of endangered species.

Ending Your Turn and Inviting Participation

How do you finish sharing your thoughts? Signal that you are finished by decreasing volume, decreasing speed, or using falling intonation. If you have nothing more important to say, don't continue to talk. To show others that you are interested in their ideas, open up the discussion by inviting participation. Here are a few expressions to end your turn and invite participation:

	Expression
Ending your turn	That's just what I think. That's all I have to say about that.
Inviting participation	What does everyone else think? Do you all agree? Does anyone else have thoughts on this?

VOCABULARY PREVIEW

Read the vocabulary items in the box. Circle the ones you know. Put a question mark next to the ones you don't know.

discovery	existed	similar	fossils	exactly	case	likely

EXERCISE 4

A. What would you do if you saw an animal that you thought was extinct?

🔊 B. Listen to a lecture and class discussion about *Lazarus taxon*. The professor asks students to share their ideas. How does each speaker signal the end of a turn? Use the descriptions from the box. More than one answer may be possible.

falling intonation	decreasing volume	asking a question
slowing down	acknowledging a speaker	

Professor: And there are many stories similar to this one. Does anyone have an idea how this might happen—how we think something is gone forever, but then it seems to reappear? (1) ....

....

The coelacanth, rediscovered after it was thought to be extinct

Student 1: One idea is that there were a lot more of the coelacanth 66 million years ago. And after that, the population began to decline. But it didn't disappear altogether. (2) ....

Student 2: Yeah, and because of the smaller population, fewer fossils were created. So, there were fewer fossils to discover. The sea *is* a big place. (3) ....

Professor: Very nice ideas. (4) ....

Glossary

Decline: (v) to become worse

C. Discuss these questions with a partner.

1. Are there other ways that the professor could encourage participation? If so, what are they?

2. Are there other ways the students could signal the end of a turn? If so, what are they?

3. Are there other ways that the professor could acknowledge the students' ideas? If so, what are they?

EXERCISE 5

🎧 A. Listen again. Complete the sentences about the rediscovery of the coelacanth.

1. The woman in South Africa thought she had discovered ....

2. She sent .... to a professor.

3. In the 1930s, scientists thought that the coelacanth had gone extinct ....

B. How does the professor define *Lazarus taxon*? ....

EXERCISE 6

A. Work with two partners. Take turns reading the excerpt in Exercise 4, Part B. Signal turns and acknowledge other people's ideas.

B. How comfortable were you using these signals? Are there any signals that are particularly easy or difficult to use?

VOCABULARY CHECK

A. Review the vocabulary items in the Vocabulary Preview. Write their definitions and add examples. Use a dictionary if necessary.

B. Complete each sentence using the correct vocabulary item from the box. Use the correct form.

case	discovery	exactly	exist	fossil	likely	similar

1. Over the next 40 years, it is .... that thousands of animal species will go extinct.

2. .... 46 species of birds live in this park.

3. Scientists have discovered a frog species they did not know ....

4. In 1965 came the surprising .... that the Caspian horse was still alive. Many thought it had gone extinct in the 7th century.

5. These two types of frogs are very .... Their bodies have almost the same shape and size. The biggest difference is their color.

6. In the .... of the loggerhead sea turtle, efforts by policymakers have prevented the species from going extinct.

7. Researchers have found many dinosaur .... in western North America, China, and some parts of South America.

🔊 Go to MyEnglishLab to complete vocabulary and skill practices, and to join in collaborative activities.

INTEGRATED SKILLS
TAKING ORGANIZED NOTES

WHY IT'S USEFUL By writing and organizing notes from a lecture, you can keep track of important information, explanations, and examples that the professor covers in class. You can study and review these notes later. Taking notes can also help you to identify key information from longer articles and papers.

University lectures are full of important information. But it isn't easy to remember everything after just listening to it once. By **taking notes**, you can bring the lecture's main ideas and important details home with you, in a notebook or on a computer file. To do this successfully, you need to write down information quickly and then **organize** that information.

CULTURE NOTE

Many professors allow students to use mobile devices, such as laptops and smartphones, to record information in class. However, some do not. Be sure to check the professor's policy before bringing these devices to class.

Using Symbols and Abbreviations

If you try to write down every word a professor says in a lecture, you may quickly fall behind and miss important information. There is no need to write down *every* word. Instead, write keywords and ideas. You can also use symbols and abbreviations to simplify the process of note-taking. The chart shows common examples, but you should feel free to create your own.

Commonly Used Symbol / Abbreviation	Meaning
=	equals, is the same
≠	does not equal
>	is more than
<	is less than
w/	with
w/o	without
#	number
+	and
!	important
b/c	because
→	causes
bef	before *(Continued)*

Commonly Used Symbol / Abbreviation	Meaning
aft	after
est	established OR estimated
govt	government
cons	conservation
pop	population
intl	international
yr	year
e.g. / ex.	for example
i.e.	that is
exp	experiment
maj	major

TIP

If there is no specific abbreviation or symbol for a word or phrase you use regularly, make up your own. For example, you can use *Lt* for Lazarus taxon and *?* for "not sure about this; need to look it up."

Organizing Notes by Outlining

Organizing notes is important in note-taking because it will help you understand how ideas relate to each other. The easiest way to do this is by **outlining**. Outlining organizes notes by using indentation. You put general information toward the left margin of the paper. You indent more specific details and examples farther to the right.

The following is an excerpt from the Skill 2 lecture on the coelacanth. On the next page, notice how the student has capitalized the main idea and indented related information below it. The student has also used dashes (-) to list the points.

Professor: So we've talked a lot about extinct and endangered species. But, as it turns out, sometimes scientists think a species is extinct—but it isn't. Which is pretty interesting. Take, for example, the discovery—or re-discovery—of a fish called the coelacanth. That's spelled c-o-e-l-a-c-a-n-t-h. In the 1930s, a woman in South Africa, out on a fishing boat, saw an unusual fish. She thought she had discovered a new species of fish. So she made drawings and sent them to a professor. The professor was confused by the drawings. How could this be? Scientists believed that this species had gone extinct millions of years ago—66 million years to be exact. But the fish was, in fact, still alive. It still existed.

… We call the case of the coelacanth and other species like it, *Lazarus taxon*—species that we thought were extinct but later discovered still exist.

COELACANTH
- rediscovered in 1930s
- scientists thought extinct bef. 66 million yrs ago
- example of Lazarus taxon

VOCABULARY PREVIEW

Read the vocabulary items in the box. Circle the ones you know. Put a question mark next to the ones you don't know.

| major (adj) | damage (n) | efforts | individuals | virus | destination |

Glossary

Industrialized: having a lot of factories and manufacturing companies

Habitat loss: a decrease or decline in an animal's living area

EXERCISE 7

A. Industrialization has improved many individuals' standard of living, but it has also caused environmental damage. Think about the factors that led to industrialization. What, if anything, might have been done differently?

CULTURE NOTE

People often measure the quality of life in a place by looking at the standard of living and life expectancy. *Standard of living* refers to the amount of wealth and comfort that a person, group, or country has. *Life expectancy* refers to the length of time that a person or animal is expected to live. Typically, people who live in countries with higher standards of living have longer life expectancies.

B. Read the passage. Then complete the outline that follows. Add your own details.

Habitat Loss

1 Over the past 250 years, human society has become more industrialized. In this time, manufacturing—that is, the making of goods in factories—has replaced farming as the heartbeat of the economy. Meanwhile, the average person's standard of living—here meaning wealth and comfort—and life expectancy have gotten better and better. These changes have led to an increase in population size. But the effect on other animal species has not been so good.

2 A major problem now for animal species is habitat loss. As human populations have grown, the need for farmland and living space has also increased. Human societies have met these needs by cutting down trees and destroying forests—forests that are home to a great number of animal species. The result is a loss in habitat for these species, leaving many very close to extinction.

3 Another reason for habitat loss is manufacturing. When factories burn fossil fuels—oil, gas, coal—for the purpose of production, they release carbon dioxide (CO_2) into the air. The increase in CO_2 causes oceans to become more acidic, which means they contain more acid. This causes major damage to habitats and the animal populations that live there.

4 According to the IUCN, habitat loss is a major threat to more than 75 percent of endangered species. With continued population growth and industrialization, it is likely that animal species and habitats will continue to decline as well.

Industrialization

I. For humans

    A. Manufacturing = i.e.: .... → Less farming

    B. ↑ standard of .... = ... and longer life expectancy

    C. Population ↑

II. For animals

    A. Habitat loss (HL) b/c of:

        1. ↑ humans, ... space for animals

           Ex. Cutting of ....

        2. Manufacturing

           Ex: Fossil fuels – ex.: ...., ..., ...

           .... → acidic oceans

    B. Extinction: ....% endangered animals threatened by HL

C. Compare notes with a partner. Did you have similar ideas? Did you organize your notes in the same way? Did you use similar symbols and abbreviations?

The island fox of South Catalina Island

D. Listen to a lecture about the conservation of the island fox. Add to the notes.

> SUCCESSFUL ANIMAL CONS.: Island Fox
>
>   –
>
>   – local groups collaborated to help fox pop.
>
>   –
>
>   –
>
>   – vaccination efforts → pop. now 1,800 +

E. Listen again. Add to your notes. Then compare with a partner.

F. Compare your notes on the lecture to your notes on the reading. Do both sources mention the same threats? Was it easier to take notes on the lecture or the reading? Discuss with a partner.

VOCABULARY CHECK

A. Review the vocabulary items in the Vocabulary Preview. Write their definitions and add examples. Use a dictionary if necessary.

B. Complete each sentence using the correct vocabulary item from the box. Use the correct form.

damage	destination	effort	individual	major	virus

1. The .... is very deadly. Many people have died from the disease it causes.

2. Conservation .... include protecting forests and endangered species.

3. There are about 3,000 people in the school's biology program. Each .... is given a university ID number.

4. The bark beetle causes .... to pinion pine trees by eating holes in the trunk and limbs. The result has been a(n) .... decline in habitat for the pinion jay.

5. To see polar bears in the wild, you must travel to .... like the Arctic Circle, northern Canada, Greenland, and Russia.

Go to MyEnglishLab to complete a skill practice and to join in collaborative activities.

LANGUAGE SKILL

IDENTIFYING SUBJECT RELATIVE CLAUSES

WHY IT'S USEFUL By identifying subject relative clauses, you can add more information about a person, place, thing, or idea. Subject relative clauses can help you to be specific when discussing complex topics.

Go to MyEnglishLab for the Language Skill presentation and practice.

VOCABULARY STRATEGY
CREATING A VOCABULARY JOURNAL

WHY IT'S USEFUL By creating a vocabulary journal, you can learn the meanings of new words as well as how to use them. This can help expand your ability to understand and talk about academic topics.

Many people find it challenging to learn vocabulary in a new language. This is especially true for university students who are trying to learn academic vocabulary. One way to develop your vocabulary is to **create a vocabulary journal** of new words that you see in your textbooks or hear in lectures. You can also use it for new words you read in articles online or hear when listening to the news. It makes you an *active learner* both in and outside of the classroom.

Here are a few things that you should do when creating a vocabulary journal:

- When you see a new word, write it in your journal and look it up in a dictionary.

- Then write down the source sentence—the sentence that you found the word in. This will help you to remember the word because you will see it in its original context.

- Next, write the part of speech (verb, noun, etc.).

- Write the definition of the word next.

- Finally, write an example sentence—your own sentence with the new word. By writing your own sentence, you will connect more deeply with the word's meaning and remember it better in the future.

Word	Source Sentence	Part of Speech	Definition	Example Sentence
habitat	A major problem now for many animal species is habitat loss.	noun (n)	the natural environment in which a plant or animal lives	We should protect plant and animal habitats so that the species that live there do not become extinct.

TIP

Bilingual dictionaries may be easy to use, but they are not always correct. Instead, use English-English dictionaries such as the *Longman Dictionary of American English*. They provide accurate and clear definitions, sample sentences, synonyms, and usage information.

EXERCISE 8

A. Scan the unit for five words that you want to remember. Then complete the chart.

Word	Source Sentence	Part of Speech	Definition	Example Sentence

B. Compare and discuss charts with a partner.

⊙ Go to MyEnglishLab to complete a skill practice.

APPLY YOUR SKILLS

WHY IT'S USEFUL By applying the skills you have learned in this unit, you will be able to actively participate in university lectures and contribute naturally to discussions.

ASSIGNMENT
Prepare and participate in a panel discussion about conservation and de-extinction. Use what you have learned about being an active participant to follow and take part in the conversation.

BEFORE YOU LISTEN

A. Discuss these questions with one or more students.

1. The woolly mammoth is an example of a species that went extinct. What are some other examples? When and why did they become extinct?

2. What are some species that are in danger of becoming extinct now? Why are they in danger?

3. What do you think the word *de-extinction* means?

B. You will listen to a lecture about de-extinction. As you listen, think about these questions.

1. How does the speaker define *de-extinction*? What is a health concern with the issue of de-extinction?

2. What is an ethical concern about de-extinction?

3. What is a hybrid animal? According to the lecture, how is one created?

C. Review the Unit Skills Summary on the next page. As you listen to the lecture and prepare for your panel discussion, apply the skills you learned in this unit.

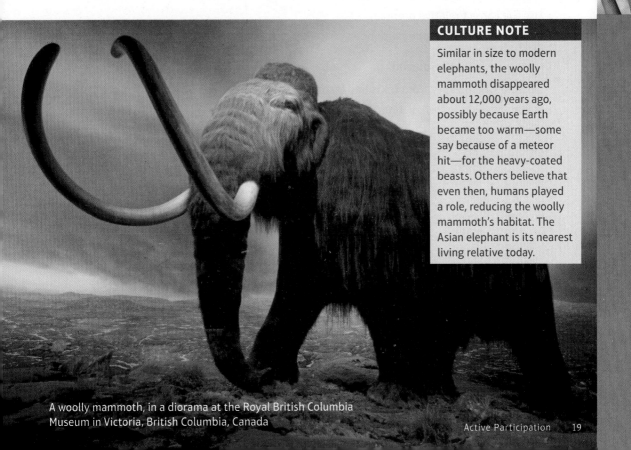

CULTURE NOTE

Similar in size to modern elephants, the woolly mammoth disappeared about 12,000 years ago, possibly because Earth became too warm—some say because of a meteor hit—for the heavy-coated beasts. Others believe that even then, humans played a role, reducing the woolly mammoth's habitat. The Asian elephant is its nearest living relative today.

A woolly mammoth, in a diorama at the Royal British Columbia Museum in Victoria, British Columbia, Canada

UNIT SKILLS SUMMARY

BE AN ACTIVE PARTICIPANT BY USING THESE SKILLS:

Listen actively to follow a lecture or discussion

- Listen for meaning, especially key content words.
- Pay attention to changes in volume, speed, and intonation.
- Notice words and phrases that speakers stress.

Take turns in a discussion

- Notice the end of other speakers' turns.
- Enter a conversation politely, using the right language.
- Encourage participation when you exit a conversation.

Take organized notes

- Note key ideas, not every word.
- Use symbols and abbreviations.
- Organize your notes.

Identify subject relative clauses

- Use them to add specific information.
- Use the correct relative pronoun.
- Make sure the verb agrees with noun.

Create a vocabulary journal

- Note new vocabulary from texts and lectures.
- Use an English-English dictionary.
- Write example sentences with new words.

Glossary

Consequence: something that happens as a result of another action

Ethical: being good, correct

DNA: deoxyribonucleic acid—a substance found in the cells of living things, that carries biological information passed from parent to child

Controversial: causing a lot of disagreement

LISTEN

🎧 A. Listen to the lecture about de-extinction. Take organized notes. Try using an outline to help you.

For an example of an outline, see Bioethics, Part 1, Integrated Skills, page 13.

B. Compare notes with a partner. Did you outline and use abbreviations in the same way?

🎧 C. Review the questions from Before You Listen, Part B. Listen to the lecture again. Work with a partner and use your notes to answer the questions.

⊙ Go to MyEnglishLab to listen more closely and answer the critical thinking questions.

THINKING CRITICALLY

Discuss these questions with another student.

1. According to the lecture, why is de-extinction controversial? Why are different people for and against it?

2. Do you think scientists and conservationists should use de-extinction to bring back extinct species? Why or why not?

THINKING VISUALLY

A. Look at the graph. Discuss the questions with a partner.

1. How did the human population change between 1800 and 2015?

2. How did extinctions change in the same time?

3. Do you think there is a connection between the two events? If so, what is it?

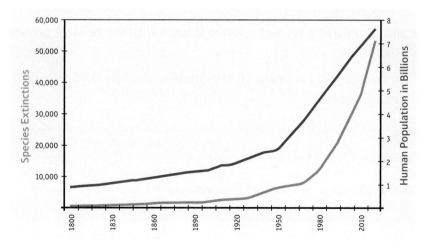

B. Work with a partner. Expand upon the line graph in Part A. Focus on the years showing the faster rates of extinction. Note major events in the world during these years. What can you conclude?

THINKING ABOUT LANGUAGE

A. Read the excerpt from the lecture. Find the sentences with subject relative clauses. Underline the relative clauses.

For help with identifying subject relative clauses, go to MyEnglishLab, Bioethics, Part 1, Language Skill.

Professor: Now, I'd like to briefly explain how the process of de-extinction works—mind you, this is one way we think de-extinction can happen; we haven't done it yet. So first, scientists examine the genome—the DNA, the whole biological set of instructions—of an extinct animal. After they've understood the extinct animal's DNA, they then compare it to the DNA of a similar living animal. Next, they genetically engineer the DNA of the existing animal so that it becomes like that of the extinct animal. That is, they use technology to change the animal's DNA. The result is a "hybrid"—an animal that gets most of its DNA from a living animal but has some DNA of the extinct animal. High-tech engineering, huh?

To summarize what I've discussed so far, de-extinction—the process of bringing extinct species back to life—is a controversial idea in conservation biology. Its supporters believe that it can help fix damaged ecosystems and also give us important knowledge about why species become extinct in the first place. On the other hand, critics say that there may be unexpected negative consequences of bringing species back to life: We don't know what will happen. So we should focus on conservation, they argue. And I agree, we should focus on traditional conservation. We've also taken a look at one way of approaching de-extinction: creating hybrid animals that have the DNA from both living and extinct animal species.

B. Combine the sentences using subject relative clauses with the relative pronouns *who*, *which*, or *that*.

1. Scientists can create hybrid animals. Hybrid animals get their DNA from both living and extinct animals.

   ....

   ....

2. De-extinction is a process. It brings extinct animals back to life.

   ....

   ....

3. There are many de-extinction critics. They say there are negative consequences to the process.

---

4. There are many de-extinction supporters. Those supporters say it will help fix damaged ecosystems.

C. Add any words from the lecture that you want to learn to your vocabulary journal.

PANEL DISCUSSION

A. You will prepare a 10–12-minute panel discussion about de-extinction. Discuss these questions with a small group.

1. What are some of the reasons that a species becomes threatened or extinct? Refer to the listenings and readings from this unit.

2. What are some examples of conservation efforts discussed in this unit?

B. With your group, choose one endangered species to research that has not been discussed in the unit. Each student has a different role:

- Student A: Find general information on the species (e.g., what type of animal it is, where it lives, its habitat).

- Student B: Find information about why the species is threatened.

- Student C: Find information about how the species can be protected.

- Student D: Act as host. Introduce the topic and panelists. Handle questions from the audience.

C. With your group, decide your roles and the speaking order. Then prepare for the discussion.

D. Listen to other groups' panel discussions. Take notes and ask questions at the end.

◑ Go to MyEnglishLab to watch Professor Greely's concluding video and to complete a self-assessment.

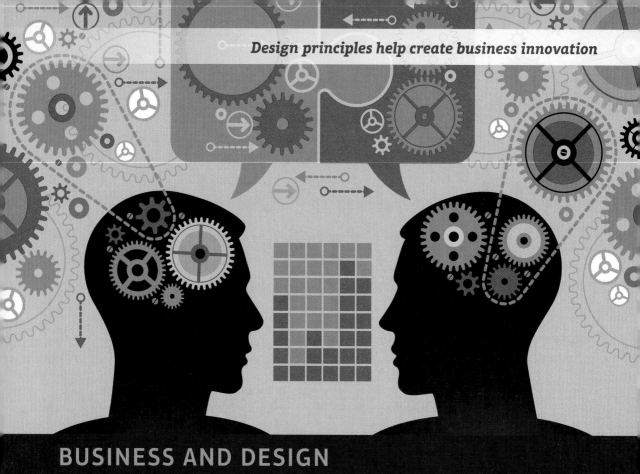

BUSINESS AND DESIGN

Idea Development

UNIT PROFILE

In this unit, you will learn about design thinking and how it is a key part of product design in the modern world.

You will prepare and participate in a brainstorming discussion about creating a new product.

OUTCOMES

- Demonstrate an understanding of ideas in a discussion
- Rephrase to clarify information
- Answer specific questions about a text
- Use tag questions to invite agreement
- Use a dictionary to improve vocabulary

For more about **BUSINESS AND DESIGN**, see ❷❸.
See also Ⓡ and Ⓦ **BUSINESS AND DESIGN** ❶❷❸.

GETTING STARTED

➊ Go to MyEnglishLab to watch Juli Sherry's introductory video and to complete a self-assessment.

Discuss these questions with a partner or group.

1. When you want to buy something, do you think about its design? Why or why not?

2. Think of a well-designed product (for example, a phone, tablet, or bag). Describe the product. Why do you think it is well designed?

3. In her introduction, Ms. Sherry says that good design can make products more innovative. Do you know any products that are innovative because of their design?

SKILL 1

DEMONSTRATING AN UNDERSTANDING OF IDEAS IN A DISCUSSION

WHY IT'S USEFUL By following the ideas in a discussion or lecture, you can understand the key ideas and others' opinions. You can also participate in discussions more effectively.

Every discussion has a **main topic**. Politics, economics, and current events are examples of main topics. Ideas within the main topic are called **subtopics**. Examples of subtopics are local election results, a change in interest rates, and a new café on campus. Consider the main topic and subtopics that are organized, or "mapped," in this mind map:

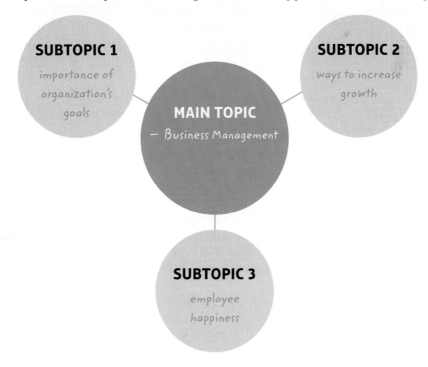

SUBTOPIC 1
importance of organization's goals

SUBTOPIC 2
ways to increase growth

MAIN TOPIC
— *Business Management*

SUBTOPIC 3
employee happiness

To **follow ideas in a discussion**, focus on the keywords that are repeated, the questions and answers, the speaker's voice, and examples.

STRATEGIES FOR FOLLOWING IDEAS IN A DISCUSSION	
Strategy	**Explanation**
Listen for keywords.	Speakers will repeat words that are important to the main idea of the discussion. Listen for these words to understand the subtopics. For example: Improving a **product's** design is all about finding **solutions** to the **problems** that **customers** have. How do you find out the **problems** that **customers** have? You ask them. You watch them. You do this to find out the **problems** that they are having while using the **product**. Then you can start to work on the **solutions**.
Focus on questions and answers.	People usually ask questions about key ideas. This gives the speaker the chance to repeat these ideas. Listen to questions and answers carefully.
Pay attention to a speaker's voice.	Speakers use speed, word stress, and pitch to signal key ideas. They slow down, emphasize keywords, and raise the volume of their voice. Listen for these cues.
Listen for examples.	Speakers use examples to bring important points to life. Listen for signposting expressions such as *for example* and *for instance*, and then pay close attention to the example in order to understand the idea better.

VOCABULARY PREVIEW

Read the vocabulary items in the box. Circle the ones you know. Put a question mark next to the ones you don't know.

solutions	services	customers	connections
patterns	make sense	creative	lead to

> **Glossary**
>
> Innovation: a new idea, method, or invention, or the use of one—innovative (adj)
>
> Prototype: a model of a new car, machine, etc., used in order to test the design before the model is produced in large numbers

EXERCISE 1

A. What does *design* mean? When you hear the word *design*, what do you think of?

B. Listen to this talk about business design. As you listen, complete the mind map.

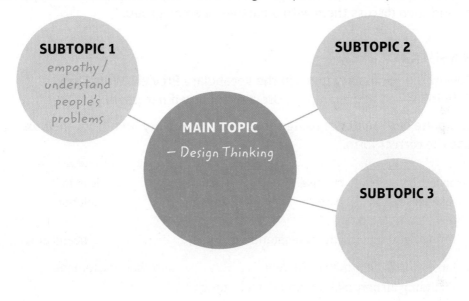

C. Was it easy to understand the topics in the talk? What strategies can you use to identify the main ideas?

EXERCISE 2

A. Listen again. What does *design thinking* mean?

....

B. Listen again. Which of the following keywords are repeated in the talk? Check (✓) them. How do these keywords help you understand the main ideas of the talk?

☐ customer   ☐ problems   ☐ change   ☐ product(s)
☐ needs   ☐ testing   ☐ organization   ☐ understanding

EXERCISE 3

A. Take turns with a partner reading this excerpt. Use speed, stress, and volume to emphasize important ideas.

> **Expert 1:** Yes. And it all starts with empathy—that means understanding someone's problems and needs. If you care to understand what your customers need, you're able to design products or services that they'll like.

B. Empathy is necessary for healthy personal relationships and it is important in business. Are you an empathetic person? Why or why not? Think about your ideas and then discuss them with a partner or small group.

VOCABULARY CHECK

A. Review the vocabulary items in the Vocabulary Preview. Write their definitions and add examples. Use a dictionary if necessary.

B. Complete each sentence using the correct vocabulary item from the box. Use the correct form.

connection	creative	customer	lead to
make sense	pattern	service	solution

1. Empathy will help you understand what your .... needs are.

2. Large hotels offer many different .... to their customers, including airport pick-up and dry-cleaning.

3. Finding the best .... to a problem can take time. It's important to be ....—the traditional answer isn't always best.

4. Customers may display certain .... That is, they will repeat a behavior, for example, using their phone at the same time every day.

5. I can't understand this idea. It doesn't .... to me.

6. Eating unhealthy foods can .... health problems in the future.

7. There is a very clear .... between the design of a product and how happy customers are with it. Well-designed products make customers happy.

🔊 Go to MyEnglishLab to complete vocabulary and skill practices, and to join in collaborative activities.

SKILL 2
REPHRASING TO CLARIFY INFORMATION

WHY IT'S USEFUL By rephrasing to clarify information, you can make your thoughts easier to understand. This can help you explain a complex idea or correct a mistake while speaking.

In discussions and presentations, we do not always say *exactly* what we want to say. Sometimes we say something complicated, and we can see from the expression on listeners' faces that the message was unclear. Or sometimes we realize that we have said something that is simply *wrong*. We know that we need to correct our mistakes in these situations, but how we do it? We can **clarify information** with a few useful expressions. Look at these examples:

> **Speaker:** I often get asked, "What is design thinking?" I always say that it's a way to be sure that innovation happens in an organization. **In other words**, design thinking is a process that starts by looking at a customer's problems and then works to find creative solutions to those problems.

> **Speaker:** In design thinking, empathy is key to understanding a company's needs. **That came out wrong. What I meant to say was** that empathy is key to understanding <u>customers'</u> needs.

In the first example, the speaker presents a confusing idea: Design thinking is a way to be sure that innovation happens. For her audience, the meaning of this might not be clear, so she clarifies her information by repeating herself, by making her point more clearly. She uses *in other words* to tell her listeners that she is presenting her idea in a different, more straightforward way.

In the second example, the speaker makes a mistake by saying *company* instead of *customer*. In this case, the speaker needs to first *alert* (to warn someone of a problem) his listeners of the mistake, and he does this with *That came out wrong*. After that, he signals that he is clarifying his idea with *What I meant to say was*. The chart on the next page contains signals that can help you **rephrase ideas** when speaking.

Alerting Listeners	Clarifying an Idea
To tell listeners you said something incorrectly: That came out wrong. That's not what I meant (to say).	**To tell listeners you were not clear:** Let me put that more simply / clearly. Let me explain that again. What I meant (to say) was …
	What I mean (to say) is … What I'm trying to say is … *What I mean by this is … *In other words, … *That is, …

***Note:** These expressions do not follow alerting expressions. They are only used to clarify a complex idea.

VOCABULARY PREVIEW

Read the vocabulary items in the box. Circle the ones you know. Put a question mark next to the ones you don't know.

define	figure out	unique	come up with
consumers	feature (n)	according to	

Glossary

Electronics: the study or industry of making electronic equipment, such as computers or televisions

EXERCISE 4

A. Do you know what the *design process* is? Define it. If not, take a guess at what it is.

B. Listen to this lecture about the design process. Check (✓) the alerting and clarifying expressions that the speaker uses.

☐ That came out wrong.　　　　☐ What I'm trying to say is …

☐ That's not what I meant.　　　☐ In other words, …

☐ That is, …　　　　　　　　　☐ What I mean by this is …

☐ Let me explain that again.　　☐ What I meant to say was …

C. Do you think it is necessary to use clarifying expressions, or can you understand the speaker without them? Why or why not?

EXERCISE 5

🔊 **A. Listen again and take notes. Then write a short description of each stage of the design process.**

1. Define Stage: ....

....

2. Ideate Stage: ....

....

3. Prototype Stage: ....

....

4. Feedback Stage: ....

....

5. Develop Stage: ....

....

🔊 **B. Listen again. The professor uses clarifying expressions when describing the Define Stage. What are the two ideas that she clarifies? Why did she need to clarify her ideas?**

1. ....

2. ....

EXERCISE 6

A. Read the excerpt from the lecture that you just heard. Look at the clarifying expressions in bold. What expressions can you use in their place?
With a partner, take turns reading the excerpt using different expressions.

> **Speaker:** First in the design process is the Define Stage. The electronics company needed to define the idea for a better phone. **What I mean by this is** it needed to figure out the "problem" with its old phones so it could decide how to create its new product. So the company did market research to figure out the problem. The company discovered that people wanted more colorful phones. Excuse me. That came out wrong. **What I meant to say was** people wanted phones that were more unique. Ones that they felt a personal connection with.

B. Think of something you have created (a poem, cookies) or have done (been a tutor, had a party). Who was your "customer"? Which stages of your process involved design thinking?

VOCABULARY CHECK

A. Review the vocabulary items in the Vocabulary Preview. Write their definitions and add examples. Use a dictionary if necessary.

B. Complete each sentence using the correct vocabulary item from the box. Use the correct form.

according to	come up with	consumer	define
feature	figure out	unique	

1. This new phone has some great .... , such as a better battery and a brighter screen.

2. The professor doesn't speak very clearly. It's often difficult to .... what he's trying to say.

3. The tablet has a really .... design—it's not like anything I've seen before.

4. Our boss didn't like our ideas, so we will have to .... some new ones.

5. Companies focus ads on .... to get them to buy things.

6. .... research, people use mobile devices more than computers to get news.

7. To find a good solution to a problem, it's best to .... exactly what the problem is. That is, you need to clearly describe the problem.

⬆ Go to MyEnglishLab to complete vocabulary and skill practices, and to join in collaborative activities.

INTEGRATED SKILLS

ANSWERING SPECIFIC QUESTIONS ABOUT A TEXT

WHY IT'S USEFUL By answering specific questions about a text, you can engage with the text more deeply—that is, become more involved with it. This can help prepare you for class lectures and discussions.

Professors commonly assign readings for upcoming classes. You are expected to read the material before class because the professor will discuss ideas from it. Professors also often assign specific questions about those readings, to guide you as you read. **Answering specific questions** can help you to better understand a text and prepare for class.

How should you answer these questions? Follow these steps:

1. Read the questions that the professor assigns. Find keywords in the questions. This will give you something to look for when you read.

2. Read the text. As you read, find the information that relates to the keywords in the questions. It is likely that the keywords in the questions will be the same words that are used in the text. Underline or highlight this information in the text.

3. Go back to the questions. Use the information that you highlighted in the text to answer them.

TIP

Professors expect that you will read texts to prepare for class, and they sometimes ask you questions about the reading before they begin their lecture. Make sure that you have an answer. Read before class!

VOCABULARY PREVIEW

Read the vocabulary items in the box. Circle the ones you know. Put a question mark next to the ones you don't know.

annoy	appearance	goal	solves
functioning	smoothly	complicated	essential

EXERCISE 7

A. Imagine that your business professor has assigned the questions and reading passage on the next page. In class, she will lecture about product design principles (the basic ideas that a plan or system is based on). Follow these steps:

1. Review Steps 1–3 above.

2. Read the assigned questions and reading passage on the next page. Mark keywords.

3. Answer the assigned questions.

Assigned Questions

1. How does bad design affect us? What about good design?

....

2. How can designers make sure a product is user-oriented?

....

3. What happens when a product's design is complicated?

....

What Makes Good Design?

1 In the modern world, design is all around us. From picking up a toothbrush to driving a car, in almost every moment of our day we come into contact with products, items, and goods that are the result of long and careful design processes. While bad design can annoy us and make our daily tasks more difficult, great design is easy to use and has the power to improve our lives. And it usually looks good, too.

2 Some people think design is the nice appearance of a product. In fact, good design is about much more than this. So what is good design and what separates it from bad design? Here are five important principles:

1: Innovation

3 Many examples of great design are developed by thinking about a problem in a new way. While innovation shouldn't necessarily be the only goal in all design work, it is often a positive by-product, a result that was not planned. Good design should also work well with innovative technology; a well-designed smartphone or tablet is a good example of this.

The Braun T1 table lighter, designed by Dieter Rams, 1968

2: Problem Solving

4 A well-designed product meets a need or solves a problem by functioning smoothly and effectively. Finding a problem to solve is the first stage of the design process and this stage is very important. Designers must look at a product or service in a new and creative way if they want to improve it. In the words of Bryan Lawson, author of *How Designers Think*, "Design is as much a matter of finding problems as it is solving them."

3: User-Oriented

5　Good design focuses on the user's experience with the product. Designers should think about how the product will be used by customers before they make it. That means that they must create a product for the user rather than the designer. Sometimes what looks like a great idea on paper can be difficult to use in reality, and it is important that the user not experience problems with the product. To prevent these problems from happening, a good design process will make use of prototype testing and user feedback.

4: Attention to Detail

6　Attention to even the smallest details is also important in good design. At the Develop Stage of the design process, designers must make sure that all details of the design have been carefully thought about and discussed so that no detail seems strange.

5: Making It Simple

7　Finally, in the words of the great product designer Dieter Rams, "good design is as little design as possible." That means that good design needs to be simple and easy to use. A complicated design often leads to problems with user experience. So, a product should not have unnecessary features; any non-essential parts should be removed. A simple design will make for a happier user, and a happier user will use the product more often.

CULTURE NOTE

Dieter Rams is a German designer whose work is associated with Functionalism, an architecture and design style. Functionalism is known for its interest in practicality, simplicity, and functionality. The documentary *Objectified*, directed by Gary Hustwit, explores the role of design in society and includes an interview with Rams.

B. Discuss your answers with a partner. Did reading the questions beforehand help you to understand the text? If so, how?

C. Listen to an excerpt from the professor's lecture on product design. Which of the five principles from the text does the professor talk about? Check (✓) them.

☐ Innovation ☐ Attention to Detail

☐ Problem Solving ☐ Making It Simple

☐ User-Oriented

D. Listen again. Which design principles are related to the Define and Ideate Stages? Which principles relate to the Feedback and Develop Stages? Take notes and discuss with a partner.

1. Define and Ideate Stages: ....

    ....

2. Feedback and Develop Stages: ....

    ....

E. How did reading the text first help you to understand the lecture? Discuss with a partner.

VOCABULARY CHECK

A. Review the vocabulary items in the Vocabulary Preview. Write their definitions and add examples. Use a dictionary if necessary.

B. Complete each sentence using the correct vocabulary item from the box. Use the correct form.

annoy	appearance	complicated	essential
function	goal	smoothly	solve

1. Our company's .... is to create innovative solutions for our customers' needs.

2. The app does not .... well and its user interface is terrible. It really .... me.

3. We have been working for hours to .... this problem, but we still haven't come up with any good ideas.

4. This device is not easy to use. It is definitely too .... for the average user.

5. What a product looks like, its .... , is not always the most important part of its design. If it looks good but doesn't work .... , people will not use it.

6. Reading assigned texts before class is .... to understanding a lecture well.

○ Go to MyEnglishLab to complete a skill practice and to join in collaborative activities.

LANGUAGE SKILL
USING TAG QUESTIONS TO INVITE AGREEMENT

WHY IT'S USEFUL By using tag questions, you can invite others to agree with you. Inviting others to agree with you is particularly useful in academic discussions and presentations.

● Go to MyEnglishLab for the Language Skill presentation and practice.

VOCABULARY STRATEGY
USING A DICTIONARY TO IMPROVE VOCABULARY

WHY IT'S USEFUL By using a dictionary, you can improve your vocabulary. When reading texts or listening to lectures, using a dictionary to look up unknown words can help you to better understand a word's meaning and how it is used in various contexts.

There are between 100,000 and a million words in the English language, depending on who you ask. (*Merriam Webster's Third New International Dictionary* puts the figure at 470,000.) Luckily for English language learners, many of those words are rarely used. However, a lot of them are important to know, especially in an academic setting. **Dictionaries** are a useful tool **to improve your vocabulary**. They not only provide you with the *meanings* of words, but they also help you to understand how to *use* those words in new contexts.

This section focuses on how to know the exact meaning of a new word that you see or hear. But words often have more than one meaning in a dictionary. How can you know which meaning is most useful for you? Follow the steps on the next page.

For information about how a dictionary is used to create a vocabulary journal, see Bioethics, Part 1, Vocabulary Strategy, page 17.

TIP

It can be difficult to hear a new word and know how to spell it. Many online talks have transcripts, which you can scan to find the new word. But it's more difficult with "live" lectures, so be sure to read before class in order to be familiar with new words you might hear.

Step 1: Look at the context.

When you encounter a new word, don't go straight to the dictionary. Take time to learn about the word from the context of the sentence.

- the word's part of speech (noun, verb, etc.)

- the subject or idea of the sentence that the word appears in

- synonyms for the word—words that have the same or similar meaning as the unknown word—found in the context

For more about guessing the meaning of unknown words, see Zoology, Part 1, Vocabulary Strategy, page 59. For more about using synonyms to understand new vocabulary, see Business and Design, Part 2, Vocabulary Strategy, page 148.

Look at this example with the unknown word, *acquired*:

Facebook has <u>acquired</u> a number of different companies in recent years, including Instagram and WhatsApp.

What does the context tell you? First, you can see that *acquire* is a verb. You can also see that it is used to talk about business. These are two important clues—pieces of information that help you to figure something out—for when you look up a new word.

Step 2: Go to the dictionary.

Once you've learned all you can from the context, go to a dictionary. There are plenty of free ones online, but a good one for English learners is the *Longman Dictionary of American English (LDAE)*. It provides easy definitions and example sentences, which you can see below.

---

ac·quire /əˈkwaɪɚ/ ●●○ W3 AWL *verb* [transitive] *formal* ◀))

ETYMOLOGY   VERB TABLE   THESAURUS

1   to buy or obtain something, especially something that is expensive or difficult to get:
◀)) *AC Transit recently acquired 70 new buses.*
◀)) *A major Hollywood studio has acquired the rights to the novel.*

2   to get or gain knowledge, skills, qualities, etc.:
◀)) *Research helps us acquire new insight on the causes of diseases.*
◀)) *Many inner cities have acquired reputations for violent crime.*

[**Origin:** 1400–1500 Old French *aquerre*, from Latin *acquirere*, from *ad-* **to** + *quaerere* **to look for, obtain**]

Step 3: Understand the use of the new word.

You can see that the first meaning is best for the example. Now you have two sentences that tell you a lot about how to use the first meaning of *acquire*: company / person + *acquire* + company / property. This is how you improve your vocabulary—coming to understand both the *meaning* (to buy a company or property) and the *use* of a word (how to put it into a sentence). If you are keeping a vocabulary journal, add the definition for *acquire* to it and write an example sentence. For example:

Word	Source Sentence	Part of Speech	Definition	Example Sentence
acquire	Facebook has acquired a number of different companies in recent years, including Instagram and WhatsApp.	verb	to buy a company or property	The company acquired a few smaller companies so that it could provide different kinds of services.

EXERCISE 8

A. Read the transcript. Notice the challenging words in bold. Then complete the chart. What parts of speech are they? Make notes about the context.

Speaker: Design is all around us. From waking up the (1) **moment** the alarm clock (2) **buzzes**, to picking up a toothbrush, to driving a car or riding a bicycle, we come into contact with (3) **objects** nearly every minute of the day. And those items and goods are often the (4) **fruit** of long and careful design processes. While bad design can annoy us and prevent us from doing our daily tasks easily, great design has the power to change our lives and (5) **inspire** us the same way a great painting can.

Word	Part of Speech	Note
moment	noun	It's used with "waking up" and followed by "clock," so it could be about time.
buzz		
object		
fruit		
inspire		

B. Check (✓) the best definition for the words in Part A. Use the sample sentences in the entries to help you.

1.

mo·ment /ˈmoʊmənt/ ••• *noun* [countable] ◀))

WORD ORIGIN   COLLOCATIONS

☐ **1 a very short period of time → minute:**
◀)) *Robert paused **for a moment**.*
◀)) *I'll be back **in a moment**.*
◀)) *Could you wait **just a moment**?*
◀)) *He was here **a moment ago**.*
◀)) *Denise arrived moments later.*

☑ **2 a particular point in time:**
◀)) *Just **at that moment**, Shelly came in.*
◀)) *I knew it was you **the moment (that)** I heard your voice.*
◀)) *He said he loved her **from the moment (that)** he met her.*
◀)) ***At that very/exact/precise moment**, the phone rang.*

☐ **3 at the moment now:**
◀)) *Japanese food is popular **at the moment**.*

2.

buzz¹ /bʌz/ •○○ *verb* ◀))

WORD ORIGIN   VERB TABLE   COLLOCATIONS

☐ **1** [intransitive] **to make a continuous noise like the sound of a bee:**
◀)) *What's making that buzzing noise?*

☐ **2** [intransitive] **if a group of people or a place is buzzing, people are making a lot of noise because they are excited:**
◀)) *The room **buzzed with** excitement.*

☐ **3** [intransitive, transitive] **to call someone by pressing a buzzer:**
◀)) *Tina **buzzed for** her secretary.*

3.

ob·ject¹ /ˈɑbdʒɪkt, ˈɑbdʒɛkt/ ••• *noun* ◀))

| WORD ORIGIN | COLLOCATIONS | THESAURUS |

☐ **1** [countable] **a thing that you can see, hold, or touch:**

◀)) *a small metal object*

THESAURUS **thing, something, item, article**

☐ **2** [singular] **the purpose of a plan, action, or activity:**

◀)) ***The object of** the game is to improve children's math skills.*

☐ **3** [countable]

a) ENG. LANG. ARTS **in grammar, the person or thing that is affected by the action of the verb, for example "door" in the sentence "Sheila closed the door."** SYN **direct object**

b) ENG. LANG. ARTS **in grammar, the person who is involved in the result of an action, for example "her" in the sentence "I gave her a book."** SYN **indirect object**

4.

fruit /frut/ ••• *noun* (plural **fruit** or **fruits**) ◀))

| WORD ORIGIN | COLLOCATIONS |

☐ **1** [countable, uncountable] SCIENCE, BIOLOGY **something that grows on a plant, tree, or bush**

◀)) *Apples and bananas are Nancy's favorite fruits.*

◀)) *Would you like **a piece of fruit**?*

☐ **2** **the fruit(s) of something the good results that you have from something, after you have worked hard:**

◀)) *Medical science is now benefiting from **the fruits of** his research.*

[**Origin:** 1100–1200 Old French, Latin *fructus*, from frui **"to enjoy, have the use of"**] → **bear fruit**

5.

in·spire /ɪnˈspaɪɚ/ ••○ *verb* [transitive] ◀))

| WORD ORIGIN | VERB TABLE | COLLOCATIONS |

☐ **1** **to encourage someone to do or produce something good:**

◀)) *The church is trying to **inspire** more young men **to** become priests.*

☐ **2** **to make someone have a particular feeling:**

◀)) *The captain **inspires** confidence **in** his men.*

[**Origin:** 1300–1400 French *inspirer*, from Latin, from *spirare* **"to breathe"**]

C. Write a new sentence with each of these words.

moment: ....

buzz: ....

object: ....

fruit: ....

inspire: ....

◆ Go to MyEnglishLab to complete a skill practice.

APPLY YOUR SKILLS

WHY IT'S USEFUL By applying the skills you have learned in this unit, you will be able to follow and share ideas as you engage in discussions in an academic setting.

ASSIGNMENT
Prepare for and participate in a brainstorming discussion about a new idea for an app. Use research and what you have learned in this unit to help you "ideate" and share your ideas with the group.

BEFORE YOU LISTEN

A. Before you listen, discuss these questions with a partner or group.

1. Review the term *design thinking*. Why is design thinking important for a user's experience with a product, app, or service?

2. Review the steps in the design process. In your opinion, which step is most important? Explain.

3. What are the key features of good design? Explain.

B. You will listen to a lecture that explains mobile-first design. As you listen, think about these questions.

1. The professor implies that the number of mobile phone users has changed in recent years. How does she do that and how has the number changed?

2. How has the change in mobile phone use affected website and app design?

3. What is mobile-first design?

C. Review the Unit Skills Summary. As you listen to the lecture and prepare for your brainstorming discussion, apply the skills you learned in the unit.

UNIT SKILLS SUMMARY

DEVELOP IDEAS BY USING THESE SKILLS:

Demonstrate an understanding of ideas in a discussion

- Listen for keywords.
- Focus on questions and answers.
- Pay attention to speed and emphasis.
- Listen for examples.

Rephrase to clarify information

- Alert listeners to mistakes or difficult ideas.
- Clarify your idea using specific expressions.

Answer specific questions about a text

- Read the question and find keywords.
- Read the text carefully.
- Go back to the questions and answer them.

Use tag questions to invite agreement

- Make a sentence.
- Use the correct auxiliary verb to form the tag.

Use a dictionary to improve vocabulary

- Look at the context and guess the meaning of the new word.
- Use a dictionary to check its meaning.
- Identify how to use the new word in a sentence.

LISTEN

🎧 A. Listen to the lecture about mobile-first design and take notes. Try using a mind map to organize the main topic and subtopics.

B. Compare notes with a partner. Do you have the same ideas? How did the unit's skills help you to understand the lecture?

🎧 C. Review the questions from Before You Listen, Part B. Listen to the lecture again. Work with a partner and use your notes to answer the questions.

TIP

It is common for speakers to say *right?* as the question tag instead of using an auxiliary verb and subject. For example, *The feedback was useful, wasn't it?* can become, *The feedback was useful, right?*

⊙ Go to MyEnglishLab listen more closely and answer the critical thinking questions.

THINKING CRITICALLY

Discuss these questions with one or more students.

1. According to the lecture, designers say that the design process is easier if you focus on designs for small screens first, and then move to bigger screens. Why do you think this is true?

2. Imagine you have a product (an app, a device) that is not selling well. What can you do to figure out the problem and then solve it?

CULTURE NOTE

According to the US Bureau of Labor Statistics, the IT / computer field is expected grow faster than any other field, totaling 4.4 million jobs in the US by 2024. The median annual pay in 2016 for one of these positions was about $83,000, compared to $37,000 for other jobs. The reasons behind the growth in IT / computer jobs include more cloud computing, increasing amounts of big data, and the phenomenon known as "the Internet of things," meaning the growing number of everyday products and services that are Internet-based.

THINKING VISUALLY

A. Look at the bar graph. Describe what it shows about smartphone sales.

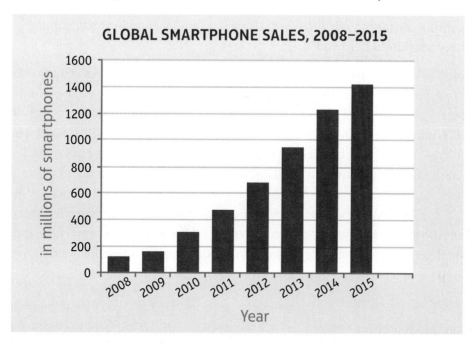

B. Look at the chart. It shows information about worldwide personal computer sales (in millions of computers). Make a bar graph using this information. Then discuss the questions that follow.

2006	2007	2008	2009	2010	2011	2012	2013	2014	2015
240	275	295	300	355	365	350	315	310	280

1. When were sales the highest? Think about changes leading up to this period.

2. Compare personal computer sales to smartphone sales between 2008 and 2015. Think about what was said in the lecture. Is this the change that you expect to see? Explain.

THINKING ABOUT LANGUAGE

A. Read the transcript. Use a dictionary to decide the meaning of the words in bold. Make sure you choose the correct meaning for the context. Then write an example sentence with the word. Use what you learned in the Vocabulary Strategy section to help you.

Speaker: In 2011, for the first time, more smartphones were sold than computers. Less than 50 years before that, a computer **required** a large room to hold it. Now, computers can be as small as a watch and we use them to **communicate** around the world. What I'm trying to say is that computer technology has become a **major** part of our lives. This is especially true of mobile devices. Mobile devices have moved very easily into our **personal** lives. There's no one in this room who doesn't have a smartphone, ... ? And most of them are probably less than two years old, ... ? Also, the look and feel of your smartphone has become important to you. And unlike a desktop computer, you can take a smartphone anywhere and **personalize** it, all while staying connected to your friends, family, the Internet, work. You're connected to everything, all the time.

1. require: _to need something_

    Example sentence: _Pets require a lot of care and attention from their owners._

2. communicate: ....

    Example sentence: ....

3. major: ....

    Example sentence: ....

4. personal: ....

    Example sentence: ....

5. personalize: ....

    Example sentence: ....

B. Complete the transcript with two tag questions.

For help with using tag questions to invite agreement, go to MyEnglishLab, Business and Design, Part 1, Language Skill.

BRAINSTORMING DISCUSSION

A. Read and discuss these questions with a small group.

People use apps on their smartphones and tablets for many different reasons.

1. Are there apps that you like to use?

2. Which apps are the most useful?

3. Which are the least useful?

4. Do apps solve problems? Explain.

B. With a small group, imagine that you are a design team in the Ideate Stage of developing an app. You can think of a completely new idea for an app, or you can make an app that is similar to one that you already know and use. Follow these steps in the discussion with your group.

1. Are there any problems in your everyday life that you want to fix? Are there apps that you think you can improve? Explain your thoughts.

2. Choose one or two ideas from the first question. *Brainstorm* about your new app— that is, explore a lot of different ideas about what it would do, how it would look and feel, and how you would market it.

3. For your best idea, discuss how you will introduce it to another group. What features of the app should you focus on when introducing it to others?

C. When you are done, share your idea with other groups.

D. Listen to other groups' ideas and take notes. Ask questions about their apps.

🔊 Go to MyEnglishLab to watch Juli Sherry's concluding video and to complete a self-assessment.

Patterns in nature can lead to advances in human medicine

ZOOLOGY

Extended Discourse

UNIT PROFILE

In this unit, you will learn about elephant behavior, elephant social structure, and the way that elephants hear sounds.

You will prepare and give an individual presentation on a specific elephant behavior.

OUTCOMES

- Formulate probing questions
- Describe conclusions
- Summarize listenings
- Connect ideas with *so* and *therefore*
- Guess meanings of unknown words

For more about **ZOOLOGY**, see ❷❸. See also R and W **ZOOLOGY** ❶❷❸.

GETTING STARTED

Go to MyEnglishLab to watch Professor O'Connell-Rodwell's introductory video and to complete a self-assessment.

Discuss these questions with a partner or group.

1. Share what you know about elephants. For example: Where do they live? How big are they? What makes them special?

2. Do you know of any elephant behaviors? Describe them.

3. In her introduction, Professor O'Connell-Rodwell says that there are different types of elephant groups: families, bond groups, and clans. What do you think the differences between the groups are?

SKILL 1

FORMULATING PROBING QUESTIONS

WHY IT'S USEFUL By asking probing questions, you can get more information from speakers about their opinions, and about why and how things happen. This will help you to understand a topic or idea better.

We ask questions whenever we want to get information. Some questions are very direct: They ask for specific details and the answers are often very short. For example:

Q: When does the lecture begin?

A: 9:30 A.M.

Q: What's the largest animal in the world?

A: The blue whale

But sometimes we want reasons, opinions, or longer, more detailed answers to get a better understanding of a subject. In this case, we **ask probing questions**. Probing questions have two key features:

• They are *open-ended*: They do not ask for a short answer. This allows the speaker to fully explain an idea. Open-ended questions usually start with *what, how,* or *why*.

• They are *reflective*: They ask for deep thoughts on a subject. This makes the speaker dig deeper to give an opinion or a different view on facts, not just more details.

Examples of Probing Questions

How has conservation policy changed since you began working in the field?

Why do you support the new law?

What do you think about the organization's efforts to protect endangered species?

Asking probing questions will increase your understanding of a subject. It will also show that you are listening closely to the speaker. Listen for probing questions in discussions, interviews, etc.

CULTURE NOTE

Lectures can sometimes be boring, with the professor speaking for long periods of time. Many professors encourage students to ask questions, especially probing questions. Ask them. They will help everyone in the class understand the subject better.

VOCABULARY PREVIEW

Read the vocabulary items in the box. Circle the ones you know. Put a question mark next to the ones you don't know.

mammal	intelligent	social	unusual	care for	come up	matter (n)

Glossary

Matriarch: a female who has the most influence or power in a family or social group—*matriarchal* (adj)

Herd: a group of a particular type of animal that lives together

---

EXERCISE 1

A. Do elephants live alone or in herds? What else do you know about elephant "society"? Discuss with a partner or small group.

B. Listen to the podcast interview. How many probing questions does the interviewer ask? Why does he ask the probing questions?

....

C. What makes a good probing question? When should you ask them?

EXERCISE 2

An Elephant Brain   **A Human Brain**

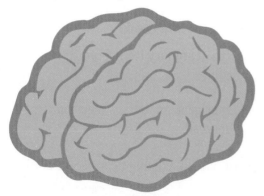   

An adult elephant's brain weighs about 4 kilograms, the largest of all land animals.
An adult human's brain weighs about 1.35 kilograms.

🔊 **A. Listen again and take notes. Then complete the sentences.**

1. Elephants have very large ...., and so they are very ....
   They are very social, and ....—grandmothers, daughters, and so on—
   live together for their whole lives.

2. Strong matriarchs build .... with others in their herd. Matriarchs need
   to have the most .... and ....

🔊 **B. Listen again. What question words does the interviewer use to ask the
probing questions?**

....

CULTURE NOTE

According to statistics, nearly 1/5 of all American adults listen to podcasts at least once a month.
Podcasts have become not only popular also very specialized. While traditional broadcast radio shows
have had to appeal to larger, more general audiences, many podcasts have smaller, particular groups
of followers. Topics range from movie reviews to soccer gossip to brain games. There are even podcasts
about zoology. Search online using the keywords "zoology podcast."

EXERCISE 3

A. Imagine you want to continue the interview with Dr. Kate Goodman. Write two
new probing questions to ask her. Share them with a partner or small group.

....

....

B. How are your questions effective probing questions? Discuss with your partner
or group.

VOCABULARY CHECK

A. Review the vocabulary items in the Vocabulary Preview. Write their definitions and add examples. Use a dictionary if necessary.

B. Complete each sentence using the correct vocabulary item from the box. Use the correct form.

care for	come up	intelligent	mammal
matter	social	unusual	

1. Humans are very .... Most of us like being near people and talking to each other.

2. Nurses are people who .... the sick and elderly.

3. Animals such as monkeys and dolphins are highly .... Some have similar behaviors to humans.

4. Examples of .... include humans, elephants, cows, and mice.

5. Some animal behaviors might seem .... , but it is completely normal to them.

6. The decisions that a matriarch makes are often a(n) .... of survival.

7. Something has .... , so I'll have to miss today's meeting.

TIP

According to research, in order for a reading or listening passage to be easily understood, you need to know 98 percent of the vocabulary in the passage. The key to knowing vocabulary is studying vocabulary. Add new vocabulary items to your notecards or vocabulary journal.

▶ Go to MyEnglishLab to complete vocabulary and skill practices, and to join in collaborative activities.

SKILL 2

DESCRIBING CONCLUSIONS

WHY IT'S USEFUL By describing conclusions, you can share your own opinions and way of thinking with others. This will help people understand you and can also be useful in convincing others of your ideas.

A *conclusion* is something that you decide after considering all of the information you have. In academic life, you receive a lot of information every day—in lectures, in discussions, in homework. But it is not enough to just receive information; you need to use it to create new ideas. And you will be asked to **describe conclusions** that you have made based on what you hear.

Describing conclusions is not very complicated, but that does not mean you can just say your conclusion and be done. You have to tell your listener *how* you arrived at your conclusion. That is, you need to give your reasons or evidence.

Reasons / Evidence

- **Facts** such as historical events and research

- **Anecdotal evidence** such as personal experiences and stories you've heard from others

- **Logic**, a set of sensible reasons

Try to cite at least two specific reasons when describing your conclusion. Explaining your reasons will help others understand your conclusion. Also, if you use very good reasons, then your conclusion will be stronger, and you will be able to convince others of your ideas.

Here are two examples of this. The conclusions are underlined:

<u>Elephant society is quite different from humans</u>. As we heard in yesterday's lecture, males leave the group around the age of 14, but this is not true for young men. Also, elephant family groups are matriarchal, which is not the case for most human societies.

Elephants have been known to use rocks as tools, throwing them at their enemies. They also understand people very well—they remember which groups have hurt or have tried to kill them, and which people are friendly. They treat different groups of people differently. <u>This shows that they are certainly intelligent</u>.

VOCABULARY PREVIEW

Read the vocabulary items in the box. Circle the ones you know. Put a question mark next to the ones you don't know.

consist of	multiple	pass	get together
maintain	memories	recognize	

EXERCISE 4

A. What have you learned about the groups that elephants live in? What do they do when they meet other groups of elephants?

B. Listen to this lecture and class discussion. Read the statements. Circle *T* (True) or *F* (False). Correct the false statements. Then explain to a partner how you made those conclusions.

T / F 1. There is only one mother in an elephant family group.

T / F 2. Bond groups are larger than family groups.

T / F 3. Elephant clans can consist of more than 100 elephants.

T / F 4. Elephants stay in the same family or bond group for life.

T / F 5. Elephants care for others even if they are from a different family.

C. When describing conclusions, is it important to explain your reasons? Why? How can this help you in academic life? Discuss with a partner or small group.

EXERCISE 5

A. Listen again and take notes. Check (✓) the two conclusions the student makes. Does she support her ideas with reasons?

☐ Elephants groups come together in good seasons.

☐ Elephants have good memories.

☐ Elephants are good with relationships.

☐ Elephants recognize others very well.

B. Listen for a third time. Then outline the two conclusions that the student describes.

1. Conclusion: ....

   Reason(s): ....

2. Conclusion: ....

   Reason(s): ....

EXERCISE 6

A. Think about the different things you have learned about elephants so far in this unit: their social structure, intelligence, matriarchs, etc. Make conclusions about the following topics. Share your ideas with a small group. Take notes on others' ideas.

- the environment elephants live in
- elephants' relationships with other living things
- why humans are so interested in elephants

B. Do you agree with the conclusions and reasons of the other students? What can they do to strengthen their conclusions and / or reasons?

VOCABULARY CHECK

A. Review the vocabulary items in the Vocabulary Preview. Write their definitions and add examples. Use a dictionary if necessary.

B. Complete each sentence using the correct vocabulary item from the box. Use the correct form.

consist of	get together	maintain	memory
multiple	pass	recognize	

1. .... friendships when you get older can be difficult, especially if you and your friends live far from each other.

2. There are .... species of elephant: the African forest elephant, the African bush elephant, and the Asian elephant.

3. About 10,000 years have .... since the disappearance of the woolly mammoth—a species similar to the elephant.

4. A recent study shows that dogs can .... human emotions, like happiness and sadness.

5. An elephant's diet—all the things it eats—........................ small plants, fruit, grasses, and tree bark.

6. Our biology professor has a terrible .... He always forgets things.

7. The two groups .... and created one larger group.

↻ Go to MyEnglishLab to complete vocabulary and skill practices, and to join in collaborative activities.

INTEGRATED SKILLS

SUMMARIZING LISTENINGS

WHY IT'S USEFUL By summarizing the information that you hear, you can use your own words to explain complex ideas. You can then use the summary to help you study for tests and write papers.

Summarizing listenings is a good way to learn. The process of summarizing makes you put pieces of information together by using your own words. This gives you a deeper connection with what you have heard in a listening.

Summarizing begins before you write. These are the first steps:

- **Take good notes** when you are listening. Listen for keywords and examples.
- Afterwards, read through your notes and **identify the main ideas**.

> For more about taking good notes, see Bioethics, Part 1, Integrated Skills, page 11.

Next, it is time to write. Here are a few tips for writing a one-paragraph summary:

- In your first sentence, include a) the name of the speaker(s), and b) the name of the class, presentation, or topic.
- Write one sentence about each of the main points that you hear.
- If possible, add a final sentence about the speaker's main conclusion.
- Keep the summary short, especially if the presentation you are writing about is short.
- Use your own words. There is no need to quote the speaker.
- Do NOT add your opinion to a summary.

⏱ Listen again to the podcast interview from Skill 1, Exercise 1, Part B.

Then look at the following example summary of that interview. You can see that it follows the rules for a one-paragraph summary. It does not include a sentence about a conclusion because there was no conclusion presented in the podcast.

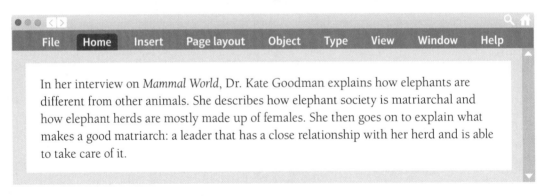

In her interview on *Mammal World*, Dr. Kate Goodman explains how elephants are different from other animals. She describes how elephant society is matriarchal and how elephant herds are mostly made up of females. She then goes on to explain what makes a good matriarch: a leader that has a close relationship with her herd and is able to take care of it.

TIP

Lectures can include a lot of information. To write better summaries, be sure to read any material assigned as homework so that you can get a better idea of a lecture's content.

VOCABULARY PREVIEW

Read the vocabulary items in the box. Circle the ones you know. Put a question mark next to the ones you don't know.

waves (n)	unit	ranges (n)	voices	tell	enemy	threat	effective

EXERCISE 7

A. Can we hear all the sounds that animals make? Do you think animals can recognize human voices? Share your ideas with a partner or small group.

🔊 B. Listen to the lecture and take notes using this T-chart.

SOUNDS THEY HEAR AND MAKE		
Humans	**Elephants**	**Other Animals**

🔊 C. Listen again and add to your notes. Then compare notes with a partner. Complete the following information together.

Main idea: ....

....

Supporting details: ....

....

....

D. Read the following summary. Is it a good summary? If not, how would you change it?

In the lecture, the professor discusses sounds that humans and elephants hear and make. She explains that each species has a different range of sounds that it can hear. Because elephants are able to hear lower-frequency sounds, they can communicate across long distances. Humans cannot hear some animal sounds because they are too low or too high in frequency. I find the sounds that animals can make and hear to be very interesting.

E. In MyEnglishLab, you will write a summary of a lecture. What makes a good summary? How can writing summaries help you study?

VOCABULARY CHECK

A. Review the vocabulary items in the Vocabulary Preview. Write their definitions and add examples. Use a dictionary if necessary.

B. Complete each sentence using the correct vocabulary item from the box. Use the correct form.

effective	enemy	range	tell	threat	unit	voice	wave

1. Sound .... travel faster through water than through air.

2. Roger has a deep and very loud ....

3. Elephants are famous for their memories, including never forgetting who is a friend and who is a(n) ....

4. We use various .... of measurement to measure mass including the stone and the pound. But the kilogram is the most common.

5. As with sounds, humans can see only a limited .... of light. This is called the visible spectrum and goes from red, at 0.7 nanometers, to violet, at about 0.4 nanometers.

6. It's difficult to .... the difference between the two species without knowing what to look for.

7. The conservation law that the local government passed five years ago is very .... Endangered species' populations have begun to increase.

8. Humans, through both hunting and development, are one of elephants' greatest ....

🔾 Go to MyEnglishLab to complete vocabulary and skill practices, and to join in collaborative activities.

LANGUAGE SKILL
CONNECTING IDEAS WITH *SO* AND *THEREFORE*

WHY IT'S USEFUL By understanding the meaning and use of *so* and *therefore*, you can better understand relationships between ideas. You can also express your ideas more clearly.

🔊 Go to MyEnglishLab for the Language Skill presentation and practice.

VOCABULARY STRATEGY
GUESSING MEANINGS OF UNKNOWN WORDS

WHY IT'S USEFUL By guessing the meaning of unknown words, you can remember the word better and improve your understanding of a text. You can also read texts more quickly.

You are reading an article for class and you see a word that you don't know. What should you do? Immediately look it up in a dictionary? Experts agree that this is not the best way to learn new words. Instead, you should **guess the meaning of the unknown word**. How do you do this? Follow these steps:

1. First, look at the grammar, or part of speech, of the word. Is the unknown word a noun, a verb, or an adjective? This will tell you how the word adds meaning to the sentence and the context in general. Then examine, or look closely at, the word. Does it look like any other words that you know? Does it have an affix (examples: *un-*, *re-*, *-less*, *-ly*) that you know?

2. Next, continue reading and study the surrounding sentences. You might see clues to the word's meaning, such as definitions and related words. Look at the following example.

   Elephant <u>tusks</u> are large teeth that come out of the front of an elephant's head, and they weigh as much as 50 kilograms. Elephants use them in a number of ways: as weapons to fight other animals such as tigers, and as tools for moving large objects. Other animals, such as walruses and pigs, also have tusks.

   Important clues to the meaning of the word *tusk* come after *tusk*, such as *large teeth*, *weapons*, and examples of other animals that have tusks.

3. Now go back to the word and make a guess. In the example, a good guess might be *the big white things on an elephant's head*. Make a note of your guess.

4. The last step is to look up the word in a dictionary. If you find *tusk* in the *Longman Dictionary of American English*, you will see that the definition is "one of the two very long teeth that stick out of an animal's mouth." This is the necessary final step in the process.

Guess Unknown Words

G   Look at the GRAMMAR

U   Try to UNDERSTAND the general meaning of the sentence

E   EXAMINE the word

S   Study the SURROUNDING sentences

S   SEARCH for the word in your dictionary

Guessing the meaning of unknown words will give you a deeper connection with them, which will help you to remember the words better. Guessing will also make you think more about the text that you are reading, increasing your understanding of it. Finally, guessing should make reading more enjoyable because you won't be stopping to look at your dictionary. Be sure to use this strategy when reading for class.

EXERCISE 8

A. Read the sentences. Use the context to write definitions for the underlined words.

1. Elephants use their long <u>trunk</u> to drink water and to smell things. They do not drink water directly through their trunk, however. They pull water into their trunk and then put their trunk into their mouth and drop the water. Then they drink it.

   ....

2. In some places, habitat loss is causing <u>trouble</u> for humans and elephants alike. For elephants, they lose their places to live. This causes them to destroy farms and homes that people use.

   ....

3. The African bush elephant can weigh up to 15,000 <u>pounds</u>, which makes it the largest land mammal. This is very small compared to the blue whale, which can weigh up to 20 times as much, about 300,000 pounds.

   ....

4. Elephants are animals with very strong feelings, which can be seen in the soft touch of a mother's trunk on her calf or in the <u>anger</u> of a bull fighting an enemy.

   ....

5. Some scientists spend years watching elephants <u>behave</u>. That's how we know about their social relationships and all of the different things they do in nature.

   ....

B. Share your definitions with a partner or small group. Do you have similar definitions? How did you use the context to create your definitions?

C. When you are finished discussing, look up the words in a dictionary. Were your definitions correct? How should you use context to guess the meaning of unknown words? Why is this a useful vocabulary strategy? Discuss with a partner or small group.

⬆ **Go to MyEnglishLab to complete a skill practice.**

APPLY YOUR SKILLS

WHY IT'S USEFUL By applying the skills you have learned in this unit, you will be able to participate in extended discourse at the university level.

ASSIGNMENT

Prepare and give an individual presentation about a particular elephant behavior or body part. Use research and what you have learned about forming conclusions and connecting ideas to help you explain your topic and make it interesting.

BEFORE YOU LISTEN

A. Before you listen, discuss these questions with a partner or group.

1. Describe the social structure of elephants.

2. Do elephants have any intelligent behaviors? Explain your ideas.

3. How is the hearing of humans and elephants similar? How is it different? Explain.

B. You will listen to a lecture and class discussion about the relationships between elephants and humans. As you listen, think about these questions.

1. Do elephants understand "who they are"? That is, do they know that they are part of a group of other elephants, each with its own identity?

2. Do elephants attack humans? Why or why not?

C. Review the Unit Skills Summary on the next page. As you listen to the lecture and discussion, and prepare for your presentation, apply the skills you learned in the unit.

UNIT SKILLS SUMMARY

IMPROVE YOUR ABILITY TO EXTEND DISCOURSE BY USING THESE SKILLS:

Formulate probing questions

- Use words such as *what*, *why*, and *how* to start the questions.
- Make the questions reflective.

Describe conclusions

- Make your conclusion clear.
- Support your conclusion with evidence, reasons, and / or logic.

Summarize listenings

- Take good notes while listening and then organize them afterwards.
- Include information on the speaker, topic, and so on.
- Keep the summary short.
- Use your own words, but don't add your opinion.

Connect ideas with *so* and *therefore*

- Guide listeners to make a "cause-effect" inference.
- Use the correct level of formality.

GUESS meanings of unknown words

- Look at the **G**RAMMAR.
- Try to **U**NDERSTAND the meaning of the sentence.
- **E**XAMINE the word.
- Study the **S**URROUNDING sentences.
- **S**EARCH for the word in your dictionary.

LISTEN

🎧 A. Listen to the lecture and discussion, and take notes. Try organizing the information in a T-chart.

B. Compare notes with a partner. Do you have the same ideas? How did the unit's skills help you to understand the lecture and discussion?

🎧 C. Review the questions from Before You Listen, Part B. Listen to the lecture and discussion again. Work with a partner and use your notes to answer the questions.

⊙ Go to MyEnglishLab to listen more closely and answer the critical thinking questions.

THINKING CRITICALLY

Discuss the questions with one or more students.

1. According to the listening, elephants attack humans because of things like stress. Do you think this is the same reason that animals like bears and tigers attack humans? Explain your thoughts.

2. Human intelligence is defined by our ability to solve problems, use tools, plan for the future, and much more. Do you think elephants are intelligent? Why or why not?

THINKING VISUALLY

A. Look at the two maps. How have the distribution ranges of the African bush elephant and African forest elephant changed? Which elephant's range has changed the most? Why do you think the elephants' ranges are changing? How did you reach these conclusions?

Distribution Range in the Early 20th Century

Distribution Range in 2016

■ African bush elephant

■ African forest elephant

B. Create a graph using the statistics from the chart. Is the elephant population increasing or decreasing? Does this information inform your answers and the maps in Part A? Explain.

ELEPHANT POPULATION					
Early 20th Century	1979	1989	2007	2016	2025 (projection)
10 million	1.3 million	800,000	500,000	352,000	160,000

THINKING ABOUT LANGUAGE

A. Read the following excerpts from the lecture. Use the context to guess the meaning of each underlined word. Write your definition and then check it with a dictionary.

1. They are animals with very strong <u>emotions</u>, which can be seen in the soft, loving touch of a mother's trunk on her calf, or in the anger of an elephant bull fighting an enemy.

....

....

2. What we're discovering is that elephants decide to <u>attack</u> after something bad has happened to them, and that's quite amazing if you think about it. For example, if a group of humans hunts a herd of elephants, the elephants will fight back.

....

....

3. Anyway, in normal situations, elephants live in nature, so living around humans isn't exactly <u>natural</u>. And sometimes people make them work. Scientists have discovered that this creates stress for them.

....

....

B. Use *so* or *therefore* to combine each pair of sentences into one sentence.

For help with connecting ideas with *so* and *therefore*, go to MyEnglishLab, Zoology, Part 1, Language Skill.

1. Elephants hear low-frequency sounds. / Elephants have very long ear canals.

   Elephants have very long ear canals; therefore, they can hear low-frequency sounds.

2. The distribution range of African bush elephants has decreased significantly. / We have to create policies to protect African bush elephants.

3. Elephants are intelligent. / Elephants use tools and plan for the future.

4. Many researchers think elephants have emotions. / Elephants touch their calves softly and they can also look very angry.

INDIVIDUAL PRESENTATION

A. Look at the list of body parts and elephant behaviors. With a small group, discuss what you know about each.

Body Part	Behavior
ear	maintain relationships
trunk	care for other elephants
skull	teach calves
tusk	communicate
brain	fight with each other
feet	attack people

B. You are going to give a 2–3-minute individual presentation on an elephant body part or behavior. Include a brief introduction and a concluding sentence. Select one of the body parts or behaviors and do more research on it, or research something that has not been discussed. Think about the following questions as you prepare.

1. What is the body part / behavior? What makes it special to elephants?

2. Is the body part / behavior unique to elephants? Or do humans or other animals have something similar?

3. Why do you find the body part / behavior interesting?

C. Listen to the other presentations and take notes. After each presenter has finished, ask questions.

◑ Go to MyEnglishLab to watch Professor O'Connell-Rodwell's concluding video and to complete a self-assessment.

HISTORY

Relationships Between Ideas

UNIT PROFILE

In this unit, you will learn about the historical sites of Machu Picchu and Olduvai Gorge. You will hear and read about their discoveries, how they have helped to improve our understanding of human history, and what else we hope to learn from studying them.

You will prepare and give a pair presentation that compares and contrasts two historical sites.

OUTCOMES

- Compare similar ideas
- Contrast different ideas
- Understand relationships between ideas
- Utilize the simple past passive
- Create flashcards to study vocabulary

For more about **HISTORY**, see ❷❸. See also ⌷R⌷ and ⌷W⌷ **HISTORY** ❶❷❸.

GETTING STARTED

⊙ Go to MyEnglishLab to watch Dr. Hunt's introductory video and to complete a self-assessment.

Discuss these questions with a partner or group.

1. Have you heard of Machu Picchu (pictured on the opposite page)? Share what you know.

2. Do you think that we can learn about modern societies by studying our past? Explain.

3. In his introduction, Dr. Hunt says that early humans were found at Olduvai Gorge in Africa. What do you know about the earliest humans who lived in Africa? Explain your ideas.

SKILL 1

COMPARING SIMILAR IDEAS

WHY IT'S USEFUL By comparing similar ideas, you can show how two or more things connect to each other. This is useful for when you want to make a point using different pieces of information.

When we make comparisons, we examine or judge two or more things in order to show how they are similar to or different from each other. Here we will focus on **comparing similar ideas**.

There are a number of ways to compare similar ideas in English. One way, which you are probably familiar with, is additive—that is, connecting one similar idea to another. In this case, we use words like *too*, *also*, and *as well*. For example:

My history professor got her PhD at Harvard University. My advisor got his PhD there **also / too / as well**.

We use these words to show two things:

• that the ideas in the two sentences are similar

• that both ideas support some kind of conclusion

We also use the words *similarly* and *likewise* to connect ideas between sentences. It is often the case that *similarly* is used when the grammatical subjects are different. *Likewise* is used when the subjects are the same. Consider these examples:

Ancient peoples built all different kinds of structures for protection. The Chinese built the Great Wall of China to protect against their enemies. **Similarly,** Canaanites constructed the Wall of Jericho, in what is today the West Bank, about 10,000 years ago to prevent floods and invasion.

European powers invaded the Americas in the 16th and 17th centuries and their influence can still be felt there. Soon after, the English took lands in what's now northern Canada, and there is a strong English cultural influence there today. **Likewise,** they took lands in what is now the United States, where today English is the native language of many of its inhabitants.

One reason that the Great Wall of China was built was to protect against invasion.

VOCABULARY PREVIEW

Read the vocabulary items in the box. Circle the ones you know. Put a question mark next to the ones you don't know.

sites	stone (n)	South America	reach (v)
centuries	proved	saw eye to eye	

Glossary

Empire: a group of countries controlled by one ruler or government

Archaeology: the study of ancient societies by examining what remains of their buildings, graves, tools, etc.—*archaeological* (adj); *archaeologist* (n)

Evolve: to slowly develop

Civilization: a society that is well-organized and developed

EXERCISE 1

A. Do you know of any historic sites in your home country? What are they? Describe them to a partner or small group.

B. Listen to a lecture about two historical sites, Machu Picchu and Olduvai Gorge. Check (✓) the comparison words you hear.

☐ also   ☐ too   ☐ as well   ☐ similarly   ☐ likewise

C. How are words like *too / as well / also* and *similarly / likewise* used differently?

Present-day Olduvai Gorge

EXERCISE 2

A. Listen again. Decide whether the following statements are about Machu Picchu (M), Olduvai Gorge (O), or both (B).

.... 1. The site was built by the Inca.

.... 2. People lived at the site for a very short time.

.... 3. The site is in Tanzania.

.... 4. The site is important for explaining human history.

.... 5. The site was discovered in the 20th century.

B. Listen again. Complete the Venn diagram. Use the phrases from the box.

located in East Africa	home to the earliest human-like species
located in South America	discovered in the 20th century
hidden for years	has changed our thinking about old human societies
difficult to reach	has taught us about ourselves

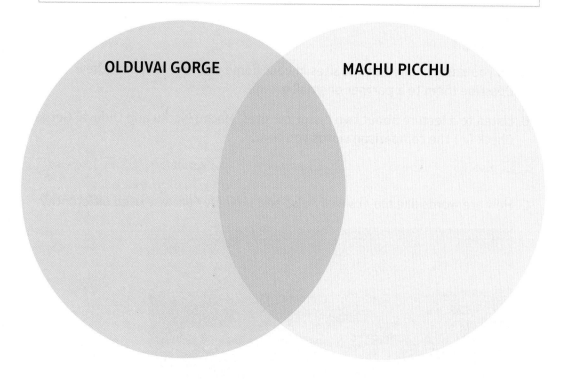

OLDUVAI GORGE   MACHU PICCHU

EXERCISE 3

A. Complete the sentences with *also, too, as well, similarly,* or *likewise*. Then read the sentences aloud with a partner.

1. Machu Picchu was discovered in the early 20th century. Olduvai Gorge was first found around that time ....

2. Archaeological discoveries can tell us about our past. Olduvai Gorge gives us ideas about how humans evolved. .... Machu Picchu tells us about the greatness of a past civilization.

B. The discoveries of Machu Picchu and Olduvai Gorge have told us a lot about our past. Do you think it is important to learn about our past? Why or why not?

VOCABULARY CHECK

A. Review the vocabulary items in the Vocabulary Preview. Write their definitions and add examples. Use a dictionary if necessary.

B. Complete each sentence using the correct vocabulary item from the box. Use the correct form.

century	prove	reach	see eye-to-eye
site	South America	stone	

1. It is difficult to know exactly when the first humans came to .... , but new discoveries hundreds of miles to the north suggest that people came to what is now the United States about 15,000 years ago.

2. Situated in northern Tanzania, Olduvai Gorge is an archaeological .... that has bones and fossils from many different human-like species.

3. Early humans used tools made of .... and animal bones.

4. It is unusual for the two archaeologists to .... on anything. They always disagree about the significance of new discoveries.

5. Traveling on the traditional Inca road, it takes four days to .... Machu Picchu.

6. Columbus first arrived in the Americas toward the end of the 15th ....

7. These fossils and tools .... that humans lived in this area over 30,000 years ago.

○ Go to MyEnglishLab to complete vocabulary and skill practices, and to join in collaborative activities.

SKILL 2

CONTRASTING DIFFERENT IDEAS

WHY IT'S USEFUL By contrasting ideas, you can give your listeners two sides from which they can identify your main point. This is useful when you want to emphasize the difference between two ideas.

In the previous section, we looked at ways to identify and use words to compare similarities. Here we focus on contrasting—or showing the difference between—ideas. When speakers **contrast different ideas**, they do so on the same topic. For example:

> Machu Picchu was an incredible piece of Inca civilization. It was built high in the Andes Mountains of modern-day Peru in the 15th century, **but** it was not known to Westerners until 1911.

Here the topic is Machu Picchu, and there are two different ideas about who knew about it, connected by the familiar conjunction *but*. This is a very basic contrast that you already know how to make.

There are many other words and phrases that can draw attention to a difference between two ideas. A few of the most common ones are presented in this chart.

Contrast Word / Phrase	Example Sentence	Notes
however	*Archaeology is an interesting subject.* **However,** *it's quite difficult because of all the reading.*	• Points out a difference • Often used between sentences and followed by a comma
while	**While** *the existence of the first site was something we've known about for a long time, we've only recently discovered that the second site exists.*	• Points out direct contrast • Used when you want to put two ideas in one sentence • Comes at the beginning or in the middle of a sentence
on the other hand	*Paris is a wonderful city to visit because of its great historical sites.* **On the other hand,** *it is not easy to see these sites because there are so many tourists.*	• Points out a difference between two ideas • Used between sentences and followed by a comma
in contrast	*The Great Wall of China has been kept in good condition over the centuries.* **In contrast,** *the Wall of Jericho was buried underground for thousands of years.*	• Used for a contrast between two different subjects (the Great Wall, the Wall of Jericho), *and* a contrast between the two ideas (kept in good condition, buried underground) • Used between sentences and followed by a comma

Speakers contrast ideas when they want to point out differences between two things. They will often point out the contrast by emphasizing the contrast word (*however, in contrast*). Listen for these words to get a better understanding of how the contrasting ideas relate to the main idea of a lecture or presentation.

VOCABULARY PREVIEW
Read the vocabulary items in the box. Circle the ones you know. Put a question mark next to the ones you don't know.

opposite	digging	layers	modern	underground	canals

Glossary

Artifact: an object such as a tool, weapon, etc., that was made in the past and is historically important

EXERCISE 4

A. Based on what you know about Machu Picchu and Olduvai Gorge, how are the two sites different?

B. Listen to the lecture about some key differences between the two sites. Check (✓) the contrast words and phrases that you hear.

- ☐ while
- ☐ in contrast
- ☐ however
- ☐ but
- ☐ on the other hand

C. How can contrasting ideas give you a better understanding of a topic?

EXERCISE 5

A. Listen again. Check (✓) the three main ideas that the speaker contrasts.

- ☐ popularity with tourists
- ☐ features of the sites and what is found there
- ☐ the people who found the sites in the early 20th century
- ☐ the things that we learn from the sites

B. Listen again and take notes. Complete the chart with contrasting information about the sites.

Olduvai Gorge	Machu Picchu
not many tourists	*popular with tourists*

EXERCISE 6

A. Use contrast words and phrases to make sentences with the information from Exercise 5, Part B. Then share that information with a partner.

1. *Olduvai Gorge and Machu Picchu are famous archaeological sites. Machu Picchu receives many tourists each year. On the other hand, very few people go to Olduvai Gorge since it is not known for its beauty.*

2. _____

_____

_____

3. ....

....

....

4. ....

....

....

B. With a partner or small group, compare and contrast Olduvai Gorge and Machu Picchu.

VOCABULARY CHECK

A. Review the vocabulary items in the Vocabulary Preview. Write their definitions and add examples. Use a dictionary if necessary.

B. Complete each sentence using the correct vocabulary item from the box. Use the correct form.

canal	dig	layer	modern	opposite	underground

1. .... humans are taller than humans that lived long ago.

2. The team of archaeologists had to .... deep to find more bones and fossils.

3. For thousands of years societies have built .... to move things more easily from place to place.

4. Archaeologists believe that some of Machu Picchu is still .... , covered by dirt and plants that have grown there in the years since it was built.

5. Several .... of soil now cover the 7,000-year-old site.

6. The entrance to the site is on the .... side of the street, facing us.

Go to MyEnglishLab to complete vocabulary and skill practices, and to join in collaborative activities.

INTEGRATED SKILLS

UNDERSTANDING RELATIONSHIPS BETWEEN IDEAS

WHY IT'S USEFUL By understanding the relationship between ideas in a text, you can get a better idea of how the individual parts of a text contribute to its meaning. This is a necessary critical thinking skill for academic life.

Professors often ask critical thinking questions. This requires you to **understand relationships between ideas**. Let's look at some common relationships:

- **General statement – specific example**: This is a general statement followed by something more specific, usually an example. Writers do this to explain more about a topic and to show support for a claim.

  History is an interesting subject. It provides us with stories from the past so that we can learn from them.

- **Chronological sequence**: This shows the order of events. Writers use chronological sequence to tell a story or to show the relationship between events.

  Construction of the Great Wall began before the Qin Dynasty, but the Qin ordered the construction of a longer wall, which connected smaller walls that existed in the 2nd and 3rd centuries BCE. Later, other family dynasties, including the Han and Ming, made the wall longer and stronger.

- **Compare – contrast**: This shows similarities and differences between ideas. Writers often state that two things are similar, but then show their difference in a later sentence. This can make two related things seem much different.

  The British and Spanish were both powerful European countries in the 16th century. But it was the British who were able to keep their power for much longer.

- **Summary of previous idea(s)**: A summarizing sentence is used to make the main point clear and easy to understand. Writers do this after they present a few ideas.

  The Wall of Jericho was big enough to prevent floods and was likely important for protection. It was also used for religious purposes. It clearly served a number of uses for the people of this early city.

Read carefully to understand how sentences are connected to each other. Then look at how these relationships give meaning to the overall text. Doing this will help you to better understand the ideas that the writer is presenting and why he is writing the text.

VOCABULARY PREVIEW

Read the vocabulary items in the box. Circle the ones you know. Put a question mark next to the ones you don't know.

ancient	origins	physical	remains	value (n)
invasion	advanced	construction	techniques	field

Glossary

Temple: a building where people go to worship

EXERCISE 7

A. Have you ever "discovered" an artifact—in the ground, at a flea market, or at a museum? What interested you? Discuss with a partner.

B. Read the title of the article. What kind(s) of relationships between ideas do you expect to find in the text? Then read the text and take notes. Answer the questions that follow.

Archaeology and What We've Learned from Olduvai Gorge and Machu Picchu

1 The word *archaeology* often makes people think of Indiana Jones movies, ancient temples, and adventure. While real-life archaeology isn't as fast-paced and entertaining, it is exciting and useful, and it can help us answer some of the most important questions about our origins.

2 In some ways, an archaeologist's work is similar to that of a historian (a person who studies or writes about history). They both want to learn about the past. But while historians look at written evidence (letters, books, journals), archaeologists study physical evidence. This physical evidence includes artifacts, remains of buildings, and lands that have been affected by people. Because of this, historians are limited to studying times for which there is written evidence. Archaeologists, on the other hand, can study times much earlier than this, even going back to the earliest humans.

3 To better understand the value of archaeology, let's look at two famous archaeological discoveries. The first of these is Olduvai Gorge. Archaeological and paleoanthropological (the study of evolution through fossils) research done here by Mary and Louis Leakey in the 1950s and 1960s taught us some important lessons about the story of our evolution. The Leakeys discovered skull and hand

fossils in an area where they were digging up ancient stone tools. Tests showed that these human-like fossils were around 1.8 million years old. The shape of the bones and teeth led Louis Leakey to the conclusion that they were of a different species from our own *Homo sapiens* (i.e., modern humans). This newly discovered early-human species was named *Homo habilis*. This discovery has become important for our understanding of how modern humans evolved.

4 The second example is the discovery of Machu Picchu in Peru. This citadel, located high in the Andes Mountains, was built around 1450 and is a great work of Inca architecture. The Inca left the site in the 1570s. Some believe they left because of the Spanish invasion of the Americas. The site was gradually covered by jungle and was hidden to all but a few local people until its "rediscovery" in the early 20th century. Yale University professor Hiram Bingham led a project to clear away the jungle growth and uncover the site. From the work at Machu Picchu, we know that the Inca were advanced engineers who used complex construction techniques in their stone buildings. A bronze alloy (mixed metal) knife was also found at Machu Picchu, showing us that the Inca had developed highly advanced metal-making technology, too.

5 These are just two of many examples of how archaeology has given us amazing lessons by which we can understand the past. As such, it is an important field of study that we will continue to learn from.

1. What is the difference between archaeology and history?

   ....

2. What did archaeological research at Olduvai Gorge lead to?

   ....

3. What did Hiram Bingham do at Machu Picchu?

   ....

C. Read these excerpts from the text. Answer the questions.

But while historians look at written evidence (letters, books, etc.), archaeologists study physical evidence. This physical evidence includes artifacts, remains of buildings, and lands that have been affected by people.

1. What is the relationship between the two sentences?

   general-specific   chronological sequence   compare-contrast   summary

Because of this, historians are limited to studying times in which there is written evidence. Archaeologists, on the other hand, can study times much earlier than this, even going back to the dawn of humanity.

2. What is the relationship between the two sentences?

   general-specific   chronological sequence   compare-contrast   summary

Archaeological and paleoanthropological (the study of evolution through fossils) research done here by Mary and Louis Leakey in the 1950s and 1960s taught us some important lessons about the story of our evolution. The Leakeys discovered skull and hand fossils in an area where they were digging up ancient stone tools.

3. What is the relationship between the two sentences?

   general-specific   chronological sequence   compare-contrast   summary

The shape of the bones and teeth led Louis Leakey to the conclusion that they were of a different species from our own *Homo sapiens* (i.e., modern humans). This newly discovered early-human species was named *Homo habilis*. This discovery has become important for our understanding of how modern humans evolved.

4. What is the relationship between the first two sentences and the last sentence?

   general-specific   chronological sequence   compare-contrast   summary

The Inca left the site in the 1570s. Some believe they left because of the Spanish invasion of the Americas. The site was gradually covered by jungle and was hidden to all but a few local people until its "rediscovery" in the early 20th century.

5. What is the relationship between the two sentences?

   general-specific   chronological sequence   compare-contrast   summary

D. **How does understanding the relationship between ideas in these sentences help you better comprehend the text?**

E. **Listen to an interview about archaeology. Take notes. Use your notes to discuss these questions with a partner.**

1. What is the Dr. Mary Benson's definition of archaeology? Of history?

2. Why is archaeology so important for studying the Inca?

F. **What ideas are described in both the reading and listening? Write a summary that connects those ideas.**

VOCABULARY CHECK

A. Review the vocabulary items in the Vocabulary Preview. Write their definitions and add examples. Use a dictionary if necessary.

B. Complete each sentence using the correct vocabulary item from the box. Use the correct form.

advanced	ancient	construction	field	invasion
origin	physical	remains	technique	value

1. They first discovered the .... of *Homo habilis* at Olduvai Gorge.

2. There is a lot of .... evidence, such as bones and tools, that suggests *Homo habilis* came to this site.

3. The .... of our species and our culture are in Africa.

4. Because of the discovery of Machu Picchu and Inca artifacts, we now know that the Inca had a(n) .... understanding of engineering.

5. The Chinese used many different .... to construct the parts of the Great Wall.

6. Many artifacts and historical records were lost because of the .... of European powers during the 16th century.

7. Stonehenge is a(n) .... structure that was built more than 4,000 years ago in Wiltshire, England.

8. History is a(n) .... that studies the past by looking at written records.

9. The .... of archaeology is in the knowledge that it gives us about earlier human civilizations and how those people lived.

10. It took about 15 years to complete the .... of the Parthenon in ancient Greece.

❖ Go to MyEnglishLab to complete a skill practice and to join in collaborative activities.

LANGUAGE SKILL

UTILIZING THE SIMPLE PAST PASSIVE

WHY IT'S USEFUL By using the simple past passive, you can use another verb form to talk about a subject. This is especially useful when you focus on a specific topic in your speaking and writing.

❖ Go to MyEnglishLab for the Language Skill presentation and practice.

VOCABULARY STRATEGY

CREATING FLASHCARDS TO STUDY VOCABULARY

WHY IT'S USEFUL By using flashcards to study vocabulary, you can practice English anywhere you go. Making flashcards for yourself will help you to better remember the words that you want know.

Flashcards are a useful tool that you can easily create to help yourself learn vocabulary. They allow you to take your study materials and use them anywhere—on the bus, at the beach, or in bed.

Making the Flashcard

The first thing you need is an index card. They are usually 3 by 5 inches, but larger sizes are also available. On the front, write the word that you want to learn, for example:

architecture

Index card

On the back, there are a number of things you can write: the part of speech (noun, verb, etc.), the definition, an example sentence with the word, a picture to illustrate the word. Consider doing the following:

- Include a definition, but write *your own* definition of each word. Do not simply copy a definition from a dictionary.

- Write an example sentence with the word, but leave a blank space—where the word should be in the sentence (see reason below).

- Draw a simple picture or image of the word on the card.

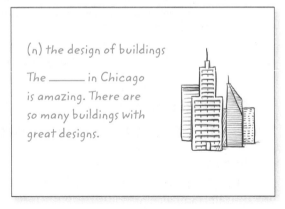

(n) the design of buildings

The _____ in Chicago is amazing. There are so many buildings with great designs.

Making your own definitions and drawing pictures will help you to create a deeper connection with the vocabulary that you want to learn, and this will help you to remember it better.

Using the Flashcard

Now that you've made your flashcards, take them anywhere. When starting to practice with a set of new words, go through the flashcards forwards, that is, by reading the side of the card with just the vocabulary word on it. Turn to the back and read the definition. Read the example sentence aloud, filling in the blank space with the new word.

After going through the flashcards forwards a few times, go through them backwards, that is by looking at the side with the definition, sentence, and picture. Read the example sentence first, and try to fill in the blank with the correct vocabulary word. If that doesn't work, look at the definition and picture to remind you. Then turn the card over to confirm. Practice with friends, too—it'll be more fun.

> **TIP**
>
> Using flashcards is only one way to learn vocabulary. Try it out, and if it doesn't work, find your own way to learn. What's most important is being an active learner and trying to practice English on your own.

EXERCISE 8

A. Go through the vocabulary in the unit. Select eight words to make vocabulary cards with. Then take a few pieces of paper and make them into flashcard size (or get index cards). Write the words on the front of the cards.

B. Write your own definitions and example sentences on the cards. Be sure to use a blank space in the example sentence. Draw a picture on each, too.

C. Take some time to practice going through the cards backwards and forwards. Then exchange your cards with a partner. Test your partner by reading the word on the front. If your partner can't remember the definition, remind him or her by reading the example sentence. Do this for all of the cards.

> **TIP**
>
> To do well on high-stakes tests like the GRE and GMAT, you need to have a strong vocabulary. The vocabulary-learning methods presented here can help you prepare for those tests.

🔾 Go to MyEnglishLab to complete a skill practice.

APPLY YOUR SKILLS

WHY IT'S USEFUL By applying the skills you have learned in this unit, you will be able to identify relationships between ideas as you participate in college-level courses.

ASSIGNMENT

Prepare and participate in a pair presentation that compares and contrasts two historical sites. Use your research and what you have learned about comparing and contrasting ideas to help the audience understand the relationship between the two sites.

BEFORE YOU LISTEN

A. Before you listen, discuss these questions with a partner or group.

1. Describe some basic similarities between Machu Picchu and Olduvai Gorge.

2. How were the people who lived at the two sites different? Explain.

3. You have learned a lot about Machu Picchu and Olduvai Gorge. Are there any questions that you still have about the sites? What are you still curious about?

B. You will listen to a lecture about some unanswered questions (questions without good answers) concerning Machu Picchu and Olduvai Gorge. As you listen, think about these questions.

1. Is there anything that we don't know about the human-like people of Olduvai Gorge? What do you think?

2. What are some of the mysteries of Machu Picchu?

C. Review the Unit Skills Summary. As you listen to the lecture and prepare for your presentation, apply the skills you learned in the unit.

UNIT SKILLS SUMMARY

RECOGNIZE THE RELATIONSHIPS BETWEEN IDEAS BY USING THESE SKILLS:

Compare similar ideas

- Show that ideas are similar with words like *similarly, likewise, as well*, etc.
- Use comparisons to make a conclusion.

Contrast different ideas

- Point out the difference between two things using contrasting words like *however, while*, etc.
- Use contrast to support a main idea or point of view.

Understand relationships between ideas

- Read the sentences to get a good understanding of their meaning.
- Identify the relationship between the sentences.
- Use the relationship to better understand the main ideas presented in the text.

Utilize the simple past passive

- Focus attention on the receiver of an action.
- Use this form when the subject of a sentences is unknown, obvious, or unimportant.

Create flashcards to study vocabulary

- Make a flashcard using the new vocabulary and include both your own definition and a sample sentence.
- Use the flashcard to study vocabulary by yourself or with others.

LISTEN

A. Listen to the lecture and take notes. Try completing the T-chart with information from the lecture.

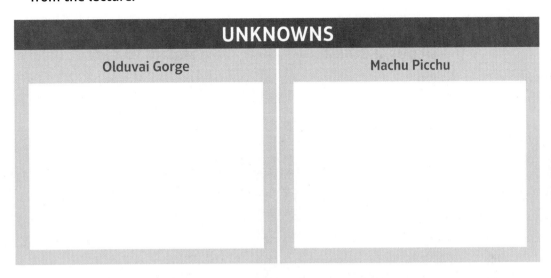

UNKNOWNS	
Olduvai Gorge	**Machu Picchu**

B. Compare notes with a partner. Do you have the same ideas? How did the skills you studied in this unit help you to understand the lecture?

C. Review the questions from Before You Listen, Part B. Listen to the lecture again. Work with a partner and use your notes to answer the questions.

Go to MyEnglishLab to listen more closely and answer the critical thinking questions.

THINKING CRITICALLY

Discuss the questions with one or more students.

1. Read the following excerpt from the listening. What is the relationship between the ideas in the two sentences? How is relationship language useful when talking about unanswered questions at Olduvai Gorge?

> **Professor:** Researchers know from fossils that modern humans evolved in Africa about 200,000 years ago. However, there aren't many fossils of *Homo sapiens*— humans—and more research needs to be done to understand our past.

2. One goal of studying our evolutionary history as *Homo sapiens* is to understand the environmental conditions that made us different from other species. We know a lot about the past, but there is a lot that we do not know about Machu Picchu, which is less than 600 years old. Do you think we will ever really know about our evolutionary history? Can we know it? Should we try to understand it? Explain your thoughts.

THINKING VISUALLY

A. Look at the Venn diagram. Describe it with a partner.

OLDUVAI GORGE   **MACHU PICCHU**

located in Tanzania

discovered in
the 20th century

hidden for years

located in Peru

B. Use information from the unit, including your notes in the Venn diagram on page 72, to add more information to the diagram. Consider things like the mysteries, location, and discoveries involved with each site. Then present the diagram to a partner. Do you both have the same information? Are Venn diagrams good for comparing and contrasting? Why or why not?

THINKING ABOUT LANGUAGE

A. Complete the sentences. Use the verbs in parentheses. Use the correct forms (tense and voice).

> For help with the simple past passive, go to MyEnglishLab, History, Part 1, Language Skill.

1. Machu Picchu .... (build) in a high location that was difficult to get to.

2. Few fossils of *Homo sapiens* .... (find) at Olduvai Gorge.

3. The Inca .... (grow) many different foods in their lands.

4. Artifacts .... (discover) near the ancient site.

B. Work with a small group. Review the vocabulary from the unit. Choose five words that you find to be the most challenging. Then write each word and its definition on an index card or a small piece of paper. Each person in the group does the same. Collect all the cards from your group. Have a student select one and read *only* the definition to everyone else. The others students then guess the word on the card. If the answer is correct, that person makes an example sentence with the word.

PAIR PRESENTATION

A. The following is a list of historical sites. With a partner, read through the list and discuss what you know about each one.

the Great Wall of China

the Palace of Versailles

Stonehenge

the Statue of Liberty

the Wall of Jericho

the Great Pyramid of Giza

The Great Pyramid of Giza

B. You and your partner will give a 2–3-minute presentation comparing two historical sites.

You can use the historical sites from Part A or you can choose others. While researching, consider the following questions:

- Where are the places located?
- Who are the people that made them?
- What was their purpose?
- Are they still in use?
- What interesting fact or insight (new and useful understanding) about the past have we learned from them?

Focus your presentation on 2–3 ideas that allow you to make interesting comparisons. Include visual aids (photos, maps, etc.) to help the audience understand. Decide what each person will present on.

C. Listen to the presentations of other pairs and takes notes. After each presentation, ask questions about what you heard.

🔾 Go to MyEnglishLab to watch Dr. Hunt's concluding video and to complete a self-assessment.

Our everyday experiences are based on how we interact with nature

CHEMICAL ENGINEERING

Presentations

UNIT PROFILE

In this unit, you will learn about lake ecology. Ecology is how plants, animals, and people are connected to each other and to their environment. You will also learn about a situation in deep water called hydrostatic pressure.

You will prepare and give an individual presentation on a process related to lake ecology.

OUTCOMES

- Identify parts of a presentation
- Plan for a presentation
- Make predictions
- Explain order with linking words
- Choose the right level of formality

For more about **CHEMICAL ENGINEERING**, see ❷❸.
See also ⬚R and ⬚W **CHEMICAL ENGINEERING** ❶❷❸.

GETTING STARTED

⟳ Go to MyEnglishLab to watch Professor Spakowitz's introductory video and to complete a self-assessment.

Discuss these questions with a partner or group.

1. Have you ever visited a lake? If so, describe it. If not, imagine a lake. What is a lake like?

2. What do you know about the nature—animals, plants, and land—around lakes?

3. In his introduction, Professor Spakowitz says that we all experience hydrostatic pressure when we swim in deep water. What pressure do you feel in deep water? What causes this pressure?

SKILL 1

IDENTIFYING PARTS OF A PRESENTATION

WHY IT'S USEFUL By identifying the parts of a presentation, you can better understand the speaker's main ideas. It also can help you organize your own presentations more effectively.

Presentations are a big part of university life and come in different forms. Students give presentations as class assignments. Professors give lectures to their classes. Both students and professors give talks at academic and professional conferences.

What exactly are presentations? At a university, a presentation is when a speaker describes an idea or subject to an audience. The audience may not know much about the idea or subject. Therefore, it is important to present the information clearly. One way speakers do this is by dividing the presentation into parts. Study the chart.

Presentation Part	Purpose
Introduction	to get the audience's attention
	to introduce the topic
	to introduce the main ideas
Body	to explain the main ideas
	to support the main ideas with details or examples
Conclusion	to restate the topic
	to summarize the main points
	to close with a conclusion

Lectures have a couple of unique features. First, while most presenters follow the organization in the previous chart, some professors in their lectures do not. They may leave out part of the introduction or the conclusion. Also, while presentations can vary in length depending on program schedule, university lectures are almost always about 50 minutes long, the length of the class. A professor may rush through some parts of the lecture. For example, she may speak more quickly toward the end of lecture if there is still a lot of information to share.

How can you understand a presentation or lecture when the speaker gives a lot of information? Listen for **signposting expressions**, words that help listeners get ready for certain types of information. See some examples in the chart.

PART	SIGNPOSTING EXPRESSION
Introduction	
Introducing focus	Today, I'll be talking about … I'll discuss … I'd like to introduce …
Introducing main ideas	First, I'll discuss … Then I'll go on to … Toward the end, I'd like to …
Body	
First main point	First … First off … The first point I'd like to make is …
Second, third, etc., main point	On to my second point … The next point I'd like to discuss is …
Last main point	That brings me to my final point … Finally, I'd like to talk about … My last point is …
Conclusion	
Restating and summarizing	I'd like to conclude by … To summarize …
Final sentences	(Are there) any questions?

CULTURE NOTE

When speakers conclude a talk, they don't usually say "Thank you." Instead, they often ask the audience or students if they have any questions. This is an invitation to ask questions about anything that is not clear.

VOCABULARY PREVIEW

Read the vocabulary items in the box. Circle the ones you know. Put a question mark next to the ones you don't know.

introduce	surface (n)	landscape	influence (n)	ponds
environments	factors	climate	planet	shallow

EXERCISE 1

A. Imagine a body of water that you have visited. What kind was it—for example, a lake, ocean, river? Did it seem healthy or unhealthy? Explain.

B. Listen to the beginning of a lake ecology lecture. Complete the chart by following these steps:

- Check (✔) the signposting expressions you hear.
- Write the idea introduced.

Part of Lecture	Signpost Language	Idea Introduced
Introduction	☑ I'm going to talk about …	lake ecology
	☐ I want to introduce …	
	☐ I'll introduce …	
	☐ I'll start with …	
	☐ To begin with …	
	☐ Then …	
	☐ After that …	
	☐ Finally …	
	☐ In conclusion …	
Body	☐ First (off) …	
	☐ Next …	

C. Did the signposting expressions help you follow the professor's ideas? What other expressions could the professor have used to help you follow the ideas?

EXERCISE 2

A. Listen again. Number the topics in the order that the professor will discuss them.

Lake Tahoe, between Nevada and California

A small pond

.... physical factors that influence lakes

.... ecological or biological processes in lakes

.... background on lakes

.... how the physical environment affects a lake's ecological systems

B. Discuss these questions in a small group.

1. Why does the professor think students should study lakes?

2. What's the difference between a lake and a pond?

EXERCISE 3

A. Think about a geographical feature—a lake or a mountain, for example—that you know well. Imagine you are going to give a presentation about it. Write three important points that you will talk about.

1. ....

2. ....

3. ....

B. Work with a partner. Give a brief introduction to your presentation using signposting expressions. Then listen to your partner's introduction and take notes.

VOCABULARY CHECK

A. Review the vocabulary items in the Vocabulary Preview. Write their definitions and add examples. Use a dictionary if necessary.

B. Complete each sentence using the correct vocabulary item(s) from the box. Use the correct form.

climate	environment	factor	influence	introduce
landscape	planet	pond	shallow	surface

1. .... are similar to lakes, but they are not as deep. They are quite ....

2. Pollution has damaged the .... , making the air, soil, and water dirty.

3. There are many physical .... that affect lakes and the surrounding .... of trees, shrubs, and other plants.

4. Changes in .... affect water temperature, especially at the .... of lakes and oceans.

5. As Earth's average air temperature gets warmer, the ....'s water temperatures will increase as well. That is just one example of industrialization's .... on our lives.

6. I'd like to .... the next presenter. She is an expert on lake ecology.

🔊 Go to MyEnglishLab to complete vocabulary and skill practices, and to join in collaborative activities.

SKILL 2

PLANNING FOR A PRESENTATION

WHY IT'S USEFUL By carefully organizing and planning your presentation, you can have a clear "road map" for what you want to say. You will feel more prepared and confident, and your audience will appreciate your preparation.

Think about a presentation or lecture you really enjoyed and still remember clearly. How many of the following things were true?

- The speaker was interested in and knowledgeable about the topic.
- The speaker understood the audience well.
- The speaker prepared for the presentation and presented the information in an organized way.

If the speaker planned for the presentation, then all of the above were probably true. The following tips can help you plan a successful presentation.

Be interested in and knowledgeable about the topic.

Choose a topic you want to share with others and are already somewhat knowledgeable about. You may have to do additional research as well. Your presentation will be stronger if you provide support and source information for your main points.

Understand the audience.

Try to anticipate (know and prepare for) who your audience is and how much they know. For example, let's say you are an expert on lake ecology. If you are giving a presentation to high school students, you should give a brief introduction about lake ecology, with a simple definition and some general ideas. However, if you are giving a presentation to other lake ecology experts, you should give information that is detailed and specific.

Prepare and organize your ideas.

Preparing for your presentation is the key to success. Preparing well includes these steps:

1. Organizing the content: Choose your main points. Then decide how to support or explain your main points (e.g., with examples).

2. Practicing your presentation: Practice your presentation a couple of times. Make sure it's not too long or too short.

Study this chart:

Dos	Don'ts
• Focus on a few main and supporting ideas. • Give clear definitions of technical terms. • Keep the presentation within time limits.	• Don't add unimportant details. • Don't forget to define technical terms. • Don't make the presentation too long or too short.

VOCABULARY PREVIEW

Read the vocabulary items in the box. Circle the ones you know. Put a question mark next to the ones you don't know.

seasons	sand	streams (n)	take place	reach (v)	creates

EXERCISE 4

A. Imagine you are at a lake on a hot summer day. Touch the surface of the water. What do you notice about the water temperature? Now reach toward the bottom. Does the temperature change? Why or why not?

B. Listen to a lecture about the water in lakes. Is the main idea clear? What does the professor say to help you understand the main idea? Look at the process diagram as you listen.

> ### Glossary
>
> Evaporation: the process of liquid becoming gas
>
> Cycle: stages of change or development
>
> Density: the relationship between an object's weight and the amount of space it fills

THERMAL STRATIFICATION

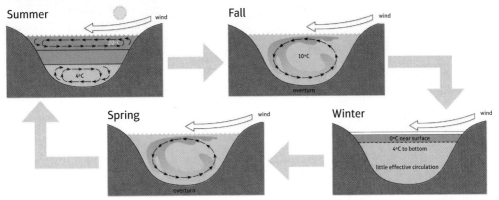

C. Discuss these questions with a partner. Give reasons for your answers.

1. Does the professor seem knowledgeable about the topic?

2. Does the professor explain the topic clearly for the audience (a class of students)?

3. Is the professor well prepared?

EXERCISE 5

A. Listen again. What topics does the professor discuss? Check (✓) them.

☐ seasonal effects on lake temperature   ☐ how water gets into lakes

☐ thermal stratification   ☐ how lakes are created

☐ the biodiversity of lakes   ☐ why some lakes are deeper than others

B. Read the statements. Circle *T* (True) or *F* (False). Correct the false statements.

T / F   1. Human use and evaporation are the two ways lakes lose water.

T / F   2. Underground water is not a water source for most lakes.

T / F   3. Warm water is less dense than cold water.

T / F   4. Light from the sun does not reach the bottom of lakes.

T / F   5. Lake water mixes in the fall more than in the summer.

EXERCISE 6

A. How might the professor's presentation be different if it were to a group of other professors? Discuss your ideas with a partner.

B. Imagine you are giving a presentation about lake ecology (or a similar topic) to two different groups—students and professors. What information would you include for each group? Write *S* (students), *P* (professors), or *B* (both). Compare answers with a partner.

.... definition of *lake*   .... why studying lakes is important

.... types of things that live in lakes   .... chemicals that affect lake water

.... new research on lake ecology   .... decreases in funding for lake ecology research

VOCABULARY CHECK

A. Review the vocabulary items in the Vocabulary Preview. Write their definitions and add examples. Use a dictionary if necessary.

B. Complete each sentence using the correct vocabulary item from the box. Use the correct form.

create	reach	sand	season	stream	take place

1. Rivers and .... bring water into lakes.

2. Temperatures change from one .... to the next. It is usually warmest in the summer.

3. The chemical engineering conference .... every April.

4. Cold water stays at the bottom of lakes because the sun cannot .... it.

5. White or gray .... is often on beaches next to rivers, lakes, and oceans.

6. Water pollution .... many problems for organisms that live in lakes.

🔵 **Go to MyEnglishLab to complete vocabulary and skill practices, and to join in collaborative activities.**

INTEGRATED SKILLS

MAKING PREDICTIONS

WHY IT'S USEFUL By making predictions about a text before you read, you can make a deeper connection with it. Also, by thinking about what you *already* know about the topic of a text, you can better understand and learn its content.

The New York Times headline on July 21, 1969, was "Men Walk on Moon." Below the headline was the subtitle "Astronauts Land on Plain; Collect Rocks, Plant Flag." There was also a picture of two men in spacesuits walking on the moon. Without reading the article, we know that the article will contain information about who the men are, when they landed on the moon, and what they did there. How do we know this information will be there? Because we predict it from the title, subtitle, and image.

Title → **MEN WALK ON MOON**

Subtitle → **Astronauts Land on Plain; Collect Rocks, Plant Flag**

CULTURE NOTE

The staking of the US flag on the surface of the moon was photographed during the first *Apollo 11* lunar landing mission. The image shows astronauts Neil Armstrong (left) and Edwin "Buzz" Aldrin Jr. (right) standing on the so-called Sea of Tranquility region of the moon. The photo was taken by a camera mounted in the astronauts' lunar module, *Eagle.* Meanwhile, the service module, *Columbia*, stayed in lunar orbit, piloted by astronaut Michael Collins.

TIP

You will need to research topics for presentations and other assignments. There is a lot of information on the Internet, and most of those articles, videos, and podcasts will have titles. Read the title and make predictions about the content to help you decide if the material will be useful for your presentation or assignment.

How can you prepare yourself for a new reading? Make predictions based on what you can see at a glance: titles, subtitles, other headings, and images. Your predictions do not have to be correct. In fact, incorrect predictions can help active readers make new predictions while they read a text. They will change their predictions and make new predictions, making more connections. This is very active reading.

What kinds of things should you preview to make predictions? Why are they useful? Study the chart.

What to Look For		Why It's Useful
Titles and subtitles	Main ideas and key content words for the whole text	Making predictions about the main ideas will help you understand what the information in the text relates to. The most important information is often in the title and subtitle.
Section headings	Main ideas and key content words for sections of the text	Longer texts have different sections. Each section focuses on one of the main ideas.
Images, graphs, and captions	Important details, concepts, and statistics	Images and graphs make complex details, concepts, and statistics easier to understand. Looking at them before you read will give you clues about important ideas. They often have captions (words that explain the image or graph) that provide clues about why the image or graph is important.

When you make guesses before and while you read, you are activating your prior knowledge about the topic. In other words, you are starting to connect the knowledge that you already have with the new information that you are reading. This can help you better understand and remember the main ideas and details.

TIP

Presentations with visuals such as PowerPoint are common at universities, and they always have titles. Just like titles of books and articles, titles of presentations can give you a good idea of what they are about. This is true of things you watch and listen to, too, such as videos and podcasts.

Read the vocabulary items in the box. Circle the ones you know. Put a question mark next to the ones you don't know.

liquid	explode	breathe	reduce	demonstrate	pressure

EXERCISE 7

A. Read the title of the article. Then look at the picture and caption. Make two predictions about the article. Tell a partner.

B. Read the first paragraph of the article. Were your predictions in Part A correct? Should you change your predictions? Discuss with a partner.

C. Read the rest of the article. Take notes on the main ideas.

Warming Waters Create Problems for Fish

1 What do we have in common with fish? Quite a bit. Among other things, fish and people need oxygen to survive. Just like humans have trouble when oxygen (O_2) concentrations in the air are low, less oxygen in water creates problems for fish. And water temperature is one of the biggest reasons for changes in oxygen concentrations.

Shaking the can adds heat to the soda, which makes the CO_2 escape. When the temperature of a liquid increases, it cannot hold as much gas.

2 At lower temperatures, water holds more gases, such as carbon dioxide (CO_2) and oxygen. (Gases in water are called *dissolved* gases.) However, as temperature increases, water molecules have more energy and push the gas out. Imagine a can of soda. Soda is mostly water, but it has dissolved CO_2 in it (the bubbles in soda are dissolved CO_2 escaping). When a can of soda is cold, the liquid soda holds the CO_2 well. However, if you shake the can and then open it, what happens?

3 The gas and liquid inside the can explode out. That's because shaking the can adds heat to the soda. As the liquid soda gets warmer, the can releases CO_2. As you open the can, the CO_2 explodes out. Although there is no explosion, gases in lake water behave in the same way. When a lake is warm, the water holds less gas. Therefore, there is less oxygen for fish to breathe.

4 Another factor that affects oxygen concentration in water is photosynthesis, the way that green plants make their food using light from the sun and dissolved CO_2. Aquatic plants release oxygen as a result of photosynthesis. When there is a lot of sun during the daytime, plants produce a lot of oxygen for the lake. At night, they produce less oxygen. However, fish and other organisms use oxygen both day and night, so there is a lot less oxygen in the water at 3 a.m. than at 3 p.m.

5 How is this a problem? Average global temperatures are increasing, and this could have a terrible effect on aquatic life. Because higher temperatures reduce the amount of dissolved oxygen and CO_2 in water, fish will be in serious danger. There will also be less oxygen from plants because plants will not have enough CO_2 for photosynthesis. Global warming will have widespread effects.

Glossary

Concentration: a large amount of something in a particular place

Dissolved: mixed in or broken up

Molecule: one or more atoms that form the smallest unit of a particular substance

Aquatic: water-related

Gills: a fish's lungs

D. Imagine that you read the above passage before class. Now in class, you hear a lecture called "Dissolved Gases in Lake Water." Make three predictions about the content of the lecture.

1. ....

2. ....

3. ....

E. Now listen to the lecture and take notes.

F. Compare your notes with your predictions from Part D. Were your predictions correct? Was it easier to make predictions about the article, or the lecture? Why? Share your ideas with a partner or small group.

VOCABULARY CHECK

A. Review the vocabulary items in the Vocabulary Preview. Write their definitions and add examples. Use a dictionary if necessary.

B. Complete each sentence using the correct vocabulary item from the box. Use the correct form.

breathe	demonstrate	explode	liquid	pressure	reduce

1. The gases in Lake Nyos in Cameroon, West Africa, built up and after some time ...., killing many people in the area.

2. To .... how the water cycle works, I'm going to start by showing you this diagram of a lake and the lakebed below it.

3. If we .... the amount of carbon we put into the air, we can possibly slow global warming.

4. The three forms the chemical substance H_2O can become are solid, gas, and .... It can also be "in-between" forms, like snow and fog.

5. Fish .... somewhat like we do. They take in water through their mouth and then the oxygen is separated out as the water passes over their gills.

6. As we swam deeper, the .... of the water became greater, causing our ears to pop.

⬆ Go to MyEnglishLab to complete a skill practice and to join in collaborative activities.

LANGUAGE SKILL
EXPLAINING ORDER WITH LINKING WORDS

WHY IT'S USEFUL By using linking words for chronological order (time), you can better explain how ideas relate to each other in a presentation. Understanding linking words can also help you follow the order of ideas in a lecture.

⬆ Go to MyEnglishLab for the Language Skill presentation and practice.

VOCABULARY STRATEGY
CHOOSING THE RIGHT LEVEL OF FORMALITY

WHY IT'S USEFUL By understanding what technical language is and when to use it, you can communicate with different audiences more effectively.

Technical language is the vocabulary that experts use to talk about their academic or professional field. You will often hear this language in specialized presentations and lectures. In contrast, nontechnical or common language is used in everyday situations, such as conversations over dinner.

To understand the difference between technical and common usage, consider a species of fish called *Thunnus albacares*, also known as the yellowfin tuna. Yellowfin tuna is often eaten as sushi. When talking to a friend about the delicious sushi you ate last night, would you say this?: *We went to a good restaurant. The Thunnus albacares sushi was amazing!* Of course not. In fact, the only situation where we hear *Thunnus albacares* is when scientists or policymakers are discussing it. For example:

Correct: Overfishing and climate change are threatening a number of tuna species, including Thunnus albacares, Thunnus obesus, and Thunnus thynnus.

In this situation, it would be strange to hear *yellowfin*:

Incorrect: Overfishing and climate change are threatening a number of tuna species, including yellowfin, Thunnus obesus, and Thunnus thynnus.

Technical Term	Common Term
Thunnus albacares	yellowfin tuna
Urocyon littoralis	island fox
stratification	layering
aquatic	water-related
solution	mixture
canine	dog
habitat	home

Thunnus albacares

How do you know when to use technical language? It mostly depends on the audience. For people who know the topic well, use technical language. With an unfamiliar audience, you should define the terms clearly when you first use them.

EXERCISE 8

A. Underline the technical term in each pair.

1. a. organism   b. living thing
2. a. canine species   b. types of dog
3. a. atmospheric pressure   b. air pressure
4. a. environment   b. ecological system
5. a. thermal stratification   b. temperature at different layers
6. a. amount   b. concentration

B. Choose the best word or phrase to complete each item. Then compare answers with a partner.

1. Lecture:

   Speaker: Good afternoon. It's an honor to be giving a lecture at the Northeast Lake Ecology Society. As you know, today I'll be talking about the importance of **biodiversity / different types of life** in this area's lakes.

2. Student conversation:

   A: We really need to protect our **ecological systems / environment**. We only have one, and we can't replace it if we destroy it.

   B: Yeah, I agree with you. So what are we going to do about it?

   A: I wish I had the answer. Anyway, want to get some lunch?

3. Presentation to lake ecology class:

   Speaker: Thermal stratification affects **organisms / living things** in lakes.

4. Discussion between two family members:

   A: What's the right **concentration / amount** of sugar in lemonade to make it taste good?

   B: Use as much as you'd like. Everybody's taste is different.

C. Work in a small group. Discuss whether you would use technical or common language in the following situations. Give reasons.

1. You are giving a short presentation on threatened species as part of a public speaking course at your university.

2. You are at an academic lecture on lake ecosystems. You want to ask the presenter a question about the lecture.

3. You are talking to your professor about aquatic plant life during office hours.

⬤ Go to MyEnglishLab to complete a skill practice.

APPLY YOUR SKILLS

WHY IT'S USEFUL By applying the skills you have learned in this unit, you will be able to identify parts of presentations and lectures, plan your own presentations, and engage in college-level courses.

ASSIGNMENT

Prepare and give an individual presentation on a process related to lake ecology. Use what you have learned about presenting to organize and deliver an effective presentation.

BEFORE YOU LISTEN

A. Before you listen, discuss these questions with one or more students.

1. Think about lake ecology. What are some physical factors that affect lakes?

2. How are living things affected by their environments?

3. The lecture is called "Water Pressure and Aquatic Life." What do you think it will be about?

B. You will listen to a lecture on hydrostatic pressure. As you listen, think about these questions.

1. What is hydrostatic pressure?

2. How does hydrostatic pressure affect people?

3. How does hydrostatic pressure affect fish ?

C. Review the Unit Skills Summary on the next page. As you listen to the lecture and prepare for your individual presentation, apply the skills you learned in this unit.

UNIT SKILLS SUMMARY

BE BETTER AT PRESENTING INFORMATION BY USING THESE SKILLS:

Identify parts of a presentation

- Listen for the main idea in the introduction and conclusion.
- Pay attention to the body for key points and details.
- Listen for signposting words to help you understand the different parts of the presentation.

Plan for a presentation

- Know your audience.
- Identify your main points and examples.
- Organize your information so it is clear.

Make predictions

- Use titles, subtitles, headings, and captions to predict the content of a lecture or text.

Explain order with linking words

- Make clear the connections between your main points by using linking words.

Choose the right level of formality

- Understand when to use technical language and when to use common language.

LISTEN

A. Listen to the lecture about hydrostatic pressure and aquatic life. Try using this outline to help you.

Hydrostatic pressure

   1. Description ....

   2. Effects on humans ....

   3. Effects on fish ....

Glossary

Organ: a part of the body that has a particular purpose

Gravity: the force that makes objects fall to the ground

Lung: one of two organs in your body that you use for breathing

B. Compare notes with a partner. Do you both have the same main ideas? What skills from this unit helped you identify main ideas?

C. Review the questions from Before You Listen, Part B. Listen to the lecture again. Work with a partner and use your notes to answer the questions.

Go to MyEnglishLab to listen more closely and answer the critical thinking questions.

THINKING CRITICALLY

Discuss these questions with another student.

1. The speaker discusses the topics in this order: definition of hydrostatic pressure, effects on living things, how aquatic animals breathe. Why do you think he organizes the topics in this way?

2. The speaker talks about the experience of swimming underwater. Why do you think he uses this example?

THINKING VISUALLY

A. Look at the diagram of two containers. Match the equations with their explanations. (Note: m=depth in meters and p=pressure)

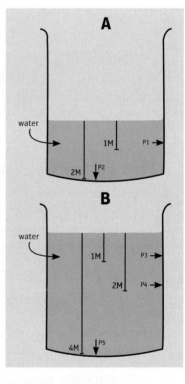

.... 1. p1 = p3

.... 2. p2 = p4

.... 3. p5 > p3 + p4

a. At the same depth, the pressure is the same in every direction.

b. At the same depth, the pressure on the outside of a container is the same.

c. Pressure is higher at lower depths.

B. The listening includes the following information: Water pressure pushes down from the top, and it also pushes out toward the sides. Look at the image of a water container with two holes in it. How does that information explain the way that water comes out of the container?

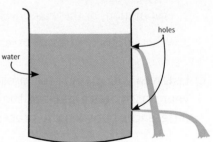

THINKING ABOUT LANGUAGE

A. Complete the partial transcript from a conference presentation. Use the correct form of the words from the box or your own ideas.

For help with explaining order with linking words, go to MyEnglishLab, Chemical Engineering, Part 1, Language Skill.

then	toward the end	organism	thing
thermal stratification	type	species	layering
concentration	to begin with	fourth	build-up

Today, I'll be discussing local lake ecology and the various (1) ....._organisms_..... that live in these lakes. First, I'll talk about (2) .... and how seasonal changes affect lake temperatures. (3) .... I'll move on to examples of specific plant and animal (4) .... in lakes. (5) .... I'll take a look at some environmental problems that lakes face, including global warming and how this affects (6) .... of oxygen and carbon dioxide, and so on.

B. Work with a partner. Take turns reading your completed transcript out loud.

INDIVIDUAL PRESENTATION

A. You will research, plan, and give a 2–3-minute individual presentation about a lake ecology process. Discuss these questions with one or more students.

What physical, chemical, and biological processes in lakes did you learn about in this unit? What other lake processes do you know about?

B. Think about the following questions as you prepare. Include examples and visuals in your presentation.

1. Do you know about any other processes in lakes, such as photosynthesis, evaporation, or the water cycle? Why are these processes important?

2. What effects do the processes have on other parts of the lake, like plants?

C. Listen to your classmates' presentations. Take notes and pay attention to how your classmates organized their presentations. Then discuss the similarities and differences between the processes your classmates presented.

⬥ Go to MyEnglishLab to watch Professor Spakowitz's concluding video and to complete a self-assessment.

Critical Thinking Skills

Part 2 moves from skill building to application of the skills that require critical thinking. Practice activities tied to specific learning outcomes in each unit require a deeper level of understanding of the academic content.

BIOETHICS

Facts and Opinions

UNIT PROFILE

In this unit, you will learn about DNA, the chemical that contains the information that decides how an organism will develop. You will also learn about how new genetic engineering technology can be used to change our DNA.

You will prepare and participate in a class debate, arguing for or against the use of genetic engineering to treat diseases.

OUTCOMES

- Identify and express facts
- Identify and express opinions
- Identify bias
- Express conditions with *if*
- Examine abbreviations

For more about **BIOETHICS**, see ❶❸. See also R and W **BIOETHICS** ❶❷❸.

GETTING STARTED

⊙ Go to MyEnglishLab to watch Professor Greely's introductory video and to complete a self-assessment.

Discuss these questions with a partner or group.

1. What is DNA? Why is it important for life?

2. Would you change your own DNA to become smarter? To have different hair? Do you think it would be safe? Why or why not?

3. In his introduction, Professor Greely introduces two terms in ethics: *consequentialist* and *deontological*. He defines the first as looking at the result of an action to judge whether the action is good or bad. He defines the second as looking at whether the action followed the rules, such as religion or cultural values. Which approach do you take when judging an action?

SKILL 1

IDENTIFYING AND EXPRESSING FACTS

WHY IT'S USEFUL By identifying facts in lectures, you can feel confident that the information is true. By expressing facts in presentations and discussions, you can appear knowledgeable and scholarly.

This is a book. It is made of paper. You are reading it right now. These are all **facts.** What are facts? They are ideas that

- we can prove: A handful of rocks is heavier than a handful of feathers.

- most people accept: Earth is round.

- we know are true: When you drop something, it falls.

- we have evidence for: **According to a recent study**, large parts of Australia's Great Barrier Reef have died off.

Facts typically include

- numbers and statistics: There was a **20 percent decrease** in HIV cases over the past decade.

- references to the past: Penicillin was discovered by Alexander Fleming **in 1928**.

- references to research studies: **Research has shown** that there are two ways that the brain forms memories.

When talking about facts, use the following kinds of expressions. They will help you signal that you are expressing a fact.

Expressions That Introduce Facts

As the facts show …	Research has shown …
As we've seen …	Researchers have learned …
According to a study …	Results from their research show …
Based on these findings …	The report concludes …
It's a known fact that …	

VOCABULARY PREVIEW

Read the vocabulary items in the box. Circle the ones you know. Put a question mark next to the ones you don't know.

cell	contains	attached	approximately
organized	twist (v)	structure	

Glossary

Hereditary: passed from parents to children

Base: (n) the main part of a substance, to which other things can be added

Molecular biology: the area of biology that studies living things at the molecular level, molecules being the smallest part of something and made up of one or more atoms

EXERCISE 1

A. What sources do you use when you want facts? How do you know the sources are credible?

B. Look at the diagram and listen to the lecture about DNA. What factual information does the speaker give? What expressions does the speaker use?

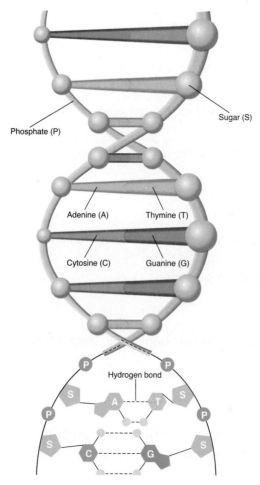

Phosphate (P)

Sugar (S)

Adenine (A)   Thymine (T)

Cytosine (C)   Guanine (G)

Hydrogen bond

DNA (deoxyribonucleic acid) and its double helix structure

1. **Kinds of information:**

    statistics ....

    years / dates ....

2. **Expressions:** ....

C. Was it easy to identify the kinds of information and expressions that the speaker used to present facts?

EXERCISE 2

🎧 A. Listen again. Then read the statements. Circle *T* (True) or *F* (False).
Correct the false statements.

T / F   1. DNA is found in all human cells.

T / F   2. DNA is the cause of some diseases.

T / F   3. Human DNA contains 13 billion base pairs.

T / F   4. DNA is made up of four bases: adenine, thymine, guanine, cytosine.

T / F   5. Each base can connect to every other base.

T / F   6. DNA was discovered in 1953.

T / F   7. Scientists are not yet able to change human DNA.

B. Compare answers with a partner.

EXERCISE 3

A. Write two facts that you know about DNA. Share them with a partner.

....

....

B. Did you use any years, dates, statistics, or expressions to express the facts?
Would adding this information make it clearer that you are stating facts? Explain.

VOCABULARY CHECK

A. Review the vocabulary items in the Vocabulary Preview. Write their definitions and add examples. Use a dictionary if necessary.

B. Complete the paragraph with the correct vocabulary items from the box. Use the correct form.

approximately	attach	cell	contain
organize	structure	twist	

Every (1) .... in every living organism (2) .... DNA. Many people consider the discovery of its (3) .... , the double helix, to be one of the most important in all of molecular biology. Human DNA consists of (4) .... 3,000,000,000 base pairs. The base pairs (5) .... to each other, adenine to thymine, and guanine to cytosine, at the center of a DNA strand. Each base pair is connected to a sugar-phosphate backbone. The backbone (6) .... , forming the double helix. Human DNA is (7) .... into 23 pairs of chromosomes. We receive one set from our mother, and the other from our father. This is why it is considered hereditary information.

⊙ Go to MyEnglishLab to complete vocabulary and skill practices, and to join in collaborative activities.

SKILL 2

IDENTIFYING AND EXPRESSING OPINIONS

WHY IT'S USEFUL By identifying opinions, you can understand the personal views of a speaker. You can use opinions to share your beliefs in discussions.

Opinions are the beliefs, viewpoints, and attitudes of the person who speaks them. In general, we express opinions in two ways: by using value and judgment words, and by using personal opinion expressions.

Using value or judgment words to express an opinion is simple: You start with a fact, and add an adjective to it.

Study these examples:

Value and Judgment Words	Example
good	This university has a **good** science program.
bad	The biology professor is **bad.**
unfair	That was an **unfair** decision.
excellent	Marie wrote an **excellent** paper on genetics.
easy	Biology 101 is a very **easy** class.
useful	Dictionaries are **useful** for learning new words.

The following are expressions that introduce opinions, followed by the opinion itself.

Personal Opinion Expression	Example
I believe …	**I believe** that we should not waste money on DNA research.
I think …	**I think** DNA research leads to many positive results.
Personally …	**Personally**, I find the history of DNA research very interesting.
In my opinion …	**In my opinion**, we need to do more to protect endangered species.

Facts and Opinions

We often express facts and opinions together. Your opinion is stronger if you can support it with facts.

> I think the discovery of DNA's double helix is the most important discovery in biology ever. It has helped scientists understand how proteins are made, and it has led to thousands of research studies.

In the example above, the first sentence is an opinion. The speaker supports his opinion with two facts in the second sentence. These facts provide evidence for his claim that the double helix's discovery is the most important in biology. If your facts are strong—that is, if they are statements based on truth and logic—they will make your opinion stronger.

VOCABULARY PREVIEW

Read the vocabulary items in the box. Circle the ones you know. Put a question mark next to the ones you don't know.

sections	cause (v)	location	crops	argument	morals	positive

Glossary

Gene: part of a cell in a living thing that controls how it develops. Parents pass genes on to their children.

Chromosome: the part of the cell that contains the genes that control things like eye color, height, etc.

EXERCISE 4

A. In what situations do you feel free to share your personal opinions? In what situations don't you? Discuss with a partner.

B. Listen to an excerpt from a lecture and class discussion about genetic engineering. Complete the discussion with the words that you hear.

Professor: What does everyone think about this?

Student 1: Well, (1) .... , I agree with the consequentialist side— (2) .... it's OK to change the genes of living things. I mean, we've been genetically engineering crops for thousands of years outside of the laboratory, right—by farming them in certain ways?

Student 2: Yeah, but that process is much more natural. And it takes a long time. (3) .... that genetic engineering is (4) .... Early studies have shown that it can cause major problems for organisms later in life.

Student 1: True.

Professor: Your ideas are (5) ....

C. Which words are value and judgment words? Which are personal opinion expressions?

EXERCISE 5

A. Listen again. Then match the concepts with the phrases to make sentences.

.... 1. Genetic mapping   a. changes genes to make organisms different.

.... 2. Genetic engineering   b. finds the location of genes.

B. Circle the correct words. Then complete the sentences with opinions.

1. The professor thinks that the discovery of DNA **was / wasn't** important
   because ....

2. People who agree with the deontological argument think
   that we **should / shouldn't** use genetic engineering because

   ....

3. People who agree with the consequentialist argument think
   that we **should / shouldn't** use genetic engineering because

   ....

EXERCISE 6

A. Circle the words that express your opinion. Then discuss each statement with a partner or small group. Use facts to support your opinion.

1. Genetic mapping **is / is not** useful.

2. Genetic engineering **is / is not** dangerous.

B. Do you feel comfortable expressing your opinion to others? Are you more comfortable using value judgment words or opinion expressions?

VOCABULARY CHECK

A. Review the vocabulary items in the Vocabulary Preview. Write their definitions and add examples. Use a dictionary if necessary.

B. Complete each sentence using the correct vocabulary item from the box. Use the correct form.

argument	cause	crop	location	morals	positive	section

1. A gene editing technology called CRISPR can cut out small
   .... of DNA and replace them.

2. The results of the study were .... ; people became healthier
   after taking the new medicine.

3. Farmers can use the technology to prevent diseases from developing in their ....

4. It is difficult to know the exact .... of a gene because there are billions of base pairs in the human genome.

5. The main idea of the consequentialist .... is that genetic engineering will help people in the future.

6. Mutations—small changes to genes—can .... disease, but they often have no effect on us.

7. What you believe is acceptable personal behavior depends on your ....

↻ Go to MyEnglishLab to complete vocabulary and skill practices, and to join in collaborative activities.

INTEGRATED SKILLS

IDENTIFYING BIAS

WHY IT'S USEFUL By identifying bias, you can evaluate the quality of information that is presented by a speaker or writer. This can help you to find the best sources and understand whether you can trust certain types of information.

Bias is the way that a person's opinions influence her actions, her writing, etc. Bias can be found in the titles, headlines, images, and statistics of an information source. Additionally, the speaker's or author's choice of words—positive, negative, or neutral—will tell you about her view on a subject.

Identifying bias is important in today's world of numerous news sources. When reading and listening to information, be sure to think about the source's bias and how it affects the information that is presented.

WAYS TO IDENTIFY BIAS

What to Notice	What to Do	Example
Title or headline	Read the title. Is it positive, negative, or neutral?	*How DNA Can Help Us* (positive) *DNA Horror Stories* (negative) *Things We Can Learn from DNA* (neutral)
Word choice	Does the speaker or writer use positive words to describe the subject? Is he presenting an opinion or trying to persuade the audience? Does he use words with positive or negative connotations to describe the subject?	*Using genetic engineering to cure diseases is challenging.* (positive / neutral) *Using genetic engineering to cure diseases is difficult.* (negative)
Statistics / Research	Does the speaker or writer present statistics or research that supports the opinion or not?	*A large government study found that smartphone use does not affect a person's ability to pay attention.* **This research supports findings from earlier, smaller studies that also found no connection between smartphone use and attention.** (positive: The sentence in bold supports the idea in first sentence.) *A large government study found that smartphone use does not affect a person's ability to pay attention.* **Other studies, however, have shown that smartphone use can reduce the amount of time a person can spend paying attention by more than 20 percent.** (negative: The sentence in bold presents an argument against the idea in the first sentence.)
Images	Does the image present the subject in a negative light or a positive light?	
Tone (for audio)	Does the speaker sound positive or negative?	

The chart shows different ways bias can appear. Use the questions to help you look for possible bias in a source. If you think that a source is biased, search for more information from other sources to get the more balanced and accurate information.

VOCABULARY PREVIEW

Read the vocabulary items in the box. Circle the ones you know. Put a question mark next to the ones you don't know.

traditional	cures (n)	editing	scissors
replace	improving	mosquitoes	

Glossary

Germline cells: the egg cells from the mother and sperm cells from the father that join to form a new organism

EXERCISE 7

A. In the media you follow, how do you recognize when information is biased? Is there any value in reading or listening to a point of view that is different from yours? Explain.

B. Listen to the first part of *Science Chat*, a podcast. The interview is about a gene editing technology called CRISPR. Circle the words that describe the tone of each speaker's voice.

Host Sana Patel: positive   negative

Dr. Xavier McMillan: positive   negative

C. Listen again and take notes. Use the notes to answer these questions.

1. Does Sana Patel use any words or phrases that show bias for or against CRISPR? If so, what are they? ....

2. Does Dr. McMillan use any words or phrases that show bias for or against CRISPR? If so, what are they? ....

TIP

Each media organization has its own point of view. But this often prevents it from giving all the information to a viewer. Read multiple sources' reports on the same event. This will give you a more complete picture, and you will start to learn about the biases of the specific media organizations. This is necessary for all research.

CULTURE NOTE

Alzheimer's is a disease that affects memory, thinking, behavior, and emotion. Approximately 50 million people around the world suffer from the disease—more women than men, and mostly people over the age of 65. Studies show that environment and genes play a role. And while some drugs are helpful in slowing the disease, there is currently no cure.

D. Now read the title of the following article. Consider these questions.

1. What can you predict about the article? ....

2. Do you think the author will have a positive, negative, or neutral point of view? Why? ....

E. Read the article. Underline positive words and phrases. Circle negative words and phrases. What does this show about the author's point of view?

The Dangers of Gene Editing

1   In recent years, science has developed a powerful new genetic editing technology: clustered regularly interspaced short palindromic repeats, also known as CRISPR. This new way of changing a person's genes works like scissors to cut out "problem" genes. It then replaces them with healthy ones. Some believe it could cure all of the world's diseases. However, because CRISPR changes our genes, we must use it carefully and think about the many negative effects it will have on our world.

2   The biggest problem is that scientists will use CRISPR on germline cells. If we allow scientists to change the genes of developing humans, then they— and their children—will have those changes for the rest of their lives. Why is this a problem? In simple terms, because we don't know what will happen. At the moment, we understand very little about the many different ways that genes work. We have no idea if humans will develop correctly with new genes. They might become very unhealthy adults. And we should not use human lives as experiments!

3   A second reason is that CRISPR may be used to give people special abilities, like making them smarter, stronger, or faster. Making people smarter is not bad, of course. But the problem is that rich people will be the only ones who will be able to pay for this technology. As a result, society will become less fair than it already is. And this is not the society that we want. Scientists must move forward slowly with genetic engineering. It is necessary both for people's safety and for the future of a fair society.

F. Discuss these questions with a partner.

1. Would an image help you understand this article? If so, what image would you like to see?

2. Compare the listening and reading. Which seems more informative? Which seems more biased? Why?

VOCABULARY CHECK

A. Review the vocabulary items in the Vocabulary Preview. Write their definitions and add examples. Use a dictionary if necessary.

B. Complete each sentence using the correct vocabulary item from the box. Use the correct form.

cure	edit	improve	mosquito	replace	scissors	traditional

1. New technologies will help us to discover .... to diseases.

2. CRISPR is like a pair of .... It can cut out genes that cause disease and then .... them with different genes. It's a tool that .... your DNA.

3. .... medicine includes drugs and surgeries. This has been used to .... the lives of people for centuries.

4. .... are found around the world and carry diseases that affect millions of people each year.

🔾 Go to MyEnglishLab to complete a skill practice and to join in collaborative activities.

LANGUAGE SKILL

EXPRESSING CONDITIONS WITH *IF*

WHY IT'S USEFUL By expressing conditions using *if*, you can show the relationship between one situation and another. This can help you write about general truths and facts, especially in science.

🔾 Go to MyEnglishLab for the Language Skill presentation and practice.

VOCABULARY STRATEGY

EXAMINING ABBREVIATIONS

WHY IT'S USEFUL By understanding the use of abbreviations, you can communicate more naturally with others, especially in presentations and formal discussions.

What do NASA, CRISPR, and SCUBA all have in common? How about the BBC, DNA, and USA? The first three are **acronyms**, words that are made from the first letter of a group of words and are pronounced as words (we say *NAsa*, not *N-A-S-A*). The second three are **initialisms**, abbreviations that are made with the first letter of a group of words. We pronounce initialisms by saying each first letter separately, as in *USA* or *UK*.

Acronym	Meaning	Pronunciation
NASA	National Aeronautics and Space Administration	NAsa
CRISPR	clustered regularly interspaced short palindromic repeats	CRISper
SCUBA	self-contained underwater breathing apparatus	SCUba
GIF	graphics interchange format	GIF
POTUS	president of the United States	POtus
UNICEF	United Nations International Children's Emergency Fund	Unicef
AIDS	acquired immune deficiency syndrome	Aids

Initialism	Meaning	Pronunciation
BBC	British Broadcasting Corporation	B-B-C
DNA	deoxyribonucleic acid	D-N-A
USA	United States of America	U-S-A
UK	United Kingdom	U-K
UN	United Nations	U-N
GPS	global positioning system	G-P-S
HIV	human immunodeficiency virus	H-I-V

Acronyms and initialisms are common, especially in science and engineering. Knowing the meaning of the individual words can help you better understand the acronym or initialism.

Speakers generally do not explain common or familiar abbreviations, such as *DNA* and *USA*. For example, if several doctors are talking amongst themselves, they don't explain *HIV* because everyone already knows the full name.

If an audience is not likely to know an acronym or initialism, the speaker may explain the meaning early in the talk. Study this example, from the lecture in Skill 1.

> **Professor:** We'll start today by taking a look at deoxyribonucleic acid—also known as **D-N-A**. **DNA** is the hereditary material in our cells that contains all the information our bodies need to grow and live. It is the reason why some people are short and others are tall. Why some people have blue eyes and others have brown. **DNA** is also the reason why some people have really terrible diseases.
>
> Research has shown that **DNA** is made up of four bases.

After speakers have mentioned the meaning of the acronym or initialism, they can then use it throughout the talk. Therefore, it is important to listen carefully for acronyms, initialisms, and their meanings so that you can follow speakers.

Sometimes speakers do not directly state what an acronym or initialism means. However, they may include the abbreviation shortly after they use the full form.

> **Reporter:** Leaders from all over the world met at **United Nations** headquarters in New York today. The leaders discussed climate change and the future of the **UN**.

How should you use an abbreviation when giving a presentation? It is best to tell your listeners its meaning when you first mention it. For abbreviations that have confusing meanings, you may need to explain it. Notice the example below from the Integrated Skills listening. The podcast host first explains the acronym CRISPR simply, saying that it is *a new gene-editing technology*. Its detailed meaning is likely too complicated for most listeners.

> **Host:** Today on the show we're discussing exciting new ways for curing disease. And we're not talking about traditional medicine. Rather, these cures use a **new gene-editing technology** called **CRISPR**. This is short for—are you ready?— **clustered regularly interspaced short palindromic repeats**.

EXERCISE 8

🔊 A. Listen to the another episode of *Science Chat*. As you listen, circle the acronyms and initialisms that you hear.

UK	US	HIV	DNA	EU	STEM
AIDS	UN	CRISPR	NASA	IPCC	

🔊 B. Listen again. Which three acronyms or initialisms does the host define? Write down the words and their meanings. Why do you think she gives the meaning for these three and not the others?

1. .... : ....

2. .... : ....

3. .... : ....

C. Research the definitions of the following abbreviations and complete the chart.

Abbreviation	Meaning	Example Sentence
USFDA		
UNESCO		
mRNA		
BP		

🔊 Go to MyEnglishLab to complete a skill practice.

APPLY YOUR SKILLS

WHY IT'S USEFUL By applying skills that you have learned in this unit, you will be able to distinguish facts from opinions and identify bias as you participate in college-level courses.

ASSIGNMENT

Prepare and participate in a class debate on whether or not scientists should use germline gene editing to treat diseases. Use what you have learned about facts and opinions to develop and deliver your argument.

BEFORE YOU LISTEN

A. Before you listen, discuss these questions with a partner or small group.

1. What are genes? How do our genes affect us?

2. What is CRISPR? How is CRISPR used to edit genes?

3. What are some arguments for and against using CRISPR to edit genes?

B. You will listen to a panel discussion about germline gene editing. Three geneticists give their opinions on the genetic engineering of human reproductive cells. As you listen to the discussion, think about these questions.

1. Does using CRISPR create any problems? If so, what are they?

2. What are the problems with editing the human germline? How can it affect a developing human?

3. What other things (besides genetic engineering) can affect human development?

C. Review the Unit Skills Summary on the next page. As you listen to the discussion and prepare for your debate, apply the skills you learned in this unit.

UNIT SKILLS SUMMARY

DISTINGUISH FACTS FROM OPINIONS BY USING THESE SKILLS:

Identify and express facts

- Identify and express ideas that are facts.
- Identify types of information in facts, such as numbers, statistics, and references to research studies.

Identify and express opinions

- Recognize adjectives that speakers use to express opinions, such as *excellent* or *useful*.
- Use cues such as *according to* to report facts.
- Recognize expressions that speakers use to express opinions, such as *I believe* or *in my opinion*.
- Support opinions with facts.

Identify bias

- Recognize how titles, headings, statistics, images, and tone can show bias.

Express conditions with *if*

- Recognize and use conditional cause-effect sentences with *if*

Examine abbreviations

- Examine acronyms and initialisms to understand what they mean.

LISTEN

A. Listen to the panel discussion on gene editing. Are these people for or against germline editing? Try using this chart to help you organize your notes.

Geneticist	Opinion (For / Against)	Reason (Fact Supporting Opinion)
Dr. Janet Kober		
Dr. Rami Said		
Dr. Ji-Young Park		

B. Compare notes with a partner. Do you have the same ideas?

C. Review the questions from Before You Listen, Part B. Listen to the discussion again. Work with a partner and use your notes to answer the questions.

CULTURE NOTE

In early 2017, the US National Academy of Sciences and the National Academy of Medicine issued a report saying that they could support germline editing of human embryos (an organism in the first eight weeks of development) to prevent a baby being born with a disease. But, the report added, more research about the risks and benefits was needed.

🔊 Go to MyEnglishLab to listen more closely and answer the critical thinking questions.

THINKING CRITICALLY

Discuss these questions with another student.

1. Why do the geneticists in the listening use facts to support their opinions?

2. Two of the geneticists say that editing germlines is risky. Should we not allow germline editing for this reason? Why or why not?

THINKING VISUALLY

A. Look at the graph. Discuss the questions with a partner.

1. What can you say about support for gene editing in the United States among adults in general?

2. What can you say about support for it among parents with children under 18 years of age? For parents with no children under 18?

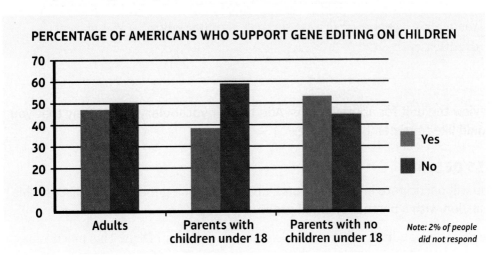

PERCENTAGE OF AMERICANS WHO SUPPORT GENE EDITING ON CHILDREN

Note: 2% of people did not respond

B. Draw a graph with the information from this chart. Then compare graphs with a partner.

Views of Gene Editing		
	Gene editing is no different from other ways of helping humans (%)*	Gene editing to reduce disease in babies is morally acceptable (%)*
Agree	51	28
Disagree	46	30
Not sure	-	40

*Note: 2–3% of people did not respond

THINKING ABOUT LANGUAGE

A. Combine the given information to make factual conditional sentences.

> For help with expressing conditions with *if*, go to MyEnglishLab, Bioethics, Part 2, Language Skill.

1. You heat ice. / Ice melts.

   If you heat ice, it melts.

2. You change an organism's genes. / You change an organism's characteristics.

3. You affect children's DNA. / You edit DNA in a parent's germline cells.

4. You replace a gene for a disease through germline editing. / You prevent the disease.

B. Review the unit for abbreviations. Add to your vocabulary journal any that you would like to remember and use.

CLASS DEBATE

A. You will participate in a class debate about germline gene editing. Discuss this question with a partner or small group.

Germline gene editing allows scientists to change human DNA. This practice has potential problems and benefits. What are they?

B. Divide the class into two teams—Team A will be for germline gene editing. Team B will be against it. Follow these steps.

With your team:

1. Research both sides of the argument.

2. Choose the best arguments for your position (for or against).

3. Choose one person to talk about each argument.

4. Write a short summary of your team's position.

5. Choose a team leader.

C. Debate the issue. Follow these steps:

1. Decide on the rules and time limits for the debate.

2. Each team presents its arguments while the other team takes notes.

3. After both teams have finished, each team will have a few minutes to respond to the other team's arguments. They may ask questions or give counterarguments.

D. As a class, discuss which team made the strongest arguments.

○ Go to MyEnglishLab to watch Professor Greely's concluding video and to complete a self-assessment.

Design principles help create business innovation

BUSINESS AND DESIGN

Inferences

UNIT PROFILE

In this unit, you will learn about business strategies. You will also learn about user experience (UX) design and how it is used to make products that people want.

You will prepare and participate in a panel discussion about business strategies.

OUTCOMES

- Make inferences
- Give oral summaries to relate ideas
- Answer inference questions
- Express present possibility with modal verbs
- Use synonyms to understand new vocabulary

For more about **BUSINESS AND DESIGN**, see ❶❸.

See also Ⓡ and Ⓦ **BUSINESS AND DESIGN** ❶❷❸.

GETTING STARTED

🎧 Go to MyEnglishLab to watch Juli Sherry's introductory video and to complete a self-assessment.

Discuss these questions with a partner or group.

1. The top goal of any company is to make enough money to stay in business. To reach that goal, a company needs a plan: detailed strategies for making money. Do you know much about business strategy? Think of a business you are familiar with. What strategies does it use to make money? Explain.

2. Think of a successful company whose product or service you use. Why is this company successful?

3. In her introduction, Ms. Sherry says that businesses add value to the world. Do you agree with her opinion? Explain.

SKILL 1

MAKING INFERENCES

> **WHY IT'S USEFUL** By making inferences, you can gain a deeper understanding of what a speaker says. This can help you to understand what a speaker thinks about a subject.

Imagine you hear this from a speaker talking about his experience creating a digital product:

> **Speaker:** Our company received feedback from users on our product, and we knew we had to change the design completely.

What does this tell you about the user feedback? The answer is clear: Users *did not* like the design. Even though the speaker did not *say* the feedback was negative, you are able to **make an inference** from the details.

Inferencing is making a conclusion based on evidence or reasoning. To do this in listening, we take the evidence from a speaker's words and then combine that with our world knowledge.

In the example above, this is how the inference was made:

1. You heard two pieces of evidence:
   a. The company received feedback.
   b. The company had to change the design.

2. You combined the evidence with your world knowledge: Companies change designs because of negative feedback. You reached this conclusion: The user feedback was negative—users didn't like the design.

Speakers, on the other hand, **make implications**. An implication is an idea that you want people to understand without you stating it directly. Sometimes a speaker will imply something casually, believing that the listener will "fill in the blanks," as with the example on the previous page. Other times, speakers use implication intentionally to avoid getting into trouble for saying something directly. For example, if a professor didn't want to directly say something bad about a university's decision to raise tuition (the cost of attending university), she might say to her class, "I hope you find today's lecture interesting. We can all agree that it will be *valuable*."

TIP

It is common to make the wrong inference. That's because we are adding our own ideas to another person's message. Make sure to listen carefully and make inferences based on not only the speaker's words and your own world knowledge, but also logic and reason.

VOCABULARY PREVIEW

Read the vocabulary items in the box. Circle the ones you know. Put a question mark next to the ones you don't know.

| management | strategy | achieve | marketing |
| advertise | market (n) | competitor | decision |

EXERCISE 1

A. Think about a goal that you had for yourself in the past. What was the goal? Did you achieve it? If not, what happened?

🎧 B. Listen to the beginning of a business lecture. Check (✓) the four strategies that the professor talks about.

☐ goal-setting ☐ mergers and acquisitions

☐ marketing ☐ manager training

☐ brainstorming ☐ pricing

C. To make good inferences, what do you need to do?

EXERCISE 2

🔊 **A. Listen again. Complete the excerpts with the words that you hear.**

1. Business management is everything a company does to make ....
   It's one of the many strategies that a business can use to reach its ....
   and to get customers.

2. Next is .... Simply offering a great product or service isn't enough
   for it to sell. Through research you learn about your customers, and through
   development, you can create your product. That's called R&D. But then you have to
   make those people want to .... your product.

B. Based on the two excerpts in Part A, what inference can be made about each? Check (✓) the best answer.

1. ☐ A business will make money if it reaches its goals.

   ☐ Business management does not focus much on making good products.

2. ☐ If a product is good, marketing might not be important.

   ☐ Research helps companies decide how to market their products.

EXERCISE 3

A. Do you think that the professor you just listened to finds the four business strategies to be important? Why or why not? What evidence do you use to make this inference? Discuss with a partner or small group.

B. Now practice inferencing with your partner. Partner A, tell about a product or service that you use. Tell just the facts. Do not give your opinion. Partner B, take notes and infer how A feels about the product or service. What led you to your conclusions? Explain.

Example

A: I recently bought a Sonos wireless speaker after reading reviews online. I only bought one because of the cost. I use it to listen to online music and podcasts. I'm thinking about saving up for a second one.

B: So, the reviews were pretty good, right? And I imagine the speaker is expensive since you have to save up for a second one. But it's clear that you like it, or you wouldn't be saving up.

VOCABULARY CHECK

A. Review the vocabulary items in the Vocabulary Preview. Write their definitions and add examples. Use a dictionary if necessary.

B. Complete each sentence using the correct vocabulary item from the box. Use the correct form.

achieve	advertise	competitor	decision
management	market	marketing	strategy

1. Through ....—for example, free samples at the supermarket—consumers became aware of the the new product.

2. Some companies spend a lot of money on TV commercials and Internet ads. They .... because they want to make sure people know about their products.

3. One of the best .... for learning is to take notes when reading and then write summaries in your own words about what you've read.

4. Our hope is that the company will .... its sales goals for next year. Otherwise, we may have to cut staff.

5. The US .... for mobile devices, made up of 95 percent of all adults, has grown significantly over the past decade or so.

6. After several closed-door meetings, the company made a(n)............................ to fire its CEO and find a new one.

7. After buying its largest .... , the company expanded and its market share increased by 8 percent.

8. Good .... will give the company's employees opportunities to develop new skills.

🔊 Go to MyEnglishLab to complete vocabulary and skill practices, and to join in collaborative activities.

SKILL 2

GIVING ORAL SUMMARIES TO RELATE IDEAS

WHY IT'S USEFUL By giving oral summaries of things you have heard, you can effectively present new information to others in discussions. This can help you to share key ideas and examples from outside of class.

At university, you are expected to attend lectures, watch videos, and go to conferences in your field of study. But it doesn't stop there. At a conference, you may see a colleague who wants to know about a presentation that you just attended. Or maybe a classmate asks about the lecture that she missed. In these situations, you **give an oral summary** of what you heard.

Oral summaries are spoken reports about something you have heard, like a lecture. They are not long speeches or presentations.

Here are some of tips for giving an oral summary:

- Start by explaining the context: the name of the speaker, when / where you saw the talk.
- Give a brief summary sentence of the **main idea**.
- Describe the **supporting details** and include interesting examples to help you illustrate these points, if possible.
- Only talk about the content of the lecture; don't give your opinion.
- Use your own words.

Generally, an oral summary should be less than 25 percent of the original's length, but it can also be much shorter than that. Include the key points and examples and then let the listener ask you questions. This way you tell about the information that the listener is most interested in or thinks is most important.

For more about listening actively to follow a lecture or discussion, see Bioethics, Part 1, Skill 1, page 3. For more about identifying main ideas, see History, Part 2, Skill 1, page 181.

Language for Oral Summaries	
To introduce the main idea	The lecture / discussion was about …
To introduce a supporting detail	One of the key points in the lecture was …
	The speaker / professor mentioned …
To introduce an example	An example of this was …
	For instance …

🔊 Listen to this example. One student is late to class and asks about what she has missed.

VOCABULARY PREVIEW

Read the vocabulary items in the box. Circle the ones you know. Put a question mark next to the ones you don't know.

taking over	competition	familiar	success
messaging	incredibly	popular	

EXERCISE 4

A. Do you use messaging apps? If so, which ones? What features of a messaging app do you like and use most?

🔊 B. Listen to the beginning of a lecture and take notes to complete the outline.

TOPIC	Strategies That Businesses Use to Grow and Sell
Main idea	Mergers and acquisitions (M&A)
Supporting detail 1	Definitions:
Supporting detail 2	Example of M&A:
Supporting detail 3	Facebook's acquisition of WhatsApp

C. Would you include the information from Part B in an oral summary? What makes a good oral summary? Explain.

EXERCISE 5

🎧 **A. Listen again. Check (✓) the sentences that are supporting details from the listening.**

☐ 1. There are many strategies that businesses use to grow.

☐ 2. Mergers and acquisitions (M&A) is a strategy where two companies agree to become one company, or one company takes over another.

☐ 3. Mergers and aquisitions happen because companies want to grow and offer more types of products or services.

☐ 4. Facebook acquired WhatsApp for $19 billion.

☐ 5. WhatsApp was Facebook's first messaging service.

☐ 6. According to the professor, Facebook wants people to use their phones more.

B. What is the main idea of the listening? Write it in your own words.

....

....

EXERCISE 6

A. Prepare an oral summary of the lecture excerpt that you just heard. Be sure to include the main idea and supporting details or examples to make the main idea clear. Make a few notes here. Then give the oral summary to a partner or small group.

....

....

....

....

....

B. Discuss these questions with a partner or small group.

1. How should you present main ideas in an oral summary?

2. For this listening, what do you think are the best supporting details or examples to include in an oral summary in order to make your idea clear?

VOCABULARY CHECK

A. Review the vocabulary items in the Vocabulary Preview. Write their definitions and add examples. Use a dictionary if necessary.

B. Complete each sentence using the correct vocabulary item from the box. Use the correct form.

competition	familiar	incredibly	messaging
popular	success	take over	

1. The new management strategies are a huge .... The company is making a lot more money now and the employees are happier.

2. The new app is quite .... Millions of people have downloaded it since it was created a few weeks ago.

3. How does our company plan to sell more than our .... sells? We need a good strategy.

4. Hadley is very .... with the mobile phone market—she knows it better than anyone else.

5. Creating a new design for the product was .... difficult because we only had a few days to do it.

6. The largest corporate acquisition in history happened in 1999 when the British company Vodafone .... Mannesmann, a German telecommunications provider, paying about $200 billion.

7. This .... app lets you send messages and pictures to friends who live here and in other countries, and it's free to download.

⊙ Go to MyEnglishLab to complete vocabulary and skill practices, and to join in collaborative activities.

INTEGRATED SKILLS

ANSWERING INFERENCE QUESTIONS

WHY IT'S USEFUL By using inference to answer questions, you can get a better idea of how a writer thinks about a topic. This is useful in academic life because professors often ask what an author would think about something that the author did not directly write about.

Making inferences about a text is similar to making inferences about something you have heard. You must reach a conclusion based on the information on the page and your own knowledge and reasoning.

In academic settings, professors often ask questions that are only loosely based on a reading passage. They do not want to directly test your comprehension (understanding) of the passage. The answers will not be directly stated in the text, which means that you will have to **make inferences**.

Inference questions usually ask for the following:

- A writer's purpose: *What is the author's purpose in writing the text?*

- Ideas suggested by the author: *The reading implies / suggests which of the following … ?*

- What the author thinks: *Which sentence would the author most likely agree with?*

- Conclusions you can make from the text: *What is a likely result of … ?;*
  What does X indicate about … ?

No matter what the question is, you will have to use evidence from the reading. Be sure to pay attention to details and use your background knowledge to support your answers.

CULTURE NOTE

Authors write with different purposes. Common purposes include:

- to explain or inform
- to persuade
- to argue
- to entertain (i.e., to do something that interests and amuses people)

VOCABULARY PREVIEW

Read the vocabulary items in the box. Circle the ones you know. Put a question mark next to the ones you don't know.

confusion	enjoyable	variety	interact	surveys (n)
observe	reactions	versions	benefits (n)	

EXERCISE 7

A. Read the passage and answer the questions that follow.

What Is UX?

1 **User experience (UX) is becoming an important part of design in many technology companies. While the number of companies with a UX specialist or a UX team is growing, there is still some confusion about what UX means.**

2 Many people think that UX is another word for the user interface of a website or product. However, the idea of UX is wider than this. It includes many areas, such as engineering, marketing, and interface design. UX is involved with all parts of a user's experience, from first visiting a website, to buying a product in a store, to taking it home and opening it, and so on. At each and every one of these stages, the goal of UX design is to make the user experience as easy and enjoyable as possible.

3 Though UX has been defined in a variety of ways, most experts agree that it focuses on the way users interact with a product or service. UX tries to make this product-user interaction enjoyable and easy to understand.

The UX Design Process

4 So what does UX design involve? Although it can be different according to the product, here are the three key stages of the UX design process:

User Research This can include face-to-face interviews with users (or potential users) and online surveys. The goal here is to get information about the user's wants and needs as well as feelings toward a product.

Design For UX, design is more focused on a product's or website's usability and functionality rather than its color or appearance. For a digital product, this may involve information architecture, i.e., deciding what things are important for the users to see, and where and when the user sees them on the site. Prototyping is another important part of this stage, which allows a UX designer to test a variety of designs before the development stage.

Testing The product or website is then tested by real users. The designers can observe users' reactions and feelings when interacting with the product and change the design of certain features if needed. Sometimes two versions of a product are sent out to users, to see which one users like better. This is known as A / B testing.

What Is UX Used For?

5 The goal of UX is to improve the user experience by making a product or website useful, easy to use, and enjoyable. This will lead to increased customer satisfaction—how happy customers are—and to more people using the product. This has clear benefits for a company: When customers have an enjoyable experience, they are much more likely to use the product again and to tell their friends about it.

1. How does the author define UX?

....

2. What is the objective of UX design?

....

3. What are the key stages of the design process?

....

B. **Read the following excerpts from the text. Circle the best answer to each question. Reread the whole text if necessary.**

1. User Experience (UX) is becoming an important part of design in many technology companies. While the number of companies with a UX specialist or a UX team is growing, there is still some confusion about what UX means.

What is the author's purpose in writing the text?

a. She wants to educate her readers about UX design.

b. She wants to explain the best UX practices.

2. The product or website is then tested by real users. The designers can observe users' reactions and feelings when interacting with the product and change the design of certain features if needed.

When users don't like a product's features, which of the following will happen?

a. The designers will talk to them about how to make the features better.

b. The designers may alter the design of the product's features.

3. The goal of UX is to improve the user experience by making a product or website useful, easy to use, and enjoyable. This will lead to increased customer satisfaction—how happy customers are—and to more people using the product. This has clear benefits for a company: When customers have an enjoyable experience, they are much more likely to use the product again and to tell their friends about it.

For a company, what is a likely benefit of having a product or service with good UX?

a. When UX is good, a company can make more money on its product or service.

b. Customers will enjoy their experience with that company's product or service.

C. Look back at the questions in Parts A and B. Which ones needed inference to answer? What evidence did you use to make your inferences? Discuss with a partner.

EXERCISE 8

A. The reading "What Is UX?" was given to students before this lecture. Listen to the lecture. Which part of UX from the reading does the professor focus on?

....

B. Listen again. The professor describes website features that create good and bad experiences. List the features.

Bad	Good

C. Using what you have learned from the reading and lecture, how does good UX lead customers to buy more of a product or service? Discuss with a partner.

VOCABULARY CHECK

A. Review the vocabulary items in the Vocabulary Preview. Write their definitions and add examples. Use a dictionary if necessary.

B. Complete each sentence using the correct vocabulary item from the box. Use the correct form.

benefit	confusion	enjoyable	interact	observe
reaction	survey	variety	version	

1. Every year there's a new .... of the GMAT, the business school entrance exam. But the content doesn't change very much.

2. The professor was not very clear when she described the idea of branding, which created a lot of .... for the class.

3. Learning about business is very .... I like reading about it and discussing it in my free time as well.

4. When the CEO heard that the company had lost $150 million, his .... was scary—you could see the anger on his face.

5. UX designers want to see how users .... with products so that they can make the products better.

6. The university offers a(n) .... of courses in the School of Business Management. There are more than 150 different choices.

7. This .... takes only 5–10 minutes to complete. Please be sure to answer all of the questions.

8. One .... of taking classes in the evening is that you can sleep late or exercise before your classes start.

9. .... the way your customers use the product. It will give you useful information about how you can make it better.

🔊 Go to MyEnglishLab to complete a skill practice and to join in collaborative activities.

LANGUAGE SKILL

EXPRESSING PRESENT POSSIBILITY WITH MODAL VERBS

WHY IT'S USEFUL By using modal verbs, you can express how certain you are about an action or situation.

▶ Go to MyEnglishLab for the Language Skill presentation and practice.

VOCABULARY STRATEGY

USING SYNONYMS TO UNDERSTAND NEW VOCABULARY

WHY IT'S USEFUL By finding synonyms in context, you can use them to understand new vocabulary. This frees you from having to rely on a dictionary to get an author's or a speaker's meaning.

When you read or listen, you will often see words that you don't know. Should you turn to your dictionary every time you see or hear a new word? No—that's too difficult. Instead, use the context to understand the unfamiliar word's meaning. The context is the words and sentences that come before and after a word. In the context, you will often find a synonym—a word with the same or nearly the same meaning. One way to **understand new vocabulary** is to **find synonyms**. Look at this excerpt:

> (Using WhatsApp) also gets people to use their phones more, which means users see more advertisements. And that means more advertising **revenues** for Facebook— it makes more money.

Here is an unfamiliar word, *revenues*. Look at the excerpt again. Which word in the context do you think is most similar to *revenues*? It will likely be a noun because *revenues* is a noun. Take a guess. If you guess *money*, then you are on the right track.

After you have guessed which word is a synonym, use other context clues to make a specific definition. In the example are the words *advertising* and *it makes more money*. This can lead you to think that *revenues* might mean "money for a business."

After you have thought about the meaning, go to a dictionary to confirm your guess. The definition for *revenue* in the *Longman Dictionary of Academic English* is "money that is earned by a company."

How to Guess Meaning Using Synonyms

1. Find a word that you think has a similar meaning to the unknown word.

2. Use the context to decide on a more exact meaning.

3. Confirm your guess by looking in a dictionary.

Finding a good synonym might not always be easy, but by guessing and thinking about a word, you will make a deeper connection with its meaning. And this will help you to remember the word.

For more about how to use context to understand new vocabulary, see Zoology, Part 1, Vocabulary Strategy, page 59.

CULTURE NOTE

It is challenging to hear new words and connect them to synonyms in real time. Luckily, many news and educational websites provide transcripts for videos, lectures, and podcasts. After listening, read the transcripts to help you learn the meanings of new words you hear.

EXERCISE 9

A. Read each sentence. Underline the word or phrase that is a synonym of the word in bold.

1. In addition to mergers, there are also **acquisitions**, that is, one company <u>buying</u> another. Companies use these strategies for a number of reasons, one of which is to increase their market share.

2. Our company's **aim** is to deliver the highest quality service to our customers. For our employees, our goal is to create a positive working environment where they can learn and develop new skills.

3. Microsoft was **founded** in 1975. Childhood friends Bill Gates and Paul Allen started the company to make computer programs for the Altair 8800.

4. One of the smartest and most creative people in word is Elon Musk. He is a **brilliant** businessperson, a successful investor, and an innovative engineer who has created companies such as SpaceX and Tesla.

5. The new laws will affect **corporations** that have more than 500 employees. These businesses will have to follow the law starting next year.

B. Use the context of the sentences in Part A to get a more exact meaning of the new words. Write your ideas.

1. acquisition: _buying a company_

2. aim: _____

3. found: _____

4. brilliant: _____

5. corporation: _____

C. Use a dictionary to check your ideas in Part B. Were you close? Then write the dictionary definitions.

1. acquisition: _the process or act of one company buying another_

2. aim: _____

3. found: _____

4. brilliant: _____

5. corporation: _____

⬆ Go to MyEnglishLab to complete a skill practice.

APPLY YOUR SKILLS

WHY IT'S USEFUL By applying the skills you have learned in this unit, you will be able to infer information and relate ideas in the form of oral summaries as you participate in academic discussions.

ASSIGNMENT

Prepare for and participate in a panel discussion about business strategies. Use research and what you have learned about giving oral presentations to help you talk about your strategy and be an engaging and informative panelist.

BEFORE YOU LISTEN

A. Before you listen, discuss these questions with a partner or group.

1. Several business strategies have been discussed in this unit: company missions, pricing, mergers and acquisitions, and marketing. What does each one mean?

2. What is UX design? What is its focus for product development?

3. Are you familiar with Apple products? What do you know about them?

B. You will listen to a lecture about Apple, the technology company. As you listen, think about these questions.

1. What is the first step in Apple's design process, according to the professor?

2. What features of the iPhone made it a great product?

C. Review the Unit Skills Summary. As you listen to the lecture and prepare for your panel discussion, apply the skills you learned in the unit.

UNIT SKILLS SUMMARY

MAKE INFERENCES BY USING THESE SKILLS:

Make inferences

- Listen carefully and connect content to your prior knowledge.
- Notice speakers' implications.

Give oral summaries to relate ideas

- Explain the context that you hear in the lecture, etc.
- Focus the summary on the key points and ideas that you heard.
- Don't give your opinion, but use your own words.

Answer inference questions

- Read the text and questions carefully.
- Connect ideas in the reading to your prior knowledge.

Express present possibility with modal verbs

- Use the correct modal verb for your degree of certainty.
- Make sure that your guess is about the current action or situation, NOT a past action or situation.

Use synonyms to understand new vocabulary

- Find a nearby word with a similar meaning to the new word, using the context to help you.
- Confirm your guess with a dictionary.

LISTEN

A. Listen to the lecture about Apple. Take notes. Try using an outline or a mind map to organize your ideas.

For an example of a mind map, see Business and Design, Part 1, Skill 1, page 27.

B. Compare notes with a partner. Did you have the same ideas? Did you make similar inferences?

C. Review the questions from Before You Listen, Part B. Listen to the lecture again. Work with a partner and use your notes to answer the questions.

Go to MyEnglishLab to listen more closely and answer the critical thinking questions.

THINKING CRITICALLY

Discuss the questions with one or more students.

1. Steve Jobs famously said, "It is not the customer's job to know what they want." How might this idea be used in the product development process?

2. Do you think that it is important for new technologies and apps to be easy to use? Do you think people will like a new product if it is useful but not easy to use? Why or why not?

THINKING VISUALLY

A. Consumers care about design, both how a product looks and how it functions. Part of a product's function is its safety. Occasionally, a product is unsafe and the company has to recall it—that is, tell consumers to return the "bad" product. Recall of cars is common.

Study the graph. What does it show? What do you think causes the numbers to change from year to year?

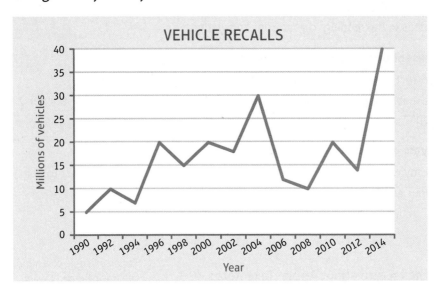

B. Look at the chart. It shows data for the number of injuries caused by different types of products in a recent year in the United States. Use the data to create a visual. Then answer the questions.

Consumer Product Type	Number of Injuries
Sports and recreation equipment	4,200,000
Toys	240,000
Packaging and containers for home goods	410,000
Home tools	340,000
Child nursery equipment (cribs)	95,000
Home furniture and fixtures	2,900,000
Home communication and entertainment (TVs, computers)	210,00

1. According to the data, which products seem to cause the most injuries? The least? Why do you think there is such a big difference between the two?

2. How do you think each type of product causes injury? Do you think it is the design of the products? Or is it because of the nature of the activities related to the product? Explain.

THINKING ABOUT LANGUAGE

A. Write sentences showing possibility in the present about the following situations. Use the modal verbs from the box.

> For help with expressing present possibility with modal verbs, go to MyEnglishLab, Business and Design, Part 2, Language Skill.

must (not)	should	may (not)	might (not)	could (not)	can't

1. Our top competitor just moved to a larger office space and hired 100 new employees. *Our competitor must be doing something right.*

2. This tablet is huge and has many useful features.

3. ElectroniCo, a technology company, is planning to buy one of its competitors in the laptop computer market.

4. A lot of people are talking about this new app made by Softeq.

B. Read the sentences. Use the skills presented in Vocabulary Strategy to understand the meaning of the words in bold.

1. Apple focuses on the product as a **whole**. The company thinks about all of the product's features and functions.

   Synonym in context: ....

   ....

   Definition: ....

   ....

2. The user interface is easy to **figure out**. New users do not need to spend much time learning about how to use the product.

   Synonym in context: ....

   ....

   Definition: ....

   ....

3. Our company **stands for** making innovative products that do not hurt the environment. We support finding innovative and environmentally friendly solutions to meet our customers' needs.

   Synonym in context: ....

   ....

   Definition: ....

   ....

PANEL DISCUSSION

A. Read and discuss these question with a small group.

A number of business strategies have been discussed in this unit: company missions, pricing, mergers and acquisitions, marketing, advertising, and branding.

1. What is the purpose / goal of each strategy?

2. Which one interests you the most?

B. You are going to participate in a 10–12-minute panel discussion about the role that various business strategies play in business. Each member of your group will focus on one business strategy, and there will be one host (i.e., the leader) of the discussion. With your group, decide on the speaking order. Then prepare for the discussion.

Consider the following points and do research to help you prepare.

– How do you define the business strategy?

– What role does the strategy play in making the company successful, i.e., making money for the company?

– Find an example of the strategy and use it to illustrate your point.

C. Listen to the other panel discussions. Take notes and ask questions at the end.

◑ Go to MyEnglishLab to watch Juli Sherry's concluding video and to complete a self-assessment.

ZOOLOGY

Synthesis of Information

UNIT PROFILE

In this unit, you will learn about the ways elephants communicate. You will also learn about the anatomical (body) features that allow both humans and elephants to make and hear sounds.

You will prepare and give an individual presentation about animal communication.

OUTCOMES

• Take notes on research lectures

• Relate source information to an audience

• Synthesize information from multiple sources

• Use complement clauses after *about*

• Recognize collocations to expand vocabulary

For more about **ZOOLOGY**, see ❶❸. See also ⬛R⬛ and ⬛W⬛ **ZOOLOGY** ❶❷❸.

GETTING STARTED

🔾 Go to MyEnglishLab to watch Professor O'Connell-Rodwell's introductory video and to complete a self-assessment.

Discuss these questions with a partner or group.

1. Do other animal species show feelings like happiness, sadness, and anger? What are some examples? What about elephants?

2. What parts of our bodies do we use to communicate and show feelings? How about other animals such as elephants, dogs, and mice?

3. In her introduction, Professor O'Connell-Rodwell says that elephants receive information via vibrations felt through their feet. How do you think they send those communications? How might the information in those vibrations be different from information communicated by air?

SKILL 1

TAKING NOTES ON RESEARCH LECTURES

WHY IT'S USEFUL By taking notes on research presented in lectures, you can look up specific information about that research after class. This lets you connect with the information on your own time, at your own pace.

Taking notes is a useful way to collect information in both readings and lectures. You can refer to your notes when you are preparing for exams, writing papers, or participating in discussions.

Especially important is **taking notes on research**. You will often hear speakers mention specific scientists and their work. This is because their work has added to understanding in their field.

For more about note-taking, including using symbols and abbreviations, see Bioethics, Part 1, Integrated Skills, page 11.

When taking notes on research and theories, include the **name** of the scientist(s), the **year** that the work was published, and the **main idea** of the research. This will give you the information that you need to follow up on the research so that you can gain a better understanding of it.

TIP

Speakers often mention the year that the important work was published so that you can get a better idea of how the research fits into the field's development.

Using a graphic organizer is one way to take notes. Graphic organizers show the relationship between ideas. Knowing this is important for synthesizing information.

Here are two examples of graphic organizers, with information about the discovery of DNA. Other common graphic organizers include T-charts, grids, and timelines.

Mind Map

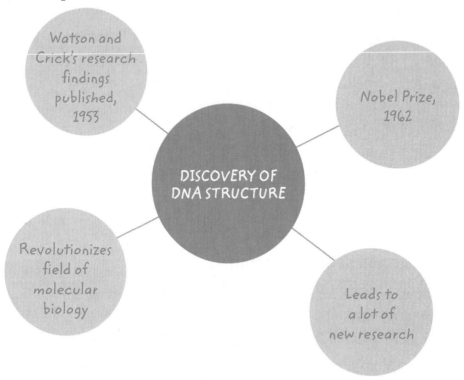

The Cornell Method

	"Discovering DNA" — Prof. Washington, 11/16/2018
SUMMARY: Discovery of DNA structure was significant at the time and continues to be a very important development in biological sciences.	- Watson and Crick publish research findings in 1953 - Nobel Prize in 1962 - Led to a lot of new research - Revolutionized field of molecular biology
QUESTION: What's the difference between a chromosome and DNA?	

VOCABULARY PREVIEW

Read the vocabulary items in the box. Circle the ones you know. Put a question mark next to the ones you don't know.

senses (n)	call (n)	gestures (n)	movements
frighten	bends (v)	series of	vibrations

EXERCISE 1

A. People talk to each other. What other ways do we communicate? Do elephants communicate in those same ways?

B. Listen to the lecture about elephant communication. Add notes to the mind map.

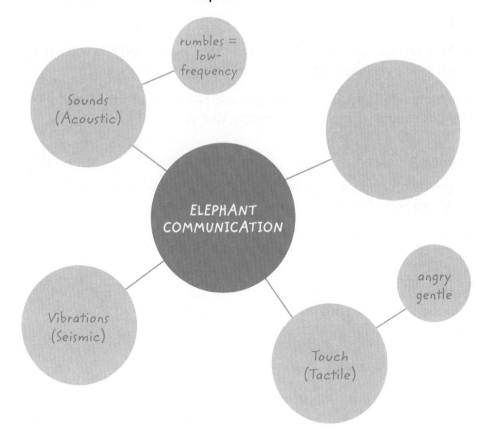

C. Why is it important to listen for the results of research?

EXERCISE 2

🔊 A. Listen again. Then read the statements. Circle *T* (True) or *F* (False).
Correct the false statements.

T / F 1. Having large social circles is normal behavior for animals.

T / F 2. Elephants can communicate at distances of up to 50 kilometers.

T / F 3. When one elephant wants to frighten another, it bends its ears.

T / F 4. Tactile communication is when elephants use gestures to communicate.

T / F 5. Using vibrations to communicate is called *seismic communication*.

B. Check answers with a partner.

EXERCISE 3

🔊 A. Work with a partner. Listen to this next part of the lecture and add notes to the
mind map on the previous page.

B. Compare notes with your partner. Did you add the same information?
Why did you choose to add the information that you did? Explain.

VOCABULARY CHECK

A. Review the vocabulary items in the Vocabulary Preview. Write their
definitions and add examples. Use a dictionary if necessary.

B. Complete each sentence using the correct vocabulary item from the box.
Use the correct form.

bend	call	frighten	gesture
movement	sense	series of	vibration

1. Through a(n) .... experiments, the researchers were able to find
   the cause of the disease.

2. Loud noises often .... smaller animals.

3. Our .... of smell is important for how we taste things.

4. Animals use their voices to make all sorts of .... For example
   some monkeys make a sound when they see a dangerous animal. This
   sound tells other monkeys to be careful.

5. The dancer's .... were beautiful, and his performance was excellent.

6. The music was so loud that you could feel the .... through the floor.

7. Elephants .... their ears when they want to make another elephant afraid.

8. Dolphins, like humans, make .... with their bodies to communicate.

CULTURE NOTE

Like elephants, humans communicate through gesture and touch. Early in life, gestures such as pointing and eye movement play an important role in language learning. And throughout life, touch is used to express love, caring, and encouragement amongst family and friends.

◐ Go to MyEnglishLab to complete vocabulary and skill practices, and to join in collaborative activities.

SKILL 2
RELATING SOURCE INFORMATION TO AN AUDIENCE

WHY IT'S USEFUL By referring to sources when speaking, you can help your audience find more information on the topic that you are discussing. Sharing your sources is important in the academic world.

In academic lectures and discussions, you will often hear professors and colleagues **refer to sources**. Why do they do this?

- First, in the academic world, it is important to tell others the source of the ideas, theories, and research that you mention in a presentation, discussion, or paper. By sharing your sources, you avoid plagiarism.

- Most importantly, mentioning a source gives listeners a place to go if they want to follow up or learn more about the topic. Oftentimes speakers will make a quick reference to the main idea of a theory or research study, but they may not give many details about it. Do they use the source correctly in making their point? What are the specific details of a theory that they mentioned? If you are interested in finding the answers to these questions, knowing the source will help you.

Best Practices

When referring to sources, remember the following:

1. Be brief: Include what you believe is the most important information. But make sure that you give enough information so that interested audience members can find the source on their own. Include important names (the author, the website, etc.) and if possible, the date of the work.

2. If using a visual aid, include the source information there.

3. Signal to your listeners that you are referring to a source. Here are common expressions for doing this:

> **In his book *The Selfish Gene*, Richard Dawkins argues** that genes are the main force behind evolution.

> **According to research by psychologists Daniel Kahneman and Amos Tversky,** people do not always act rationally when making decisions.

> **Watson and Crick, in their often-cited 1953 paper "A Structure for Deoxyribonucleic Acid,"** detail their model for the structure of DNA.

> **The IUCN website provides** information on threatened mammal species. Their statistics show that nearly a quarter of the world's mammals are threatened.

It is also useful to refer to lectures, whether the source is the class that you are in or something that you saw online.

> Professor, **in yesterday's lecture you mentioned** that elephants make gestures. Can you give us some examples of those gestures?

TIP

It is best to briefly reference sources while speaking. But when giving more formal presentations, you must provide a list of your sources. Each field has its own format for this, and universities have websites explaining how to make reference lists. Be sure to visit these sites and add a reference slide to the end of your presentation.

VOCABULARY PREVIEW

Read the vocabulary items in the box. Circle the ones you know. Put a question mark next to the ones you don't know.

through	turn into	suddenly	apparently	wonder (v)	articles

EXERCISE 4

A. Refer back to your lecture notes from Exercises 1 and 3. How would you explain seismic communication in your own words?

🔊 B. Listen to the class discussion. The teaching assistant makes two references to sources of information. Complete the excerpts with the expressions she uses.

> 1. ... . , Professor Nicks discussed elephant seismic communication ...

> 2. .... Caitlin O'Connell-Rodwell, elephants understand what these calls mean by sensing them through their feet and trunk.

C. Why should you refer to sources and authors in discussions?

EXERCISE 5

🔊 A. Listen again and take notes. Write the main idea of the discussion.

....

....

🔊 B. Listen again. Use the information from the discussion to complete these sentences.

1. At the beginning of the discussion, a student asks a question about

....

2. Elephant rumbles are .... sounds.

3. In addition to elephants, ... can also sense low-frequency vibrations.

4. Elephants sense these calls through their ....

5. Elephants can sense calls from .... away.

EXERCISE 6

A. Use the expressions from this section to make references to sources. Use the given sources and ideas. Say your sentences aloud to a partner.

TIP

Style guides are publications that offer rules for academic writing. They can help you to use the correct format for citing sources. Two common ones are the *Chicago Manual of Style* and the *Publication Manual of the American Psychological Association*.

1. Source: The book *The Selfish Gene* by Richard Dawkins

   Idea: Genes are the main force behind evolution.

   > A: In his book *The Selfish Gene*, Richard Dawkins argues that genes are the main force behind evolution.

2. Source: Dolphin Research Center website

   Idea: Dolphins make more frequent calls to others when they find food.

3. Source: The article "Elephant Communication" by W.R. Langbauer

   Idea: More research needs to be done to understand the details of the different messages that elephants communicate.

4. Source: The group African Wildlife Foundation

   Idea: Bonobos—an animal similar to chimpanzees—live in matriarchal societies, just like elephants.

5. Source: The book *A Natural History of Human Thinking*, by Michael Tomasello

   Idea: Humans have the ability to think complex thoughts because we are social. Because we know that other people have thoughts and that we can share the same goals, we are able to think in unique ways.

CULTURE NOTE

Many animals can sense vibrations through the ground. Scientists at the US Geological Survey think that some animals including birds and rodents (like rats and squirrels) can sense vibrations from earthquakes. These vibrations, called P-waves, do not cause damage, but they are the first signs of an earthquake. Unlike these small animals, humans cannot feel P-waves without special equipment.

B. Have you read, watched, or listened to anything interesting recently? What was it about? Discuss with a partner or small group. Be sure to reference the source as best you can.

VOCABULARY CHECK

A. Review the vocabulary items in the Vocabulary Preview. Write their definitions and add examples. Use a dictionary if necessary.

B. Complete each sentence using the correct vocabulary item from the box. Use the correct form.

apparently	article	suddenly	through	turn into	wonder

1. Carolyn .... if dolphin gestures communicate complex meanings. She is now doing an experiment to test her idea.

2. .... lots of hard work and many hours at the library, Alex was able to complete his PhD.

3. The discussion about elephant habitats quickly .... a discussion about conservation policy.

4. Our professor has written dozens of .... on economic policy.

5. We were doing research in the forest when we .... heard a loud noise. We looked over and there was a huge bear about 50 feet away.

6. The test was really difficult. .... only one student received an A on it.

🔊 Go to MyEnglishLab to complete vocabulary and skill practices, and to join in collaborative activities.

INTEGRATED SKILLS

SYNTHESIZING INFORMATION FROM MULTIPLE SOURCES

WHY IT'S USEFUL By synthesizing information from multiple sources, you can form new ideas that draw on the work of others. This will help you to gain a deeper understanding of the subject and write interesting research papers.

A key skill at university is being able to **synthesize information**. Synthesizing is taking information from one or more sources and organizing it in a new way. You make connections between the sets of information in order to answer a specific question or to develop your own idea in a longer research paper.

You can synthesize information from different types of sources, for example: academic journals, textbooks, lectures, podcasts, newspapers. When synthesizing, you first have to understand the source material well.

While Reading or Listening to a Source

- Carefully annotate the text you are reading—that is, add short notes to it or highlight important parts.

- Take notes while you read or listen.

- After reading or listening, organize your notes in a way that connects similar ideas.

For more examples of graphic organizers, see pages 157–158.

After you have gathered your information, it is time to write, synthesizing information into a paragraph or short essay.

How to Synthesize

- Ask yourself, what idea will you will explain?

- Outline, or make a plan for, your paragraph or essay. Use notes from what you have read and listened to.

- Start your writing with a strong topic sentence or introductory paragraph.

- For a paragraph, write one or two sentences for each main idea. For an essay, write a paragraph for each main idea.

- Use examples to illustrate your important points.

- Write a concluding sentence to your paragraph that ties the information together. For an essay, write a short conclusion.

- Be sure to cite your sources where necessary.

On the next page is a paragraph that synthesizes information from two lecture excerpts in Skill 1. The notes have a lot of the information from the lectures, but the paragraph does not include all of it. Instead, it focuses on the way that elephants use gestures to communicate.

Notes

Lecture 1
- elephants communicate in many ways
  - sound—low frequency
  - gestures—bend ears to frighten others
  - touch
  - seismically—use their feet to feel vibrations

Lecture 2	
GESTURES	TOUCH
– elephants create about 160 signals / gestures	– use trunk, head, legs, ears, and tail to communicate
– "let's go" gesture—elephant lifts leg and points, others follow	– trunks are very sensitive

Synthesis

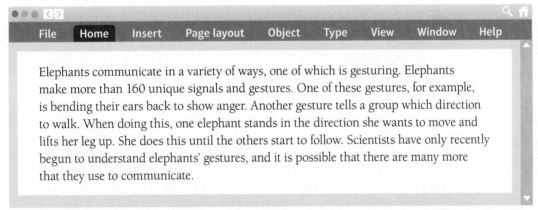

Elephants communicate in a variety of ways, one of which is gesturing. Elephants make more than 160 unique signals and gestures. One of these gestures, for example, is bending their ears back to show anger. Another gesture tells a group which direction to walk. When doing this, one elephant stands in the direction she wants to move and lifts her leg up. She does this until the others start to follow. Scientists have only recently begun to understand elephants' gestures, and it is possible that there are many more that they use to communicate.

VOCABULARY PREVIEW

Read the vocabulary items in the box. Circle the ones you know. Put a question mark next to the ones you don't know.

thunder	decades	looser	instruments
strings	length	wider	

EXERCISE 7

A. Based on an article and a lecture, you will write a paragraph that explains how elephants hear and make different sounds. First, discuss these questions with a partner or small group.

Are there differences between the sounds that humans and elephants make?

What are they?

B. Read the article. Think about the writing assignment in Part A as you read. Annotate the text.

How Elephants Produce Sound

1   The loud trumpet-like sound made by elephants through their trunks is one of the most famous noises of the animal world; but it is not the only sound that elephants make. Elephants can make many different sounds from deep, very low-frequency rumbles (like the sound of thunder) to higher-frequency roars and cries. Over the last few decades, scientists have learned more and more about how elephants make all these sounds.

2   Though humans and elephants look very different on the outside, they both have similar body parts for making sounds. Like humans, elephants have a larynx (or voice box) in their throat. Air that is pushed out from the lungs travels over the larynx and makes the vocal cords (which are part of the larynx) move—similar to the way a flag moves in the wind. This movement makes sound, which can then be changed by the tongue, mouth, and trunk to make more exact sounds for communication.

3   There are also differences in the ways elephants and humans make sounds. Most importantly, the vocal cords in an elephant's larynx are much longer, thicker, and looser than a human's. When the elephant's vocal cords are moved by the passing air, it can make very low-frequency rumbling noises—often so low that people cannot hear them. This is similar to how frequency works with musical instruments: the short, tight strings on a violin make a high-frequency sound; the long, thick, and looser strings of a bass violin make a deep, low-frequency sound.

A violin has short, tight strings that produce higher-frequency sounds.

A bass violin has long, thicker strings that produce lower-frequency sounds.

4 While an elephant's call starts with air passing over the larynx, other parts of the animal's body are also important in controlling the sound. Scientists believe that elephants move their head, neck, and ears to change the position of the larynx so they can create different sounds. Of course, the elephant also has a very large body, and this means the sounds can strongly vibrate through the body and be amplified (i.e., the sound's volume increases). When the trunk is fully extended, stretched out to its full length, the sound is amplified even more powerfully. This means that the low rumbling noises that elephants make can travel long distances. These long-range rumbles are not only useful for communication, but they can also tell the listening elephant how far away the sender is.

C. **Complete the top row of this graphic organizer using your annotations from the reading.**

	Elephants	Humans
How they make sounds		
How they hear sounds		

🔊 D. **Listen to the lecture and add notes to the graphic organizer. When you are finished, compare notes with a partner.**

E. Read the following paragraph about how humans make and hear sounds. Does it synthesize information from the reading and the listening well? Where does the information in each sentence come from: the reading, the listening, or both? Discuss with a partner. As you discuss, keep in mind that in MyEnglishLab, you will write your own paragraph, synthesizing information from these same two sources.

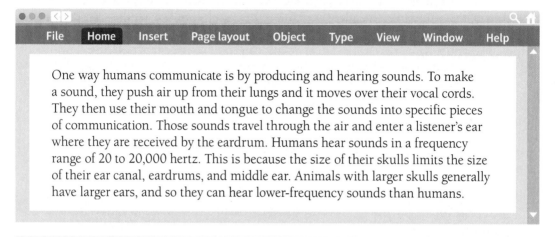

● ● ● ⟨ ⟩   🔍 🏠

| File | Home | Insert | Page layout | Object | Type | View | Window | Help |

One way humans communicate is by producing and hearing sounds. To make a sound, they push air up from their lungs and it moves over their vocal cords. They then use their mouth and tongue to change the sounds into specific pieces of communication. Those sounds travel through the air and enter a listener's ear where they are received by the eardrum. Humans hear sounds in a frequency range of 20 to 20,000 hertz. This is because the size of their skulls limits the size of their ear canal, eardrums, and middle ear. Animals with larger skulls generally have larger ears, and so they can hear lower-frequency sounds than humans.

VOCABULARY CHECK

A. Review the vocabulary items in the Vocabulary Preview. Write their definitions and add examples. Use a dictionary if necessary.

B. Complete each sentence using the correct vocabulary item from the box. Use the correct form.

decade	instrument	length	loose
string	thunder	wide	

1. The 1960s was a(n) .... of great social change in many countries throughout the world.

2. The green anaconda is the largest snake in the world. Found in South America, it can weigh up to 100 kilograms and its average .... is about 4 meters.

3. A bass violin has four ....

The green anaconda

4. During a storm, ... is the loud sound you hear several seconds after you see a bright flash of lightning in the sky.

5. When the strings on a violin are too ...., the violin does not make a good sound.

6. The Amazon River in South America is very .... at some points, measuring 180 kilometers at its mouth, the place where it meets the ocean.

7. Ji-Young knows how to play three .... : violin, trumpet, and guitar.

● Go to MyEnglishLab to complete a skill practice and to join in collaborative activities.

LANGUAGE SKILL

USING COMPLEMENT CLAUSES AFTER *ABOUT*

WHY IT'S USEFUL By using *about* followed by a complement clause, you can better explain the main idea of something you have heard or read.

● Go to MyEnglishLab for the Language Skill presentation and practice.

VOCABULARY STRATEGY

RECOGNIZING COLLOCATIONS TO EXPAND VOCABULARY

WHY IT'S USEFUL By recognizing collocations, you can better understand which words are commonly used together. This can help you to sound more natural when speaking and writing.

Collocations are combinations of words that are frequently used together. For example, we say *take a break* instead of *do a break*, and *a large amount* instead of *a big amount*.

To learn collocations, you have to make a focused effort. This means doing a lot of reading and listening on your own and paying attention to the patterns of words that are used together. This is how you **recognize collocations**. The more effort you make, the more frequently you will notice collocations.

For example, look at this paragraph from the Integrated Skills reading. What verb collocates with the word *sound*?

> The loud trumpet-like **sound** made by elephants through their trunks is one of the most famous noises of the animal world; but it is not the only **sound** that elephants make. Elephants can make many different **sounds** from deep, very low-frequency rumbles (like the **sound** of thunder) to higher-frequency roars and cries. Scientists have learned more and more about how they can make all these **sounds** over the last few decades.

It is easy to see that the answer is *make*. There is no verb form for this sense of the word *sound*, so knowing its collocation is necessary. These word combinations are natural; using an unnatural combination such as *a big amount* or *do a sound* is awkward.

> **TIP**
>
> There are many websites that give lists of collocations for different subject areas, and dictionaries often list very common collocations under the definition for some words. Use these resources to help you learn.

EXERCISE 8

A. Match the words within each of the three groups to form collocations. Use a dictionary if necessary.

1. take	a lecture	5. have	a class	9. do	a challenge
2. give	a look	6. make	research	10. face	a discovery
3. make	competition	7. take	a decision	11. make	an experiment
4. face	a sound	8. do	a discussion	12. take	action

B. Use the collocations in Part A to complete the sentences. Use the correct form.

1. There are so many classes to choose from. It's impossible to .... about which one to take.

2. I like to .... with my friends each semester. It makes the class more interesting.

3. Our professor .... on elephants. She spends her summers observing them in Africa.

4. Horizons Cell Co. .... in the cell phone market. There are many different companies that sell similar products.

5. In the lab section of our biology class, we have to .... and write lab reports with our partners.

C. Read the groups of sentences. Each sentence has a common collocation in
   bold. Then choose the best collocation to complete the final sentence. Use the
   correct form. Use a dictionary if necessary.

1. a. Consumers are often interested in **brand name** clothing such as Burberry,
      Gucci, and Dior.

   b. **Brand loyalty** is important for businesses; they want their customers to come
      back and buy more of their products.

   c. Companies try to create a good **brand image**. Even if the customers don't buy
      the product, they will still think highly of it.

   People pay thousands of dollars for the best .... bags and accessories.

2. a. Our product has a lot of **international competition** in the local market for
      cell phones.

   b. Our school's team had a lot of **stiff competition** in the tournament.

   c. It's good for students to experience a bit of **healthy competition** from
      their classmates.

   We faced some .... in the contest, but we still did well enough to
   finish in second place.

3. a. The speaker presented a few **difficult concepts** in class today.

   b. Design thinking is a fairly **new concept** in product design and business.

   c. The book points out a number of **key concepts** in bioethics.

   Einstein's theory of relativity is a .... in physics. The ideas behind it
   are very complex.

4. a. Your ideas don't **make sense**. Nobody understands them.

   b. If this product doesn't **make** a lot of **money**, then we will have to close down
      the factory.

   c. It's important for Jonathan to **make a strong argument** in the next debate.

   This plan doesn't .... There is no way you can slow climate change
   and use more oil and gas at the same time.

🔾 Go to MyEnglishLab to complete a skill practice.

APPLY YOUR SKILLS

WHY IT'S USEFUL By applying the skills you have learned in this unit, you will be able to synthesize information and acknowledge sources as you participate in college-level courses.

ASSIGNMENT

Prepare and give an individual presentation about the ways a particular animal communicates. Use research and what you have learned in this unit to help you inform the audience and make connections between different sources of information.

BEFORE YOU LISTEN

A. Before you listen, discuss these questions with a partner or group.

1. In this unit, you have looked at the different ways that elephants communicate using sounds, gestures, touch, and seismic communication. Do people also communicate in these ways? Are any unique to elephants / people? Explain your answers using examples.

2. What is seismic communication? Why is it special? How do elephants communicate this way?

3. When humans and elephants produce vocalizations (i.e., sounds) to communicate, they need to make the sound and hear the sound. What are the features of human and elephant anatomy that make this communication possible? What causes the differences in the sounds humans and elephants produce?

B. You will listen to a lecture comparing elephant and human communication. As you listen, think about these questions.

1. Signals are things—like sounds and words—that represent a complex meaning. How do humans use signals to communicate?

2. Do elephants communicate about things that happened in the past?

3. Is communication more important to human survival or elephant survival?

C. Review the Unit Skills Summary on the next page. As you listen to the lecture and prepare for your presentation, apply the skills you learned in the unit.

UNIT SKILLS SUMMARY

SYNTHESIZE INFORMATION AS YOU USE THESE SKILLS:

Take notes on research lectures

- Include the researcher's name, year of publication, and main ideas.
- Use graphic organizers to better understand relationships between ideas.

Relate source information to an audience

- Be brief—include only the most important information.
- Use expressions such as *according to*, etc.

Synthesize information from multiple sources

- Take notes while listening or reading to get a good understanding of the material.
- Plan your writing by focusing on one or two main ideas.
- Cite sources where necessary.

Use complement clauses after *about*

- Give more information on a topic.
- Use the correct word order and *wh-* words.

Recognize collocations to expand vocabulary

- Make an effort to read and listen in your free time.
- Notice words that are often used together.
- Use other resources such as websites and dictionaries to learn collocations.

LISTEN

A. Listen to the lecture and take notes. Try using a mind map to organize your thoughts.

B. Compare notes with a partner. Do you have the same ideas?

C. Review the questions from Before You Listen, Part B. Listen to the lecture again. Work with a partner and use your notes to answer the questions.

Go to MyEnglishLab to listen more closely and answer the critical thinking questions.

THINKING CRITICALLY

Discuss the questions with one or more students.

1. In the lecture, the professor says that our ability to communicate "has led us to where we are today." What exactly does this mean? How has human communication changed the world that we live in?

2. There are many different definitions of *language*, but scholars agree that three key features make human language unique:

   • Humans can talk about things that are not "here and now," that is, they are in the distant past and future, or in a different place.

   • Humans can communicate an infinite (limitless) number of ideas using a finite (limited) system of words and grammar.

   • The sounds of words often have no relation to their meaning.

   By this definition of *language*, is elephant communication a language? How about computer languages? Explain.

THINKING VISUALLY

A. Work with a partner. Look at the elephant gestures. Describe what is happening in each picture. What do the gestures mean? Match the meanings to the pictures.

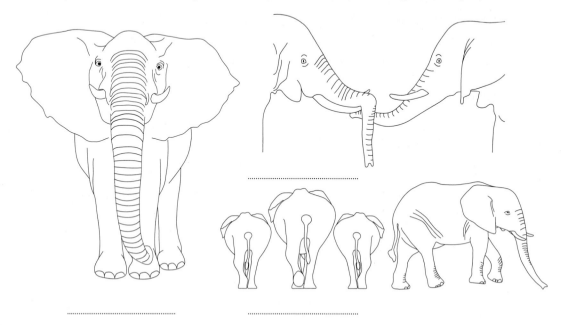

| anger / aggression | Hello. | Let's go! |

B. Think about the gestures that humans use to communicate. Draw 2–3 gestures in the space below. Then describe them to a partner. You partner will have to listen to your description and guess the meaning of the gesture that you describe.

THINKING ABOUT LANGUAGE

A. Combine the sentences using *about* and a complement clause.

> For help with complement clauses after *about*, go to MyEnglishLab, Zoology, Part 2, Language Skill.

1. Our professor wrote a book. Its topic is the importance of conservation.

   Our professor has written a book about why conservation is important.

2. Mira is giving a presentation. The topic is the way that elephants communicate.

3. On his podcast, Sam Harris interviewed Siddhartha Mukherjee. They discussed the reasons for genetic research's usefulness to human health.

4. I read an interesting book. It explains the way that human language evolved over time.

B. Read the sentences with common collocations in bold. Then use the best collocation to complete the final sentence.

1. a. These days, most people **communicate by** email or text message.

   b. He is very good at **communicating** his ideas **to** his colleagues.

   c. I **communicate** well **with** my wife—we always seem to understand each other.

   Elephants .... each other in a variety of ways.

2. a. When working in the wild, some researchers **carry a gun** with them in case they are attacked by animals or other humans.

   b. The hunter **pointed the gun** at the animal, but it ran away just before he could shoot it.

   c. When he **fired the gun**, it made an incredibly loud sound.

   It is illegal to .... in New York City, even in your car.

3. a. I make sure that my **daily schedule** always includes 45 minutes of exercise.

   b. The project is on a very **tight schedule**; we really have to finish everything quickly and on time.

   c. My **class schedule** is full of difficult science classes and long lab hours.

   Let's try not to waste any time. We have a ....

INDIVIDUAL PRESENTATION

A. You have learned a lot about elephants. Other animals also communicate using gestures, vocalizations, or other methods. These include chimpanzees, bonobos, bottlenose dolphins, bats, and bees. What do you know about how these animals communicate? What would you guess?

B. You are going to give a 2–3-minute individual presentation on an animal's way of communicating. You can do research on one of the animals in Part A, or choose a different one. Use these questions as you prepare.

- What is the social organization of the animal?
- How does it communicate (gestures, vocalizations, other signals)? Describe them. What do they mean?
- How did scientists discover the animal's communication?
- Make reference to other people's work / research and consider using visuals in your presentation.
- Be sure to cite your sources.

C. Listen to the presentations and take notes. When your classmates are finished presenting, ask them questions.

◉ Go to MyEnglishLab to watch Professor O'Connell-Rodwell's concluding video and to complete a self-assessment.

The past is full of new discoveries

HISTORY

Main Ideas

UNIT PROFILE

In this unit, you will learn about two more archaeological discoveries: the Dead Sea Scrolls and the Tomb of 10,000 Warriors. You will learn how they were discovered and why they are important to our understanding of the past.

You will prepare and give an individual presentation about an historical site, document, or artifact from your own culture or home country.

OUTCOMES

- Identify main ideas
- Paraphrase to relate main ideas
- Rephrase to simplify ideas
- Construct the present perfect passive
- Utilize a dictionary to understand grammatical behavior

For more about **HISTORY**, see ❶ ❸. See also ⬛R⬛ and ⬛W⬛ **HISTORY** ❶ ❷ ❸.

180 HISTORY PART 2

GETTING STARTED

⬩ Go to MyEnglishLab to watch Dr. Hunt's introductory video and to complete a self-assessment.

Discuss these questions with a partner or group.

1. Do you know any historical sites that are important to understanding human history or culture? Explain.

2. Have you heard of the Dead Sea Scrolls or the Tomb of 10,000 Warriors? If so, share what you know.

> **TIP**
> A scroll is a document that is rolled up, especially an official document from the past.

3. In his introduction, Dr. Hunt asks if you would want to travel to see great historical sites such as the Tomb of 10,000 Warriors. Would you? What famous sites would you like to see in the world?

SKILL 1

IDENTIFYING MAIN IDEAS

WHY IT'S USEFUL By identifying the main ideas in things you read and hear, you can better identify what's important. This will help you to participate in class and to understand related information.

When you listen to a lecture, podcast, or news report in your first language, what do you listen for to **identify the main idea**? The title? Some words or sentences? You probably listen for a few different things.

Whether you know it or not, you are actively doing several things to understand the main idea, and not just *while* listening, but also before and after. Although we learn how to do this at a very young age in our first language, it is not as obvious how we should do it in a second language. Use the strategies on the next page to help you identify the main idea.

Before You Listen

- Activate the knowledge that you already have by making predictions about what you're going to hear. This will prepare you for the keywords and topics that will be discussed.

- Use the context of the listening to guess its purpose (to educate, entertain, persuade). Knowing the purpose will help you to figure out how the main idea is presented.

While Listening

- Pay attention to the beginning. The speaker may state the main idea directly, but more often the speaker will start with a story or "hook" to try to catch your attention and get you interested. After the hook, the speaker will often state the main idea.

- Listen for sentences that clearly express the main idea(s).

- As always, take notes!

> For cues speakers use to emphasize main ideas, see Bioethics, Part 1, Skill 1, page 3.

After Listening

- Read through your notes and organize them. This will help you to identify information the speaker highlighted, emphasized, or repeated—and thus, the main idea(s).

VOCABULARY PREVIEW

Read the vocabulary items in the box. Circle the ones you know. Put a question mark next to the ones you don't know.

statues	ruler	military	placed	buried	damaged

Glossary

Terracotta: hard red-brown baked clay

Jars and flower pots are often made of terracotta.

EXERCISE 1

A. A tomb is the place where a dead body is put and is usually above ground. Do you know of a famous tomb? Explain where it is, whose body is there, and what that person was known for.

B. You are going to listen to a lecture titled "Accidental Discoveries in Archaeology." What do you think the lecture will be about? What will its purpose be? Make a prediction or two with a partner. Then listen and take notes.

C. Were your predictions correct? What other strategies can you use to get the main idea of a lecture or news story?

EXERCISE 2

A. Listen again. Check (✓) the excerpt that is most closely related to the main idea.

☐ It was the first piece of the Terracotta Army, one of the greatest archaeological finds of the 20th century and part of the world's largest tomb—the Tomb of 10,000 Warriors.

☐ Over the years, archaeologists have slowly dug up a huge army from three different places.

☐ When the emperor died, he was buried with this Terracotta Army because he believed that it could protect him in the afterlife—the place some people believe they go after death.

B. Listen again. Then read the statements. Circle T (True) or F (False). Correct the false statements.

T / F   1. Yang Zhifa first discovered the tomb of Qin Shi Huang.

T / F   2. The Tomb of 10,000 Warriors is located near Beijing, China.

T / F   3. All of the soldiers' faces look different from each other.

T / F   4. Other things, such as weapons and horses, were also found in the tomb.

T / F   5. The tomb where Qin Shi Huang is buried is now open to the public.

EXERCISE 3

A. In your own words, state the main idea of the lecture excerpt. Share your idea with a partner. Do you and your partner have similar ways of describing the main idea?

....

B. Do you find the ideas in the lecture to be interesting? Why or why not? How is the tomb similar to / different from other tombs that you know? Discuss with a partner or small group.

VOCABULARY CHECK

A. Review the vocabulary items in the Vocabulary Preview. Write their definitions and add examples. Use a dictionary if necessary.

B. Complete each paragraph using the correct vocabulary items from the box. Use the correct form.

bury	damage	military	place	ruler	statue

Qin Shi Huang was the first emperor of China and he was its (1) .... for 11 years. During his life, he made people build a tomb for him, and later, when he died, his body was (2) .... inside the tomb. With his body, there were all kinds of things such as weapons, terracotta (3) .... of soldiers, and much more.

For centuries, the tomb and everything in it were (4) .... underground until a farmer found the remains of a terracotta warrior while working in a field. In the years since, archaeologists have dug farther and found all the things Qin Shi Huang was buried with. The soldiers were not (5) .... much, and many of the weapons were still in good condition. It seems that his (6) .... support was able to protect him over the years. Archaeologists have yet to enter the part of the tomb where his body is, and it is unlikely that they ever will.

◑ Go to MyEnglishLab to complete vocabulary and skill practices, and to join in collaborative activities.

SKILL 2

PARAPHRASING TO RELATE MAIN IDEAS

WHY IT'S USEFUL By paraphrasing, you can present the main points of another person's ideas using your own words. This can help you to communicate an idea you've heard.

Imagine you heard something interesting in a podcast or lecture and wanted to tell someone else about it. What do you say? Do you quote the speaker's words exactly as he or she said them? Probably not. Instead, you **paraphrase** the original information, that is, you share the meaning of what you heard using different words.

Paraphrasing is an important academic skill. We use it in things like presentations and discussions to share the opinions of important scholars, to support our arguments, and to tell others what we have heard.

Look at two examples of paraphrasing. This first example changes the word form of *discovery* from the original, or source, quote and makes the quote shorter.

> For more about rephrasing to simplify ideas, see History, Part 2, Integrated Skills, page 189.

> For more about word forms, see History, Part 2, Vocabulary Strategy, page 195, and Chemical Engineering, Part 2, Vocabulary Strategy, page 216.

Original: A Chinese farmer made an archaeological <u>discovery</u>: He found the first pieces of terracotta from Qin Shi Huang's Tomb of 10,000 Warriors.

Paraphrase: The speaker said that a Chinese farmer <u>discovered</u> some pieces of the Tomb of 10,000 Warriors.

TIP

Use your own words when paraphrasing. But remember: Don't use words that suggest your opinion or change the speaker's meaning.

In the following example, the paraphrase uses similar words to the source. Notice that it still keeps the same meaning and makes it shorter.

Original: The tomb's exact location was unknown for <u>centuries</u>.

Paraphrase: The tomb's location was unknown for <u>hundreds of years</u>.

Changing word forms and using similar words or synonyms are the two most common ways to paraphrase when speaking.

Additionally, it is common to hear **reporting verbs** that introduce a paraphrase. Below is a short list. Each has a specific meaning.

Common Reporting Verbs That Introduce Paraphrases						
argue	claim	mention	report	say	suggest	state

Read the vocabulary items in the box. Circle the ones you know. Put a question mark next to the ones you don't know.

hid	stated	recent	doubt (v)	claims (n)	running away

Glossary

Scholar: someone who studies a subject and knows a lot about it

Manuscript: an old book written by hand

EXERCISE 4

A. What are the Dead Sea Scrolls? With a partner, share what you already know. If you don't know what they are, do light research online.

🎧 B. Listen to the lecture excerpt about the Dead Sea Scrolls. Check (✓) the reporting verbs you hear.

☐ argue   ☐ claim   ☐ mention   ☐ report

☐ say   ☐ suggest   ☐ state

The Cave of the Dead Sea Scrolls, known as Qumran Cave 4, is one of the caves in which the Dead Sea Scrolls were found, at the ruins of Khirbet Qumran, the West Bank.

C. What's the purpose of paraphrasing? What are different ways to paraphrase?

The Dead Sea Scrolls, as we now know, were ancient texts of the Jewish people. The Jewish people lived in the areas in and around modern-day Israel, western Turkey, Iraq, and northern Egypt, all areas controlled by the Roman Empire (27 BCE–476 CE). At first, they lived peacefully under Roman rule, but eventually they fought each other, with the Romans destroying the Jewish city of Jerusalem and their Second Temple in 70 CE.

EXERCISE 5

🎧 **A. Listen again. Answer these questions.**

1. What is the main idea of the excerpt?
   a. The Dead Sea Scrolls were a big discovery, but people disagree about who wrote them.
   b. The Dead Sea Scrolls were discovered in the 1940s and they are important for history.

2. How many scrolls have been found?
   a. 981
   b. 1,949

3. Some scholars, such as Roland de Vaux, think that the scrolls were _____ .
   a. written by the Essenes
   b. hidden by the Romans

4. Others, such as Yuval Peleg, think that were written by _____ .
   a. only a few people
   b. many different groups

🎧 **B. Listen again. Write the words you hear. Then compare the professor's statement (from the beginning of the listening) to the student's paraphrase (toward the end of the listening). What changes were made? Complete the chart.**

> **Professor:** Let's take a look at two of the ideas and how either could affect our .... of the scrolls.
>
> **Student:** Professor, you mentioned that these two .... could .... how we understand the scrolls. What did you mean?

Professor		Student
ideas	→	
affect	→	
	→	how we understand

EXERCISE 6

A. Read the following excerpts from the lecture. Paraphrase the text. Then share your paraphrases with a partner or small group.

1. The first scrolls were discovered in 1946, and until today, archaeologists have found a total of 981 in 11 Qumran caves.

....

....

2. Roland de Vaux began working in Cave 1 in 1949. He thinks that a religious group called the Essenes lived in Qumran and were the authors of the scrolls.

....

....

3. But more recent discoveries have made some scholars doubt these claims.

....

....

B. Do you and your partner(s) have similar paraphrases? How did you decide to paraphrase the statements? Did they keep the same or similar meanings?

VOCABULARY CHECK

A. Review the vocabulary items in the Vocabulary Preview. Write their definitions and add examples. Use a dictionary if necessary.

B. Complete each sentence using the correct vocabulary item from the box. Use the correct form.

claim	doubt	hide	recent	run away	state

1. The reporter made two .... in her story that were not true.

2. The professor's most .... book presents a new idea about how Stonehenge was built. The book was published last month.

3. You .... that the temple was constructed in only a few years. How were you able to figure out how long it took?

4. They had to .... away from their land because they were afraid that they would be killed.

5. Yuval Peleg argued that people decided to .... the Dead Sea Scrolls because they were afraid that the Romans might destroy them.

6. I .... that she will be able to finish her history paper in time. She just started it this morning, and it's due tomorrow.

⊙ Go to MyEnglishLab to complete vocabulary and skill practices, and to join in collaborative activities.

INTEGRATED SKILLS
REPHRASING TO SIMPLIFY IDEAS

WHY IT'S USEFUL By simplifying ideas, you can share information from sources more effectively. This can help your readers to understand how others' ideas contribute and relate to the points that you are making.

As mentioned in Skill 2, paraphrasing is a key skill for academic life. And this skill is equally important in reading and writing. It helps the reader to understand the main idea of a complex process or thought.

A good author wants the reader to understand her point, so she will **rephrase to simplify ideas**. To do this, you will use many of the same strategies that were presented in Skill 2.

- First, you have to get a deep understanding of the text. Read it a few times and look up words that you don't know.

- Then take the complex idea presented in the text and think about how you can make it simpler. You may not need to include everything that was in the original to make your point—include only the information that is most important for you. Oftentimes, this will make the paraphrase shorter than the original.

- As with speaking, writing can still use similar words as the original.

- Remember to keep the author's original tone; do not introduce your own opinion.

Study these examples:

> **Original (Vanessa Detrie, author):** My claim is that the Essenes hid the Dead Sea Scrolls in the caves outside of Qumran in order to prevent them from being destroyed by the Romans.

> **Paraphrase:** Author Vanessa Detrie (2012) has suggested that the Essenes hid the Dead Sea Scrolls to protect them from the Romans.

In the example, suppose that the paraphrasing author only needs to focus on *why* the Dead Sea Scrolls were hidden, and not *where* they were hidden. She does not include "the caves outside Qumran" because it is not necessary to make her point. This is how paraphrasing can make a thought simpler and shorter—sometimes unnecessary information is not included.

- Lastly, when writing, *use your own words.* Otherwise, you might be accused of plagiarizing—using someone else's words or ideas, pretending that they are your own. Plagiarism has very serious penalties at universities, and professors will fail their students if they plagiarize.

VOCABULARY PREVIEW

Read the vocabulary items in the box. Circle the ones you know. Put a question mark next to the ones you don't know.

complex (n)	project (n)	manufacturing	estimated	period
preserved	analysis	methods	dug up	

EXERCISE 7

A. Read the passage. Then chose the best paraphrases for the excerpts that follow.

What We Have Learned About the Technology of Ancient China from the Tomb of 10,000 Warriors

1   In 1974, a group of Chinese farmers were digging in the fields outside Xi'an, China. A few meters down one of them suddenly found a large chunk of old terracotta. These were ancient statues, the first of many to be found. This has become one of the most extraordinary and mysterious sites of the ancient world.

Arrowhead

---

2 After the discovery, archaeologists quickly arrived at the site. They found that these statues were part of the tomb complex that was built in the 3rd century BCE for the first emperor of China, Qin Shi Huang. The construction of the tomb was a huge project, which had thousands of people working on it. The total area is estimated to be over 35 square miles, and the complex contains the Terracotta Army—about 10,000 statues of Qin's soldiers. These statues are there to protect the emperor in the afterlife. Research at this site has given us new knowledge about the technological developments of this period of ancient Chinese history.

3 The soldiers of the Terracotta Army carried real metal weapons, such as swords and axes. Many of these weapons were stolen not long after the emperor's death, but some remained and have been studied by archaeologists. Usually made of bronze, many of the remaining weapons have been well preserved because of their chrome plating, a thin layer of metal that protected them from damage. Archaeologists thought that this plating technique was first used in Germany and the United States in the mid-20th century. But from this discovery, we now know that the ancient Chinese were using this advanced metal-making technology thousands of years earlier.

4 Over 40,000 arrowheads have also been found at the site. "Chemical analysis has shown," says archaeologist Dr. Frank Vandenberg, "that some groups of these arrowheads have the same chemical composition, which shows that they were made using a *cellular* manufacturing process. By *cellular* we mean that small production teams make the whole arrowhead all at one time, and then they make something completely different. Today, companies like Toyota use the same kind of manufacturing methods." In other words, these ancient Chinese weapon makers used advanced production methods way ahead of their time.

5 These are just two examples of what we have learned from Emperor Qin's tomb about ancient Chinese technology. After 40 years of research, scientists have dug up only a small amount of the tomb complex, so we can look forward to learning more fascinating things in the future.

1. The total area is estimated to be over 35 square miles, and the complex contains the Terracotta Army—about 10,000 statues of Qin's soldiers.

a. The author states that the tomb is more than 35 square miles and includes approximately 10,000 statues of soldiers.

b. The author states that the tomb is home to Qin Shi Huang, the first emperor of China.

2. Archaeologists thought that this plating technique was first used in Germany and the United States in the mid-20th century. But from this discovery, we now know that the ancient Chinese were using this advanced metal-making technology thousands of years earlier.

   a. According to the author, plating techniques were developed in the US and Germany in the 20th century.

   b. According to the author, the ancient Chinese developed plating techniques that were highly advanced for their time.

B. Paraphrase the following excerpts to make them simpler. Then read them to a partner. As you listen to your partner's ideas, compare them to yours.

1. They found that these statues were part of the tomb complex that was built in the 3rd century BCE for the first emperor of China, Qin Shi Huang.

Your paraphrase: ....

....

2. Many of these weapons were stolen not long after the emperor's death, but some remained and have been studied by archaeologists.

Your paraphrase: ....

....

3. After 40 years of research, scientists have dug up only a small amount of the tomb complex, so we can look forward to learning more fascinating things in the future.

Your paraphrase: ....

....

C. Do you and your partner have similar paraphrases? What strategies did you use to write the paraphrases? Discuss.

CULTURE NOTE

The abbreviation BCE means Before the Common Era. This is commonly used for ancient time periods before the year 0. CE, which means Common Era, is sometimes used with years from 1 to the present.

D. Listen to this excerpt from a podcast about the Tomb of 10,000 Warriors.
Take notes using the chart.

Key Idea	Notes
Qin Shi Huang's history	
Information about the tomb	
Technologies in the tomb	

E. Use the information from the reading and the listening to complete the timeline.

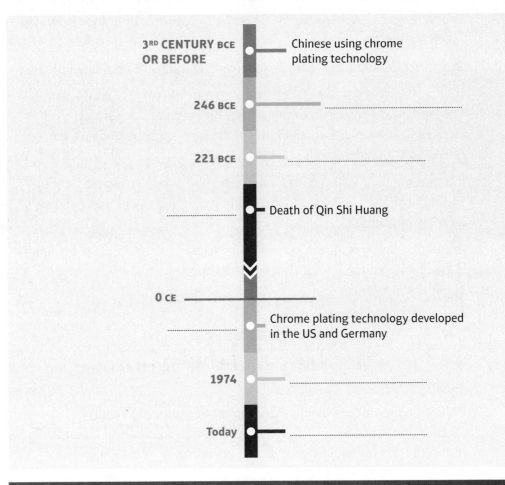

TIP

Timelines are a useful way of organizing the order of events over a period of time. They can help you to understand relationships between events and how they connect to each other.

VOCABULARY CHECK

A. Review the vocabulary items in the Vocabulary Preview. Write their definitions and add examples. Use a dictionary if necessary.

B. Complete each sentence using the correct vocabulary item from the box. Use the correct form.

analysis	complex	dig up	estimated	manufacture
method	period	project	preserve	

1. Researchers are not sure exactly how long it took to complete the building of Stonehenge, but it is .... that local people worked on it and made changes to it for about 1,500 years.

2. The .... between the 5th and 15th centuries in Europe is known as the Middle Ages.

3. The ancient stadium at Olympia, in Greece, is thought to be one of the first sports .... in the world.

4. The Duryea Motor Wagon Company first began to ....
automobiles—or cars—in 1893. It was the first company to do so, but closed a few decades later.

5. It is amazing how early civilizations were able to create complex farming and production ...., including building canals and growing a variety of plants.

6. Archaeologists working at Olduvai Gorge have .... many long-buried tools and remains of early hominid species.

7. The local government wants to construct a new library. The ....
will cost about $13 million.

8. Researchers have completed their .... of the data, and they now believe that early humans lived in all parts of Africa before moving to other places.

9. UNESCO, the United Nations Educational, Scientific, and Cultural Organization, tries to .... the world's natural and cultural history by providing money for its conservation.

🔊 Go to MyEnglishLab to complete a skill practice and to join in collaborative activities.

LANGUAGE SKILL

CONSTRUCTING THE PRESENT PERFECT PASSIVE

WHY IT'S USEFUL By using the present perfect passive, you can say how a situation or action in the past is important to the present. This can help you to speak and write more precisely.

◐ Go to MyEnglishLab for the Language Skill presentation and practice.

VOCABULARY STRATEGY

UTILIZING A DICTIONARY TO UNDERSTAND GRAMMATICAL BEHAVIOR

WHY IT'S USEFUL By understanding grammatical behavior, you can speak and write with more variety. This can help you to paraphrase and communicate more accurately.

As mentioned in Skill 2, one way to paraphrase is to use different word forms. In that section, you saw the following example, where the noun *discovery* was changed to *discovered*, the past tense form of the verb *discover*:

> **Original:** A Chinese farmer made an archaeological <u>discovery</u>: He found the first pieces of terracotta from Qin Shi Huang's Tomb of 10,000 Warriors.

> **Paraphrase:** The speaker said that a Chinese farmer <u>discovered</u> some pieces of the Tomb of 10,000 Warriors.

But for some words the noun and verb are the same, such as the noun / verb *report*. How do we know how to change the noun to a verb and the verb to the noun? It can take years of reading and writing practice to do this as easily as a native speaker, but luckily there are dictionaries to help you. Dictionaries have the noun and verb forms of a word in the same place, so if you look one up, you will find the other close by.

---

dis·cov·er /dɪˈskʌvəʳ/ ••• *verb* [transitive] ◀))

| WORD ORIGIN | VERB TABLE | COLLOCATIONS | THESAURUS |

1 to find something that was hidden or that people did not know about before:
◀)) *The Vikings may have discovered America long before Columbus.*
THESAURUS **find, detect, trace, locate, track somebody/something down, turn something up, unearth**
2 to find out something that is a fact, or the answer to a question:
◀)) *Doctors **discovered that** her left wrist was broken.*
◀)) *Did you ever **discover who** sent you the flowers?*
[Origin: 1300–1400 Old French *descovrir*, from Late Latin *discooperire* "to uncover"]
—**discoverer** *noun* [countable]

(Continued)

---

dis·cov·er·y /dɪˈskʌvri, -vəri/ ●●○ *noun* (plural **discoveries**) ◀))

COLLOCATIONS

1   [countable] **a fact, thing, or answer to a question that someone discovers:**
◀)) *Einstein* **made an** *important scientific* **discovery***.*
◀)) *the* **discovery that** *bees can communicate with each other*

2   [uncountable] **the act of finding something that was hidden or not known before:**
◀)) *the* **discovery of** *gold in 1848*

---

con·fuse /kənˈfyuz/ ●●○ *verb* [transitive] ◀))

WORD ORIGIN   VERB TABLE   COLLOCATIONS

1   **to make someone feel that s/he is unable to think clearly or understand something:**
◀)) *His directions really* **confused** *me.*

2   **to think wrongly that a person or thing is someone or something else:**
◀)) *It's easy to* **confuse** *Sue* **with** *her sister.*

3   **to make something more complicated or difficult to understand:**
◀)) *His questions were just* **confusing** *the* **issue***.*

---

con·fu·sion /kənˈfyuʒən/ ●●○ *noun* ◀))

COLLOCATIONS

1   [uncountable] **a state of not understanding what is happening or what something means:**
◀)) *There's a lot of* **confusion about/over** *the new rules.*
◀)) *The changes in the schedule have* **created confusion***.*

2   [uncountable] **a situation in which you wrongly think that a person or thing is someone or something else:**
◀)) *To* **avoid confusion***, the teams wore different colors.*

3   [singular, uncountable] **a very confusing situation, usually with a lot of noise and action:**
◀)) *With all* **the confusion***, nobody noticed the two boys leave.*
◀)) *The country is in a* **state of confusion***.*

You will notice that the dictionary also includes example sentences with each word. By reading the examples, you can see how each word is used in a sentence. Entries may also show the most common collocation for the word, that is, words that are often used together (e.g., *make a discovery*).

How to use a dictionary to understand grammatical behavior:

- Look up the word that you want to change: *discover*

- Look at its other forms (parts of speech): *discovery*

- Notice the collocations of the new form: *make a discovery*

- Rewrite using the new form: *The research team made an important <u>discovery</u>.*

When you are learning to use words, a dictionary is a valuable resource; use it to understand the form, meaning, and use of different words.

EXERCISE 8

A. Notice the two grammatical categories. Then complete the chart.

Verb	Noun
place	
	belief
argue	
suggest	
	claim
state	
permit	
	analysis
preserve	
estimate	

B. Circle the correct form of the word.

1. The Chinese government has not given archaeologists **permit / permission** to enter the tomb of Qin Shi Huang because they might damage what's inside.

2. I **estimate / estimation** that there are about 150 statues and monuments in the park.

3. Marin **argued / argument** that the Essenes were not the only ones to write the Dead Sea Scrolls.

4. The conference organizers **placed / placement** the presentation table in a bad location.

5. Tom's **suggested / suggestion** was to visit the remains of the palace because he thought they would be educational.

C. Rewrite the sentences from Part B. If the word you circled is a verb, then paraphrase the sentence using a noun. If it is a noun, paraphrase the sentence using a verb.

1. ....

....

2. ....

....

3. ....

....

4. ....

....

5. ....

....

◐ Go to MyEnglishLab to complete a skill practice.

APPLY YOUR SKILLS

WHY IT'S USEFUL By applying the skills you have learned in this unit, you will be able to identify and paraphrase main ideas as you engage in discussions in an academic setting.

ASSIGNMENT

Prepare and give an individual presentation on a historical site, document, or artifact from your own culture or home country. Use your research and what you have learned in this unit to make your topic clear and engaging.

BEFORE YOU LISTEN

A. Before you listen, discuss these questions with a partner or group.

1. Were the Dead Sea Scrolls and the Tomb of 10,000 Warriors discovered because people knew they existed? Explain how they were discovered.

2. Who wrote the Dead Sea Scrolls?

3. How were the Terracotta Army and its weapons made? What does this tell us about technology in the 3rd century BCE?

CULTURE NOTE

Christianity is a religion that is based on the life and teachings of a figure known as Jesus of Nazareth. It is a religion that was influenced by Judaism, the religion of the Jewish people.

B. You will listen to a lecture about two discoveries that have changed our understanding of history. As you listen, think about these questions.

1. Do the Dead Sea Scrolls inform us about Christianity? Explain.

2. What two insights about ancient China have we gained from the discovery of the Tomb of 10,000 Warriors?

C. Review the Unit Skills Summary. As you listen to the lecture and prepare for your presentation, apply the skills you learned in the unit.

UNIT SKILLS SUMMARY

COMMUNICATE MAIN IDEAS BY USING THESE SKILLS:

Identify main ideas

- Predict the content and purpose before listening.
- Listen for verbal cues to the main idea while listening.
- Read and organize your notes after listening.

Paraphrase to relate main ideas

- Make information clear or easy to understand.
- Change word forms if necessary.
- Use reporting verbs.

Rephrase to simplify ideas

- Make sure you understand the source text.
- Use your own words; don't plagiarize.

Construct the present perfect passive

- Use for a situation / action that is continuing.
- Use for a situation / action that has ended recently.

Utilize a dictionary to understand grammatical behavior

- Use a dictionary to find the verb or noun form of a word.
- Look at the examples for common collocations.
- Write a sentence using the alternative part of speech.

LISTEN

A. Listen to the lecture and take notes. Try using a Venn diagram or a T-chart to organize your thoughts.

For an example of a Venn diagram, see History, Part 1, Skill 1, page 72.

B. Compare notes with a partner. Do you have the same ideas? How did the unit skills help you to understand the lecture?

For an example of a T-chart, see Zoology, Part 1, Integrated Skills, page 57.

C. Review the questions from Before You Listen, Part B. Listen to the lecture again. Work with a partner and use your notes to answer the questions.

Go to MyEnglishLab to listen more closely and answer the critical thinking questions.

THINKING CRITICALLY

Discuss the questions with one or more students.

1. Have you gotten any insights about history from this unit? Do you think we should study history? Explain.

2. Marcus Garvey, a black political activist, writer, and publisher from Jamaica said, "A people without the knowledge of their past history, origin, and culture is like a tree without roots." What does this mean? Do you think it is true for humans in general? How about your culture specifically?

THINKING VISUALLY

A. Jesus lived in the same part of the world as where the Dead Sea Scrolls were written. He likely taught in Aramaic, one of the languages that the scrolls were written in. Look at the timeline. Consider these questions.

1. Describe the order of events.

2. How does the order of events relate to the hiding of the Dead Sea Scrolls?

3. Based on the timeline, how might the Dead Sea Scrolls give insights into the start of Christianity?

> ### CULTURE NOTE
>
> The New Testament is the part of the Bible that is about the life of the historic figure Jesus of Nazareth and what he taught.

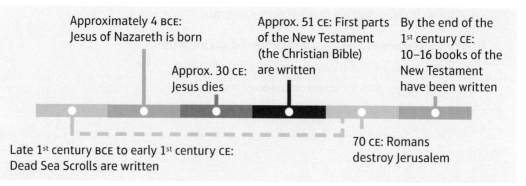

Approximately 4 BCE: Jesus of Nazareth is born

Approx. 30 CE: Jesus dies

Approx. 51 CE: First parts of the New Testament (the Christian Bible) are written

By the end of the 1st century CE: 10–16 books of the New Testament have been written

Late 1st century BCE to early 1st century CE: Dead Sea Scrolls are written

70 CE: Romans destroy Jerusalem

B. Present your ideas from Part A to a partner. Then listen to your partner's ideas and ask questions.

THINKING ABOUT LANGUAGE

> For help with the present perfect passive, go to MyEnglishLab, History, Part 2, Language Skill.

A. Use the verbs in parentheses to complete the sentences. Use the present perfect passive or simple past passive.

1. Fossils .... (find) at Olduvai Gorge in 1911.

2. A book .... (write) recently about the history of the Dead Sea Scrolls.

3. The Tomb of 10,000 Warriors .... (study) for decades.

4. Archaeologists are still not sure why the ancient site .... (build).

B. Read the following excerpt from the listening. Use your knowledge of grammatical behavior to choose the best form of the word. Do not listen again.

> Perhaps more interesting is that some historians have (1) **claim / claimed** that the art styles of the Terracotta Army possibly came from the Greeks. This would (2) **suggest / suggestion** that the Greeks and the Chinese (3) **communicated / communication**, or at least their cultures came into contact during that time. … Maybe a future (4) **discover / discovery** will tell us more about the past and how people were in contact with one another across the world.

INDIVIDUAL PRESENTATION

A. Are there interesting historical sites, documents, or artifacts in your culture or home country? Make a list. Then give a partner a basic description of each.

B. You are going to give a 2–3-minute individual presentation on one of the historic finds you discussed in Part A. Choose the topic. Then use these questions to help you prepare.

- What's the name of your site, document, or artifact? Describe it.

- Who made it? Why did they make it?

- Why is it significant today? Find a quote from an expert and report or paraphrase it.

> For more about presentation structure, see Chemical Engineering, Part 1, Skill 1, page 91.

- Choose a good visual to help your classmates understand.

C. Listen to your classmates and take notes. When they are finished, ask questions.

⬤ Go to MyEnglishLab to watch Dr. Hunt's concluding video and to complete a self-assessment.

CHEMICAL ENGINEERING

Processes

UNIT PROFILE

In this unit, you will learn about fluid dynamics, the way that gases and liquids move. You will also learn about saturation, the process of a solution becoming completely full of a substance.

You will prepare and participate in a pair presentation on a weather condition, including the process that creates the condition and the effect global warming may have on the process.

OUTCOMES

- Interpret and list steps in a process
- Utilize visual aids in a presentation
- Explain a scientific process
- Show sequence with time adverbs
- Develop vocabulary by understanding word families

For more about **CHEMICAL ENGINEERING**, see ❶❸.
See also R and W **CHEMICAL ENGINEERING** ❶❷❸.

GETTING STARTED

◑ Go to MyEnglishLab to watch Professor Spakowitz's introductory video and to complete a self-assessment.

Discuss these questions with a partner or group.

1. A boat floats in water, but a car sinks. Why does this happen? Share your ideas.

2. Describe the way that waves move at the beach. Why do they move that way?

3. In his introduction, Professor Spakowitz says that gravity can affect the flow of fluids like water. What does this mean? How does gravity affect the flow of fluids?

SKILL 1

INTERPRETING AND LISTING STEPS IN A PROCESS

WHY IT'S USEFUL By understanding steps in a process, you can better follow and comprehend the series of actions in an event. In addition, you can give instructions more effectively.

Think of the last thing that you learned to do. Maybe it was how to drive a car. Maybe it was how to get to your friend's house. Every day we learn how to do things by **interpreting steps in a process**, and we explain things by **listing steps in a process**.

Take the example of explaining how to make a cup of tea.

- First, explain the **purpose or outcome** of the process (making a cup of tea) so that the listener understands **why** the process is important. If you say, "Fill that kettle with water" without any other information, the listener might be confused. Therefore, the first part of a process explanation is a brief introduction. It explains the purpose or outcome of the process (making a cup of tea) or its importance (tea is nice to drink).

- Next, tell what equipment is needed. For making tea, this includes a kettle, water, a teapot, a tea bag, and cups.

- Then move on to explaining each step in the process.

- After explaining the steps, give a brief conclusion. Mention the purpose and its importance again.

Notice in this example how the speaker includes this information:

Tea is an easy drink to make and is quite healthy, too. First, you'll need a kettle, some water, a teapot, some tea bags, and some cups. Fill the kettle with water and then heat it. While you are waiting for the water to boil, put the tea bags in the teapot. After the water in the kettle starts to boil, turn off the heat. Next, pour the hot water into the teapot and let the tea dissolve in the water for a few minutes. Finally, pour the tea into the teacups and enjoy. It's an easy process and tea is a healthy alternative to other drinks, like soda.

You can see the parts of the process in this chart:

Process:	how to make a cup of tea
Purpose or Outcome:	a cup of tea
Things You Need:	kettle, water, teapot, tea bag, cups
Steps:	Fill the kettle with water.
	Heat the water.
	Put the tea bags in the teapot.
	After the water boils, turn off the heat.
	Pour the hot water into the teapot.
	Let the tea dissolve in the water.
	Pour the tea into the teacups.
	Enjoy the tea.

VOCABULARY PREVIEW

Read the vocabulary items in the box. Circle the ones you know. Put a question mark next to the ones you don't know.

float (v)	solid (adj)	sinks	weighs
displaces	experiment (n)	bucket	

Glossary

Force: (n) power

Water level: location and position of the water

EXERCISE 1

A. Have you ever been on a boat? How do you think boats stay on top of the water?

B. Listen to a lecture about fluid dynamics. Check (✓) the process(es) the speaker explains.

☐ fluid dynamics

☐ buoyancy

☐ displacement

C. Was it easy or difficult to understand the steps in the process(es)? What words helped you? What did the speaker do to make it easier?

EXERCISE 2

A. Listen again. Write explanations for these terms.

1. fluid dynamics ....

2. buoyancy ....

3. displacement ....

B. Outline the displacement process in the chart.

Process:	Measuring displacement of objects in water
Purpose or Outcome:	
Things You Need:	
Steps:	1. ....
	....
	2. ....
	....
	3. ....
	....
	4. *Pour out the water that is in the bucket and weigh that water.*
	5. ....
	....
	6. ....
	....

EXERCISE 3

A. Choose a simple process that you are familiar with (e.g., making coffee, using an ATM card, downloading an app to your phone). Use the chart to prepare a short explanation of the process. Then explain the steps to a partner.

Process:	
Purpose or Outcome:	
Things You Need:	
Steps:	

B. Did your partner explain all parts of the process? What parts of the explanation were clearest? What parts were less clear?

VOCABULARY CHECK

A. Review the vocabulary items in the Vocabulary Preview. Write their definitions and add examples. Use a dictionary if necessary.

B. Complete the paragraph using the correct vocabulary items from the box. Use the correct forms.

bucket	displace	experiment	float	sink	solid	weigh

There is an easy (1) .... to demonstrate buoyancy. First, fill a glass of water. Put the glass of water into a(n) (2) .... Then take a(n) (3) .... object such as a coin and place it in the glass of water. You will notice that the coin will (4) .... to the bottom of the glass; it will not (5) .... The coin (6) .... some water in this process. Use a scale to (7) .... that water, and you will see that it is less than the weight of the coin.

🔊 Go to MyEnglishLab to complete vocabulary and skill practices, and to join in collaborative activities.

SKILL 2

UTILIZING VISUAL AIDS IN A PRESENTATION

WHY IT'S USEFUL By using visual aids when presenting, you can make your ideas clearer to your audience. That way, they can understand your ideas better. It can also help you to explain the content and remember the main ideas of your presentation.

A **visual aid** is something a speaker shows the audience to help explain an idea in a presentation. In a traditional classroom, teachers may write notes and diagrams on the board to help students understand material. They also might show short videos or provide handouts. In universities and businesses, professors and businesspeople usually use presentation software such as PowerPoint and Prezi, especially when there is a large audience. This software can display text, videos, charts, graphs, and pictures.

Why Use Visual Aids?

- Visual aids make a presentation more interesting. Pictures and videos can bring life to a presentation.

- Visuals also help speakers to communicate their ideas better and remember their main points.

- Lastly, people remember and understand things better when they can hear *and* see them.

What Kinds of Visual Aids Should I Include in My Presentation?

Most presentation software breaks information into separate slides. These are the most common types of visuals used in presentations:

- text-only slides

- charts and graphs

- images and diagrams

Text-Only Slides

Text-only slides are simple: They have only text. The title slide of a presentation is often text-only. It might have the title of the presentation, the presenter's name, and the date. Presenters use text-only slides to do the following:

- outline the presentation

- highlight the main points and key supporting details

- define important terms, provide useful quotes

- ask questions of the audience

When creating text-only slides, don't put too much information on one slide. As a general rule, use one slide for a main point and its basic supporting points. Remember the slide is there to give an outline, not to give details.

Tsunamis

● **Causes:**

　○ Earthquakes

　○ Underwater landslides

　○ Volcanic eruptions

Text-only slide

TIP

The text on a slide should guide the presenter and the audience through the presentation. Too much text is hard to read. Limit the text on your slides to three or four bullet points. Aim for no more than 25 words per slide.

Charts and Graphs

Charts and graphs can be useful when presenting numbers and statistics. Pie charts and line graphs are common.

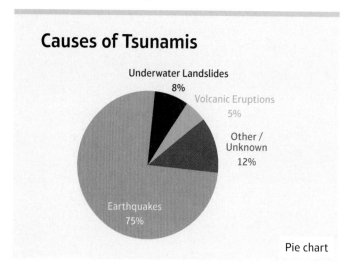

Causes of Tsunamis

Pie chart

Choose a graph that makes sense for your subject matter. For example, pie charts are better for percentages and line graphs are better for changes over time.

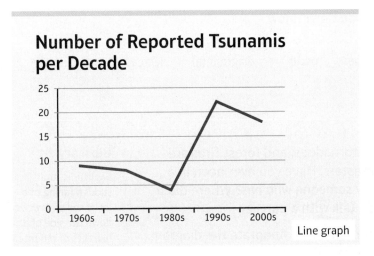

Line graph

Images and Diagrams

Images and diagrams bring words to life. They show your audience what you are talking about by giving a picture of complex concepts and processes. You can make them clearer by adding a few words. Adding a title and labels to the important parts will help your audience follow along.

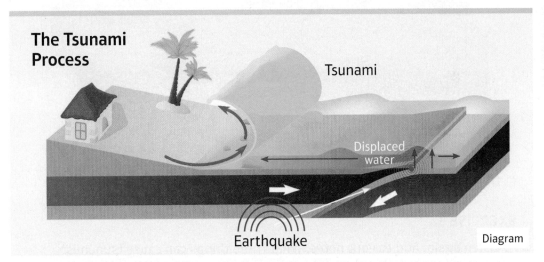

Diagram

TIP

Visual aids add life to presentations and make them more interesting. However, too many slides, words, or visuals can make a good presentation less interesting. Remember that the audience wants to get ideas and information from *you*, not only your slides. Having *fewer* slides leads to *more* understanding.

EXERCISE 4

A. Tsunamis, earthquakes, tornadoes, and forest fires are examples of natural disasters. Have you ever been in a natural disaster or know someone who has? Where did it occur? What happened? Talk with a partner.

Glossary

Landslide: the sudden falling of a lot of soil and rocks down the side of a hill, cliff, or mountain

🕕 B. Listen to a lecture about tsunamis. Annotate the diagram. Why did the speaker use this visual?

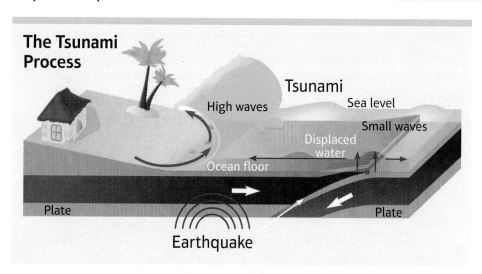

The Tsunami Process

C. Did the visual help you understand the lecture? If so, how?

EXERCISE 5

🕕 A. Listen again. Add to your notes. What three things can cause tsunamis?

....

B. Complete the sentences using information from the lecture, the visual, and your notes.

1. When an earthquake causes a tsunami, the .... moves.

2. This releases a lot of energy into the ....

3. The energy moves across the surface of the water in .... , sometimes moving at the speed of ....

4. They slow down because of .... , which makes them ....

EXERCISE 6

A. Work with a partner. Take turns using your notes from Exercises 4 and 5 to explain how tsunamis start. Point to parts of the diagram in Exercise 4 as you speak.

B. Was it easier to explain or listen? Was the diagram helpful?

VOCABULARY CHECK

A. Review the vocabulary items in the Vocabulary Preview. Write their definitions and add examples. Use a dictionary if necessary.

B. Complete each sentence using the correct vocabulary item from the box. Use the correct form.

decrease	destroy	diagram	earthquake	occur	volcano

1. Tsunamis are often caused by .... They happen underwater when the ocean floor moves, which results in a release of energy.

2. Occasionally, landslides or .... cause tsunamis. Like earthquakes, volcanoes can .... far out at sea.

3. The biggest tsunamis can .... towns that are along the water.

4. As you can see in the .... on Slide B, the distance between waves .... as the waves get close to land.

○ Go to MyEnglishLab to complete vocabulary and skill practices, and to join in collaborative activities.

INTEGRATED SKILLS

EXPLAINING A SCIENTIFIC PROCESS

WHY IT'S USEFUL By learning how to explain scientific processes, you can feel more confident talking and writing about experiments and research findings.

Explanations of processes are common in science textbooks, lab reports, and research papers. They are also common in science lectures and presentations.

For a student in any scientific field, explaining a process is a necessary skill. Most scientific reports are organized the same way.

1. A process explanation begins with an **introduction**. In the introduction, state the goal or outcome of the process. Also, explain why the process is important. For complex processes, you can also preview the most important steps of the process.

2. Then move on to the **process explanation**. Depending on the purpose of your explanation, you may use different voices:

   - When **giving instructions** (explaining how to do something), it is common to use the imperative voice: *Heat the solution to 50°C.*

   - When **reporting a process** used in an experiment, it is common to use the passive voice. When you explain the process, be as detailed as possible. Include every step and every measurement. That way, if readers want to do the same experiment themselves (an important part of scientific research), they will have all the necessary information.

3. Finally, include a brief **conclusion**. Restate the significance of the process. If you are reporting an experiment, include your results or what you learned.

Report Part	Purpose	Example
Introduction	Explain the goal or outcome of the process Explain why the process is important	*The purpose of this process is to …* *… is important because …* *We aim to …*
Process explanation	Explain how to do something Report a process used in an experiment	*First, heat the solution to 50°C. Then cool the solution to …* *First, the solution was heated to 50°C. After that …* *Finally, we measured …*
Conclusion	Explain the significance of the process Present results of the process	*As a result, you will find that …* *The results of our experiment showed that …*

VOCABULARY PREVIEW

Read the vocabulary items in the box. Circle the ones you know. Put a question mark next to the ones you don't know.

mixture	substance	powder	stir	limited	measured	steel

EXERCISE 7

A. Think of a scientific experiment you took part in. What was memorable about it?

B. Read the text. Then answer the questions on the next page.

Solutions, Saturation, and an Experimental Process

1 A solution is a type of mixture in which one substance is dissolved into another. Many types of solutions that we see in daily life involve water. For example, take a substance such as a spoonful of coffee powder (the solute) and mix it into a cup of water (the solvent). As you stir the coffee into the water, the solid coffee granules eventually disappear. This is because the coffee is water soluble; the coffee powder has dissolved into the liquid, and now you have a solution in the cup: liquid coffee. We can see the same process when other solutes, such as sugar and salt, are mixed into water.

2 The amount of a solute that can dissolve into a solvent is limited. For example, if you keep adding salt to a glass of water, eventually the water will not be able to absorb any more salt, and you will start to see undissolved salt granules in the bottom of the glass. When this happens, the solution has reached its saturation point and has gone through a process we call *saturation*.

3 The saturation point is different for every substance. This is called a substance's *solubility*. Solubility is usually measured by the number of grams of a substance that can dissolve in a certain amount of water at a given temperature.

4 A simple experiment can demonstrate the different levels of solubility of two substances: salt and sugar. First, take two glasses of water of equal size. In one glass, add a spoonful of sugar, and in the other a spoonful of salt. Then stir the solutions for a minute or two so that the sugar and salt mix in completely. After that, add another spoonful to each glass, and stir again. Keep going until the water in each glass cannot absorb any more of the solute, that is, until they reach their saturation points (you will know this when you see the sugar or salt stay in the bottom of the glass). Finally, you will find that the salt solution will reach its saturation point sooner than the sugar solution. So now we know that in water, sugar is more soluble than salt.

(Continued)

5 The examples we have looked at so far are all liquid solutions with solid solutes dissolving into liquid solvents. But solutions can also be made with gases. For example, carbon dioxide dissolved in liquid makes sparkling soda drinks. There are also solutions that are solids, such as steel.

CULTURE NOTE

Carbonated drinks were first created 1767 in Leeds, England, by Joseph Priestley, who added carbon dioxide to water to make the liquid fizzy. Today the sale of soft drinks—carbonated water with sugar and other flavors added—is big business with an estimated 950 billion liters sold in 2017. At around 40 grams of sugar per can, however, the product has become a target of children's health organizations.

1. Paragraph .... describes an experiment.

2. The writer includes this experiment in order to ....
....

3. What are the steps in this experiment? Write them. ....
....
....
....

C. Do you think an image or diagram would help you understand this text better? If so, what would you like it to show? If not, why not?

D. Listen to the explanation of how to make a supersaturated solution of sugar and water. As you listen, study the following line graph. Take notes in the process diagram on the next page.

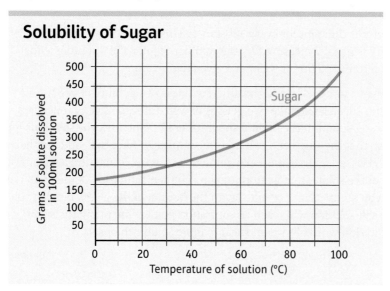

Solubility of Sugar

Grams of solute dissolved in 100ml solution

Sugar

Temperature of solution (°C)

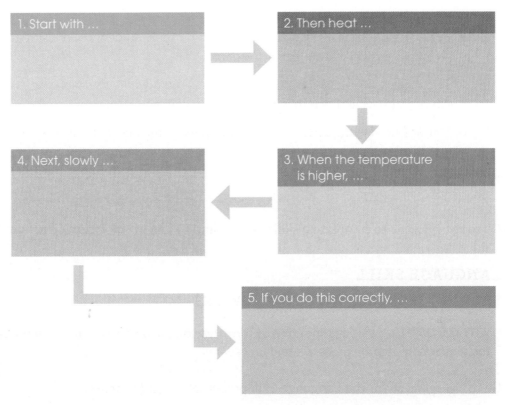

1. Start with …

2. Then heat …

4. Next, slowly …

3. When the temperature is higher, …

5. If you do this correctly, …

🎧 E. **Listen again. Then compare notes with a partner. Were the steps easy to follow? Was the speaker's line graph helpful? What could be added to the presentation to make the concept easier to understand?**

F. **Work with a partner. Starting with a glass of water and sugar, how would you make a supersaturated sugar-water solution? Use information from the reading and lecture.**

VOCABULARY CHECK

A. **Review the vocabulary items in the Vocabulary Preview. Write their definitions and add examples. Use a dictionary if necessary.**

B. **Complete each sentence using the correct vocabulary item from the box. Use the correct form.**

limit	measure	mixture	powder	steel	stir	substance

1. There is some white .... at the bottom of the cup. I think it is sugar.

2. .... the salt into the water until it dissolves completely.

3. Many car parts are made of ....

(Continued)

4. Registration for the class is .... to 50 students, so be sure to sign up early while space is still available.

5. There was a strange green .... on my bike this morning. I'm not sure what it was, but it felt like jelly and it smelled strange.

6. You will need to .... the water in the bucket to see how much was displaced.

7. Keep adding salt to the .... until it is saturated.

⊙ Go to MyEnglishLab to complete a skill practice and to join in collaborative activities.

LANGUAGE SKILL

SHOWING SEQUENCE WITH TIME ADVERBS

WHY IT'S USEFUL By using time adverbs correctly, you can be clearer when describing the sequence of steps in processes and procedures.

⊙ Go to MyEnglishLab for the Language Skill presentation and practice.

VOCABULARY STRATEGY

DEVELOPING VOCABULARY BY UNDERSTANDING WORD FAMILIES

WHY IT'S USEFUL By learning about word families, you can improve your range of vocabulary and become a more accurate speaker and writer.

Many English words have similar meanings and roots. However, they are different parts of speech. For example, the word *different* is an adjective, *difference* is a noun, and *differ* is a verb.

All of the above words have the same root word (*differ*). The suffixes (endings) of the words make them different parts of speech. Word families often have a different word for each part of speech: a noun, adjective, and verb. In some cases, they have more than one word for a part of speech. For example, there are two verbs in the *differ* word family, *differ* and *differentiate*. Study the chart on the next page.

Root	Verb	Noun	Adjective
differ-	differ / differentiate	difference	different
norm-		norm	normal
experiment-	experiment	experiment	experimental
balance-	balance	balance	balanced
limit-	limit	limit / limitation	limited / unlimited
measure-	measure	measure / measurement	measured / measuring

How can you learn different word forms in a word family? The best way is by reading actively. First, look at the root. Does it look like a word you already know? Then look at its location in the sentence. Its location will tell you what part of speech it is. For example, in Skill 2, you learned the word *destroy*. Now look at the underlined word in this sentence:

The 2004 tsunami was the most <u>destructive</u> in history.

First, notice the root, *destr-*. Then notice where it is in the sentence. It follows *the most*, so you might correctly guess that *destructive* is an adjective. It means *causing damage or harm*. Now look at how the noun form is used:

The <u>destruction</u> that was caused by the 2004 tsunami was some of the worst in history.

Again, notice the root, *destr-*. *Destruction* is the subject of this sentence, so you might correctly guess it is a noun. *Destruction* is the process of being destroyed.

CULTURE NOTE

English itself is a "family" of languages, with contributions from some 350 other languages. It is most closely related to Frisian (a language spoken in an area of northern Germany), German, and Dutch / Flemish. Many of the roots of English words are Germanic, Greek, and Latin in origin. Though learners have trouble with the "exceptions to the rules" of English, the language is, in fact, easier to use today than it was when it began some 5,000 years ago. One of the biggest changes: Words that were once a single part of speech (verbs: *act, show, mark*) can now be used as both noun and verb.

EXERCISE 8

A. Complete the chart with the missing words. Use a dictionary if needed.

Root	Verb	Noun	Adjective
destr-	destroy	destruction	destructive
know-	know		
creat-	create	/	
dens-		density	
			illustrative
	survive	/	

B. Complete the sentences. Use the correct form of the root in parentheses. Use the chart above to help you.

1. Using visual aids is important when you want to .... complex ideas or processes. But do not use too many .... or your audience could get bored. (illustrat-)

2. An object's .... will determine whether it sinks or floats. Objects that are less .... than water will float. (dens-)

3. How do birds .... in the cold months? Different bird species have different .... techniques. (surv-)

4. Rodrigo is a very .... artist. He likes to .... all sorts of things, from paintings to music. (creat-)

5. Julie .... a lot about physics. She is very .... on the subject. (know-)

C. Work with a partner. Complete the chart with other new words you have learned in this unit. Use a dictionary if needed.

Root	Verb	Noun	Adjective

◐ Go to MyEnglishLab to complete a skill practice.

APPLY YOUR SKILLS

WHY IT'S USEFUL By applying the skills you have learned in this unit, you will be able to understand and explain processes as you participate in college-level courses.

ASSIGNMENT
Prepare and participate in a pair presentation on a weather condition and the process that creates it. Use what you have learned about explaining a process and using visual aids to explain the process and weather condition.

BEFORE YOU LISTEN

A. Before you listen, discuss these questions with a partner or group.

1. Have you heard of the term *global warming*? What is it?

2. What causes global warming?

3. What effects does global warming have on the weather?

B. You will listen to a lecture about water vapor (water in the air) and global warming. As you listen, think about these questions.

1. What is evaporation? How does temperature affect it?

2. What is dew? Why does it form? How does it form? Describe the process.

3. What are some possible effects of global warming on the weather?

C. Review the Unit Skills Summary on the next page. As you listen to the lecture and prepare for your pair presentation, apply the skills you learned in this unit.

UNIT SKILLS SUMMARY

IDENTIFY PROCESSES BY USING THESE SKILLS:

Interpret and list steps in a process

- Identify the introduction to a process or procedure.
- Identify the main steps in the process or procedure.
- Identify the conclusion of the process.

Utilize visual aids in a presentation

- Use visual aids that focus on main points or illustrate difficult concepts.
- Choose the best type of visual aid for your information.
- Add images and diagrams.

Explain a scientific process

- Recognize the parts of a scientific process explanation.
- Understand the difference between a process explanation and reporting a process.
- Explain the different parts of a scientific process.

Show sequence with time adverbs

- Understand the purpose and placement of time adverbs and adverbials.
- Use time adverbs and adverbials to describe a process.

Develop vocabulary by understanding word families

- Understand how the same roots are used in different parts of speech.
- Choose the correct parts of speech in speaking and writing.

Glossary

Atmosphere: the mixture of gases that surrounds Earth and other planets

Scale: the size or level of something, when compared to what is normal

LISTEN

🎧 **A.** Listen to the lecture about water vapor and global warming. Take notes on key ideas. Try adding notes to the diagram below.

Dew on grass

A forest fire

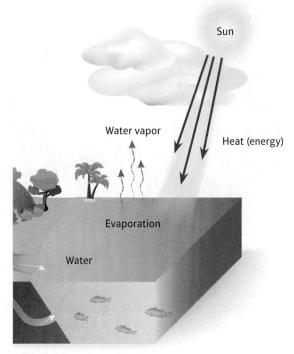

The process of evaporation

B. Compare notes with a partner. Do you have the same ideas?

🎧 **C.** Review the questions from Before You Listen, Part B. Listen to the lecture again. Work with a partner and use your notes to answer the questions.

🡪 Go to MyEnglishLab to listen more closely and answer the critical thinking questions.

THINKING CRITICALLY

Discuss these questions with one or more students.

1. During the cold months in many climates, air is often much drier. Why is this? Why don't we see much dew when it's cold?

2. Based on your knowledge of fluid dynamics and weather, do you think the size or frequency of tsunamis will change because of global warming? If yes, explain. If no, give an example of a weather event that will change because of global warming.

THINKING VISUALLY

A. Look at the line graph. Discuss these questions with a partner.

1. What does the graph show?
2. What was the change in average global temperature between 1880 and 2005?
3. Do you think temperatures will continue to increase in the future? Why or why not?

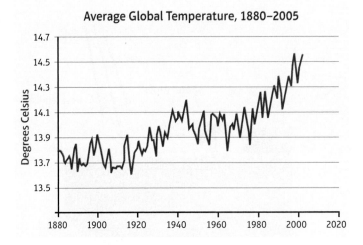

Average Global Temperature, 1880–2005

B. Use information from the following chart to add to the line graph above. Then compare and discuss line graphs with a partner.

Predictions for Increases in Average Global Temperatures

Year	Low Estimate (change in temperature °C from 2005)	High Estimate (change in temperature °C from 2005)
2065	+1.4	+2.0
2100	+1.8	+3.7
2200	+2.3	+6.5
2300	+2.5	+7.8

THINKING ABOUT LANGUAGE

A. Complete the lecture excerpt with the correct parts of speech.

> **Professor:** These processes (1) **explain / explanation / explainable** why global (2) **warm / warming / warmth** — the increase in average global temperatures—is so (3) **problematic / problem / problematize**. For instance, most scientists, myself included, (4) **predict / prediction / predictable** that there will be stronger rainstorms because of this. This is climate change, and it will likely (5) **create / creative / creation** more floods. Also, higher temperatures cause more (6) **evaporate / evaporating / evaporation**, which makes the land in these places drier. This is especially bad for people with little water to begin with—they need it for food, for life. And in places like California, drier land is part of the reason for terrible forest fires.

B. Choose words from the unit that you would like to use in your own speaking and writing. Create a word family chart for each.

C. Work with a partner. Explain the steps in a scientific or everyday process you are familiar with. Describe the sequence using time adverbs.

> For help with showing sequence with time adverbs, go to MyEnglishLab, Chemical Engineering, Part 2, Language Skill.

PAIR PRESENTATION

A. You will work with a partner to give a 5-minute presentation on a weather condition and the process that creates it. Read this short passage, look at the images on the next page, and then respond to these questions.

Fog, clouds, hurricanes, and drought are weather conditions. They are all the result of the amount of water in the atmosphere. Global warming can affect the processes that create these weather conditions. What do you know about these conditions? What about the processes that create them? What do you know about global warming and its effects?

Fog

Clouds

Hurricane

Drought

B. With your partner, follow these steps:

1. Choose one weather condition and research it.

2. In your talk, discuss both the process that creates the weather condition and how global warming may affect the process.

3. Outline your presentation and practice it.

4. Use at least one visual aid in your presentation.

C. Listen to each presentation. Take notes and think about your classmates' use of time adverbs / adverbials and visual aids. How did they help you understand the presentation?

● Go to MyEnglishLab to watch Professor Spakowitz's concluding video and to complete a self-assessment.

Extended Lectures

Part 3 presents authentic content written and delivered by university professors. Academically rigorous application and assessment activities allow for a synthesis of the skills developed in Parts 1 and 2.

BIOETHICS

Bringing Back the Dead

UNIT PROFILE

In this unit, you will watch a lecture about de-extinction. You will learn what it is, how it could happen, and which extinct animals could possibly come back to life. You will also think about the advantages and disadvantages of this process.

You will prepare an individual presentation on an extinct animal and explain why you believe it would be good for the world if it existed again.

For more about **BIOETHICS**, see **1** **2**. See also R and W **BIOETHICS** **1** **2** **3**.

EXTENDED LECTURE

BEFORE YOU VIEW

Think about these questions before you view the lecture "Bringing Back the Dead." Discuss them with another student.

1. What animals once lived on our planet but are no longer alive today?

2. What do you think scientists could do to bring back these animals?

3. What are the advantages and disadvantages of bringing back extinct animals?

LECTURE—SECTION 1

Glossary

Woolly mammoth: an extinct mammal that was covered in thick hair and lived in cold northern regions

Ice Age: a period of time thousands of years ago, when ice covered a large part of the Earth

Cattle: cows and bulls that are used for milk or meat

Descendant: someone (or something) who is related to a person (or animal) who lived a long time ago

DNA: deoxyribonucleic acid—a substance found in the cells of living things, that carries biological information passed from parent to child

Cloning: making an exact copy of a plant or animal by taking a cell from it and developing it artificially

Embryo: an organism in the first eight weeks of development

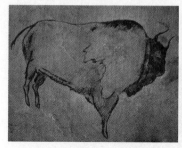
Cave painting of an auroch

Dolly the cloned sheep

An ibex in the French Alps

◐ Go to MyEnglishLab to view the first section of Professor Greely's lecture. Use the outline on the next page to take notes while you listen. Then answer the questions in Check What You've Learned.

TIP

Outlining is an effective way to take notes. It allows you to see the main points, supporting ideas, details, and examples clearly. See Bioethics, Part 1, Organizing Notes by Outlining, page 12.

I.

   A.

      1.

      2.

   B.

      1.

      2.

II.

   A.

      1.

      2.

   B.

      1.

      2.

   C.

      1.

      2.

CULTURE NOTE

Jurassic Park is a popular science fiction movie that was released in 1993. In the movie, a scientist has successfully brought dinosaurs back to life on an island. He hopes to make an amusement park for visitors to see the live dinosaurs. However, the dinosaurs become out of control, and cause many problems for the scientists on the island.

CHECK WHAT YOU'VE LEARNED—SECTION 1

Think about the lecture you have just viewed and refer to your notes.
Choose the best answers.

1. According to Professor Greely, what is de-extinction?

   a. the process animals and plants experience when they are dying
   b. the process of bringing something that was once extinct back to life
   c. the process of getting a virus
   d. the process dinosaurs went through millions of years ago

2. What three methods does Professor Greely explain?

   a. back-breeding, DNA analysis, and gene editing
   b. cloning, DNA analysis, and gene editing
   c. back-breeding, cloning, and gene editing
   d. none of the above

3. Which method does Professor Greely feel is the most possible way to bring back extinct animals?

   a. gene editing
   b. cloning
   c. DNA analysis
   d. back-breeding

Go to MyEnglishLab to watch Section 1 again. Check your answers and add details to your outline. Then continue to the next section of the lecture.

LECTURE—SECTION 2

Glossary

Advantage: a good or useful feature that something has

Disadvantage: a negative or bad feature that something has

Risk: the possibility that something bad, unpleasant, or dangerous may happen

Harm: to have a bad effect on something

Moral hazard: making a poor choice because you feel protected

Ecosystem: the living things in a place and their relationship to the environment

Awe: a feeling of great respect and admiration

Fund: to provide money for something

Pleistocene: a period of time, millions of years ago, when much of the planet was frozen

Wolves in Yellowstone National Park

An elk in Yellowstone National Park

Cliffs in Yosemite Valley

⬥ Go to MyEnglishLab to view the second section of Professor Greely's lecture. Use the outline to take notes while you listen. Then answer the questions in Check What You've Learned.

	(Continued from page 228)

III.

  A.

    1.

  B.

    1.

  C.

    1.

    2.

IV.

  A.

    1.

  B.

    1.

  C.

    1.

    2.

V.

  A.

  B.

  C.

CULTURE NOTE

Natural selection is the belief that some animals have the skills or characteristics to survive and adapt while others do not. Many biologists believe that natural selection could be a reason some animals disappear.

CHECK WHAT YOU'VE LEARNED—SECTION 2

Think about the lecture you have just viewed and refer to your notes. Choose the best answers.

1. What three disadvantages, or risks, does Professor Greely talk about?
   a. We may experience something like *Jurassic Park.*
   b. Those species could harm the environment.
   c. Humans should not decide what lives and what dies.
   d. Those species could carry disease that would affect humans or other animals.
   e. De-extinction could make people less concerned about endangered species.
   f. These new species could have health problems which would be a moral hazard.

2. What four advantages does the professor describe?
   a. Bringing back species could benefit the environment.
   b. Some species could change the ecosystem.
   c. People want to see the woolly mammoth.
   d. Scientists could do research.
   e. Animals could inspire awe or wonder.
   f. People could be more interested in the environment.

CULTURE NOTE

Yosemite Valley is a national park in the western Sierra Nevada Mountains of Northern California. It is 1 mile deep and over 8 miles long. It attracts many visitors from around the world who enjoy the natural beauty of the valley.

3. What are three reasons why Professor Greely feels it is important to ask questions about de-extinction?
   a. Although studying these species might be helpful, the government cannot afford it.
   b. Although bringing back extinct species is interesting, it may take funds from other important research.
   c. Although studying once-extinct animals may benefit humans, it may not benefit other animals.
   d. Although seeing once-extinct animals would be amazing, we need to think about the well-being of those animals.
   e. Although bringing back once-extinct species might be interesting, we need to protect our existing natural resources.
   f. Although seeing once-extinct animals would be very cool, it could bring back dangerous diseases as well.

● Go to MyEnglishLab to watch Section 2 again. Check your answers and add details to your outline. Then complete a script analysis activity.

THINKING CRITICALLY

Look back at your notes, and answer the questions with another student.

1. In addition to the advantages and disadvantages Professor Greely discusses, are there other advantages and disadvantages to de-extinction? If so, what are they?

2. Based on the overall lecture, do you think the advantages of de-extinction are greater than the disadvantages? Why or why not?

3. What can you infer from Professor's Greely's comment, "We don't want *Jurassic Park* to happen. But Pleistocene Park might be a very nice place indeed."?

● Go to MyEnglishLab to complete a critical thinking activity.

THINKING VISUALLY

A. Work with a partner. Look at the diagram. Take turns paraphrasing each step in the process. Which method of de-extinction appears in this diagram?

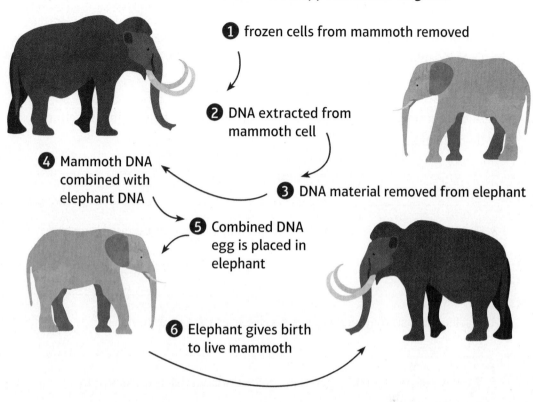

1 frozen cells from mammoth removed

2 DNA extracted from mammoth cell

3 DNA material removed from elephant

4 Mammoth DNA combined with elephant DNA

5 Combined DNA egg is placed in elephant

6 Elephant gives birth to live mammoth

B. Without looking at the diagram, take turns summarizing each step of the process.

THINKING ABOUT LANGUAGE
IDENTIFYING SUBJECT RELATIVE CLAUSES

Use a relative clause to combine the sentences.

TIP

Subject relative clauses use relative pronouns (*who, which, that*) and give more information about the subject of a sentence. For help with subject relative clauses, go to MyEnglishLab, Bioethics, Part 1, Language Skill.

1. Extinct animals have descendants.
   Descendants carry DNA.

   ....

2. The government supports programs. Some programs involve investigating de-extinction.

   ....

   ....

3. CRISPR is a gene editing method. It has made gene editing much cheaper.

   ....

   ....

4. A scientist is studying new methods. He lives next door to me.

   ....

5. We have to protect endangered animals. Endangered animals live in our community.

   ....

   ....

6. Woolly mammoths were large animals. Woolly mammoths are now extinct.

   ....

   ....

EXPRESSING CONDITIONS WITH *IF*

Complete each sentence with either a condition or result clause.

1. .... , many people would want to see it.

2. If scientists could find frozen dinosaur DNA, ...

3. If we do more to protect endangered species, ...

4. .... , taxes may increase.

5. .... , scientists could learn a lot.

6. If the government creates laws on de-extinction, ...

INDIVIDUAL PRESENTATION

GUIDED RESEARCH

A. Professor Greely discusses several extinct animals that could be brought back to life through de-extinction methods. What are the requirements for de-extinction? Working alone or with a partner, brainstorm a list of animals that meet the requirements for de-extinction.

Extinct Animals That Meet Requirements for De-Extinction

B. Working with a partner, choose an animal from the list on the previous page that you would like to make de-extinct. Find out as much as you can about that animal. Use these questions to help you with your research:

- When did the animal live?

- What did it look like? What was the size of the animal?

- What did the animal eat?

- When did the animal go extinct?

- Why did the animal go extinct?

PRESENT

A. Prepare your presentation. Describe the extinct animal using facts. Then give your opinion on why this animal should be considered for de-extinction. Be sure to introduce your facts and opinion with cues. Support all your opinions with facts.

B. Practice presenting to a partner. Listen carefully to your partner. Identify when your partner's intonation rises or falls. Listen for changes in speaking rate.

C. Listen to your classmates' presentations. As you listen, complete the chart, which continues on the next page.

Animal	Fact About the Animal	Possibility of De-Extinction

Animal	Fact About the Animal	Possibility of De-Extinction

D. After the presentations, have a class discussion on which animal would be the best for de-extinction. Be sure to take turns and to support your opinions with facts given in each presentation.

TIP

In class discussions, it is important to use turn-taking strategies to know when it is all right to begin speaking. These strategies include listening for falling intonation, decreased speaking speed, and a drop in volume. See Bioethics, Part 1, Skill 2, page 7.

⬥ Go to MyEnglishLab to complete a collaborative activity.

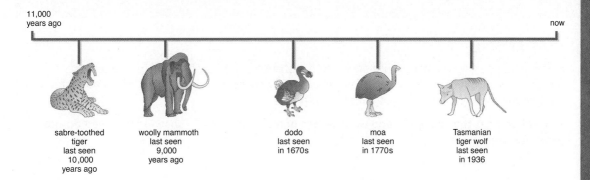

11,000 years ago   now

sabre-toothed tiger last seen 10,000 years ago

woolly mammoth last seen 9,000 years ago

dodo last seen in 1670s

moa last seen in 1770s

Tasmanian tiger wolf last seen in 1936

Design principles help create business innovation

BUSINESS AND DESIGN

Design Strategy

UNIT PROFILE

In this unit, you will watch a lecture about design strategy and how it can help businesses develop their products and services. You will also hear how one business grew into a powerful multinational company by applying design strategies.

You will present the strengths and weaknesses of a product design showing how well design principles were used.

For more about **BUSINESS AND DESIGN**, see ❶❷.

See also R and W **BUSINESS AND DESIGN** ❶❷❸.

EXTENDED LECTURE

BEFORE YOU VIEW

Think about these questions before you view the lecture "Design Strategy." Discuss them with another student.

1. Think of a successful business. How are its products different from other businesses' products or services? What makes its products special?

2. Many businesses today follow design thinking. Design thinking principles are connected to the guidelines or steps a company follows to develop a new product or service. What steps do you think a business follows to develop a new product?

3. Airbnb® is a successful business that allows people to rent short-term lodging including vacation rentals, apartment rentals, or even rooms in homes. What need do you think a business like this meets?

LECTURE—SECTION 1

Glossary

Differentiate: to recognize the difference between things

Principles: the basic ideas that a plan or system is based on

Case study: a detailed description of how a business developed over a period of time

Market-focused: concerned with the needs of the product's buyers

Framework: a set of rules, ideas, or beliefs used to develop something

Laser-focused: to focus intensely on something

Value: the importance or usefulness of something

Latent needs: real needs that may be hidden, or not yet seen

◐ Go to MyEnglishLab to view the first section of Juli Sherry's lecture. Use the organizer on the next page to take notes while you listen. Then answer the questions in Check What You've Learned.

> **TIP**
>
> When listening to a lecture on a new topic, it is important to take clear notes. One useful note-taking method is mapping. See Business and Design, Part 1, Skill 1, page 25.

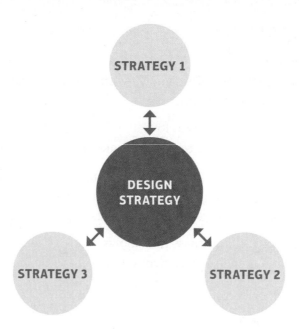

STRATEGY 1

DESIGN
STRATEGY

STRATEGY 3

STRATEGY 2

CHECK WHAT YOU'VE LEARNED—SECTION 1

Think about the lecture you have just viewed
and refer to your notes. Choose the best answers.

> **TIP**
>
> Identifying the main idea and
> subtopics of a lecture can be difficult
> when the subject is new. See Business
> and Design, Part 1, Skill 1, page 25.

1. Which set of ideas does Ms. Sherry present in
   her lecture?

   a. what design strategy is, how it is different
      from business strategy, and how Airbnb used design strategy to create a
      successful business
   b. what design strategy is, how it can help a business, and how Airbnb used
      design strategy to create a successful business
   c. what business strategy is, how it can help a business, and how Airbnb used
      business strategy to create a successful business
   d. what design strategy is, how businesses are innovative, and how using business
      strategies can lead to success

2. Which statement best defines "design strategy"?

   a. It is an innovative strategy that helps grow a business.
   b. It is a creative plan that helps an organization.
   c. It is a business strategy that uses design principles.
   d. It is a plan that uses designers to help create customer value.

3. Which statement best shows the difference between design strategy and business strategy?

    a. Design strategy is more focused on customer need and creates more value for the customer.

    b. Business strategy is more focused on customer need and creates more value for the customer.

    c. Design strategy is more innovative, and creates a better solution for the customer.

    d. Business strategy is more innovative and creates a better solution for the customer.

◐ **Go to MyEnglishLab to watch Section 1 again. Check your answers and add details to your notes in the organizer. Then continue to the next section of the lecture.**

LECTURE—SECTION 2

Glossary

Mind-set: a way of thinking about things and making decisions

Empathy: the ability to understand other people's feelings

Dig deep: to try very hard

Insight: a very clear understanding of someone or something

Problem definition: defining the problem to be solved by combining results from interviews

Analyze: to study something deeply in order to understand it

Ideation: the process of developing ideas

Prototyping: developing a model or first design of something

◐ **Go to MyEnglishLab to view the second section of Juli Sherry's lecture. Use the organizer on the next page to take notes while you listen. Then answer the questions in Check What You've Learned.**

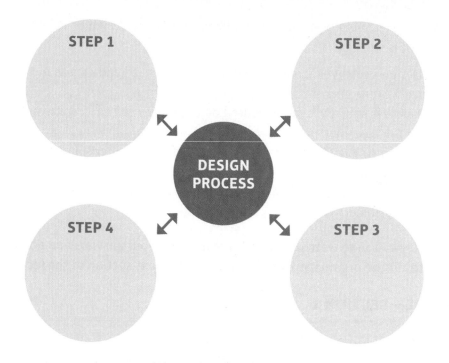

CHECK WHAT YOU'VE LEARNED—SECTION 2

Think about the lecture you have just viewed and refer to your notes.
Choose the best answers.

1. What are the four stages of design thinking strategies that Juli Sherry talks about in the lecture?

   a. empathy / research
   b. observe business
   c. define the problem
   d. ask other businesses what they need
   e. develop ideas
   f. develop a model (prototype) and test

> **TIP**
>
> Speakers often paraphrase or restate key ideas after they introduce them to clarify their information. See Business and Design, Part 1, Skill 2, page 29.

2. How does Ms. Sherry restate each strategy using everyday language? Match each strategy with its paraphrase or restatement.

   .... 1. Empathy / Research   a. Build ideas and get feedback

   .... 2. Problem definition   b. Understand the needs of customers

   .... 3. Ideation   c. Decide what people need or what is missing

   .... 4. Prototype and testing   d. Work in groups to develop designs

🔊 Go to MyEnglishLab to watch Section 2 again. Check your answers and add details to your notes in the organizer. Then continue to the next section of the lecture.

LECTURE—SECTION 3

Glossary

Realization: when you understand something that you had not understood before

Host: (v) to provide a place for guests to stay at or work in

Convince: to make someone feel certain that something is true

Generated: made or created

Iteration: a new, improved form of a product

Hosts: (n) the people who provide the rooms to the guests

Awkward: a feeling of embarrassment or discomfort

Down in the dumps: sad

Revenue: money that a business makes over time

Growth: an increase in the value of goods or services

● Go to MyEnglishLab to view the third and final section of Juli Sherry's lecture. Use the organizer to take notes while you listen. Then answer the questions in Check What You've Learned.

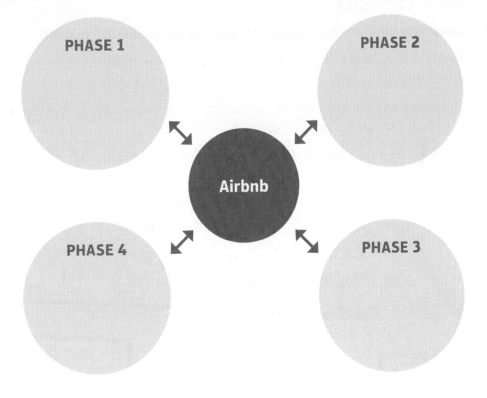

CHECK WHAT YOU'VE LEARNED—SECTION 3

Think about the lecture you have just viewed and refer to your notes.
Answer each question.

1. Juli Sherry gives the background of the founders of Airbnb. What are two important details regarding their backgrounds?

2. How did their idea for renting out the extra space in their apartment come about?

3. What are two examples of how they used design strategy to develop and grow their business?

CULTURE NOTE

Craigslist is an online classified advertisement website which allows users to offer and look for jobs, housing, cars, and other items.

⬆ Go to MyEnglishLab to watch Section 3 again. Check your answers and add details to your notes in the organizer. Then complete a script analysis activity.

THINKING CRITICALLY

Look back at your notes and answer the questions with another student.

1. Why do you think Juli Sherry chose to use the example of Airbnb to illustrate her main ideas?

2. What inferences can you make about the instructor's decision to include descriptions of Brian and Joe's failed businesses?

3. In your opinion, which stage of design strategy most helped Brian and Joe develop their business?

⬆ Go to MyEnglishLab to complete a critical thinking activity.

THINKING VISUALLY

A. Work with a partner. Look at the timeline. Using your notes, add the events to the timeline.

Events

- Brian joins Joe in San Francisco.
- They need to change their business model.
- They get a friend to design their website.
- They go to New York to take photos of hosts' homes.

- They make money selling cereal boxes.
- They meet Paul, who helps them.
- They rent out space in their own apartment.

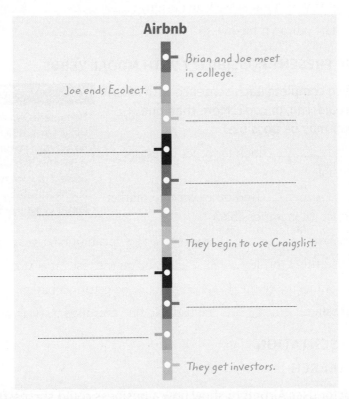

Airbnb

Brian and Joe meet in college.

Joe ends Ecolect.

They begin to use Craigslist.

They get investors.

TIP

Summarizing involves giving the main ideas. See Business and Design, Part 2, Skill 2, page 139.

B. Using the questions to help you, take turns summarizing the events on the timeline.

1. When did Joe and Brian take their business to the next level?

2. When did Joe and Brian decide they needed a fleshed-out website?

3. When did Joe and Brian find their path?

THINKING ABOUT LANGUAGE
USING TAG QUESTIONS TO INVITE AGREEMENT

Add a tag question to each statement.

TIP

When you are in an academic conversation, it is common to ask for agreement. One way speakers ask for agreement is by using a tag question. For help with tag questions, go to MyEnglishLab, Business and Design, Part 1, Language Skill.

1. Brian and Joe were very innovative, ... ?
2. You don't think they invested too much of their own money, ... ?
3. Airbnb is popular with travelers today, ... ?
4. She shouldn't advertise her business until everything is well-organized .... ?
5. They weren't very good at website design, ... ?
6. We can start our own business, ... ?

EXPRESSING PRESENT POSSIBILITY WITH MODAL VERBS

Use the cues to complete each sentence with *must, may, might, could, can,* or *can't.* More than one correct answer may be possible.

TIP

Modal verbs can express possibility in the present. Different modals show how certain you are that something is possible or probable. For help with present possibility with modals, go to MyEnglishLab, Business and Design, Part 2, Language Skill.

1. They .... look for other investors. (It is possible.)
2. Brian .... find other ways to market his product. (It is impossible.)
3. Our company .... move to a new location next year. (It is possible.)
4. We studied this a lot. It .... be on the test. (It is very possible.)
5. The boss wants to see me. I .... be getting a pay raise. (It is possible.)
6. Their website .... be bad. No one ever uses it. (It is very possible.)

GROUP PRESENTATION
GUIDED RESEARCH

A. The instructor uses Airbnb to show how a business could successfully use design strategy principles to identify weaknesses in its service and improve them. Working in a small group, use your notes to complete the chart.

Airbnb	
What problem does its service solve?	
How does its service solve the problem?	
Are there any problems with its service?	
How can its service be improved?	

B. With your group members, brainstorm a list of other innovative and successful companies. What products or services do they offer?

C. Together as a group, choose one company that all of you know. Select one product or service that company offers. What are the strengths of that product or service? What are the weaknesses?

PRESENT

A. Work together with your group members to develop a presentation analyzing the strengths and weaknesses of a product or service. Use the questions to help you prepare:

- What problem does the product or service solve?

- How does the product or service solve that problem?

- In what ways does the product or service fail to solve the problem?

- How could the product or service be improved to be more helpful for consumers?

B. Practice presenting with your group. Be sure to clarify your ideas and summarize your findings.

C. Listen to each group's presentation. As you listen, complete the chart.

Product or Service	Strength	Weakness

D. After the presentations, have a class discussion on the different products or services. Which products or services do you think are most successful? What need do they meet? What problem do they solve?

🔊 Go to MyEnglishLab to complete a collaborative activity.

ZOOLOGY

Elephants Inspire Medical Device

UNIT PROFILE

In this unit, you will watch a lecture about how elephants inspired a medical device. You will learn about elephant behavior, and how vocalizations and vibrations are an important part of elephant communication.

You will participate in a group discussion on solutions to everyday problems that have been inspired by nature and animals.

For more about **ZOOLOGY**, see ① ②. See also Ⓡ and Ⓦ **ZOOLOGY** ① ② ③.

EXTENDED LECTURE

BEFORE YOU VIEW

Think about these questions before you view the lecture "A Study of Elephants and Sound Communication." Discuss them with another student.

1. What are some ways animals may communicate with one another?

2. How do you think elephants communicate? What do they communicate about?

3. How do you think scientists study animal communication? Why is studying animal communication important?

LECTURE—SECTION 1

Glossary

Vibration: a continuous, slight shaking movement

Matriarchal societies: groups ruled or controlled by females

Dominant: more important, powerful, or noticeable than other people or things

Ritual: a series of actions that are always done in the same situation, each time

Rumble: to make a series of long, low sounds

Vocalization: making sounds with your voice

Emit: to send something out, usually sound or light

Monitor: to carefully watch and check a situation in order to see how it changes over a period of time

---

🔊 Go to MyEnglishLab to view the first section of Professor O'Connell-Rodwell's lecture. Use the organizer on the next page to take notes while you listen. Then answer the questions in Check What You've Learned.

TIP

The Cornell Method of note-taking is an effective way to take and organize notes for study. Divide your paper into two columns: the second column on the right is twice as large as the first column on the left. Take notes in the larger section of the paper and then note all the keywords, phrases, and main ideas of the lecture in the smaller column. See the organizer on the next page for an example.

Keywords / phrases, Main ideas	Your notes

CHECK WHAT YOU'VE LEARNED—SECTION 1

Think about the lecture you have just viewed and refer to your notes. Choose the best answer.

1. Based on the lecture, what three things are true about elephants?
   a. They are social animals.
   b. Males stay with their families their entire life.
   c. Females lead the family.
   d. Elephants greet one another through vocal noises.

2. What are two examples Professor O'Connell-Rodwell uses to support her ideas about elephant behavior?
   a. an elephant male leaving his family group when he is 50
   b. two elephants drinking water where one, Stoli, shows his power
   c. elephants greeting one another through loud rumbles and stamping of feet
   d. elephants at a watering hole and the sounds made to warn one another about possible trouble

3. Which statement describes something new the professor learned at Etosha?
   a. She learned that elephants prefer to put their ears against their heads.
   b. She learned that elephants feel and identify sounds that travel in the ground.
   c. She learned that elephants use their trunks to communicate with one another.
   d. She learned that elephants raise their ears to hear loud sounds.

⏵ Go to MyEnglishLab to watch Section 1 again. Check your answers and add keywords and ideas to your notes in the organizer. Then continue to the next section of the lecture.

LECTURE—SECTION 2

Glossary

Malleus: large bone in the ear that helps to identify vibrations

Vibration-sensitive: easily affected or damaged by a vibration (a continuous, slight shaking)

Wave: the form in which some types of energy such as light and sound travel

Frequency: the number of waves that pass any point per second

Geophone: a machine that notices vibrations passing through the ground

Broadcasted: sent out signals by radio, television, phone, or internet

Signal: a series of sound waves or light waves that carry sound, or a message

Detected: to have noticed or discovered something

⏵ Go to MyEnglishLab to view the second and final section of Professor O'Connell-Rodwell's lecture. Use the organizer to take notes while you listen. Then answer the questions in Check What You've Learned.

Keywords / phrases, Main ideas	Your notes

CHECK WHAT YOU'VE LEARNED—SECTION 2

Think about the lecture you have just viewed and refer to your notes.
Choose the best answers.

1. According to Professor O'Connell-Rodwell, which animals use vibrations in communication? Check (✓) the animals on the list.

   ☐ bulls   ☐ elephant seals

   ☐ crocodiles   ☐ mice

   ☐ dogs   ☐ spiders

2. The professor mentions experimenting with an elephant in a zoo in Oakland, California. Which of these facts about the experiment does she mention?

   a. The experiment was just like a human hearing experiment.
   b. The experiment tested if the elephant, Donna, could feel the vibration.
   c. The experiment was conducted by three scientists.
   d. Donna touches a target if she feels the vibration.
   e. Donna shakes her head if she feels the vibration.

3. What are three benefits for elephants of identifying sound through vibrations?

   a. Elephants can use vibrations to decide if it is going to rain.
   b. Elephants can use vibrations to tell how far away something is.
   c. Elephants can identify where a sound is coming from.
   d. Vibrations in the ground can travel farther than sounds in the air.
   e. Vibrations could help elephants understand where they should travel to.

⬆ Go to MyEnglishLab to watch Section 2 again. Check your answers and add keywords and ideas to your notes in the organizer. Then complete a script analysis activity.

THINKING CRITICALLY

Look back at your notes and answer the questions with another student.

1. Throughout the lecture, Professor O'Connell-Rodwell directly states and implies many social behaviors of elephants. What are they?

2. Professor O'Connell-Rodwell describes two separate ways she researched and proved her idea. What are they?

3. Why has Professor O'Connell-Rodwell studied elephants and sound vibrations? How does she want to use this information in the future?

⬆ Go to MyEnglishLab to complete a critical thinking activity.

THINKING VISUALLY

A. Work with a partner. Look at the photos and complete the Venn diagram.

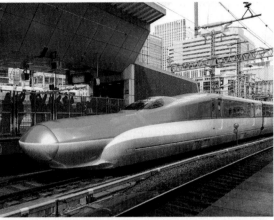

NATURE-INSPIRED DESIGN

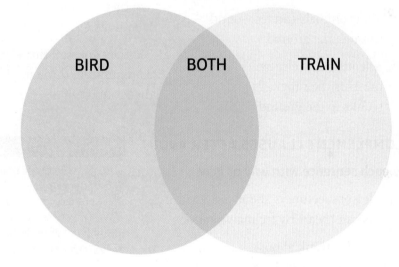

BIRD   BOTH   TRAIN

B. Using the Venn diagram, take turns describing what is the same about the bird and the train.

C. Think of another animal and something that is used in our everyday lives. What is similar about these two items? Do you think the animal inspired the development of the product? Why or why not?

THINKING ABOUT LANGUAGE
CONNECTING IDEAS WITH *SO* AND *THEREFORE*

Match the sentence halves.

TIP

So and *therefore* are often used to help listeners understand the reason for something. For help with connecting ideas, go to MyEnglishLab, Zoology, Part 1, Language Skill.

.... 1. The scientists observed elephants moving in social groups

.... 2. More and more animals are becoming endangered

.... 3. Donna, the zoo elephant, hit the target every time she felt a vibration

.... 4. Elephants have a very large malleus bone in their ears

.... 5. Many animals can feel sound through the ground

.... 6. Scientists saw elephants pressing their toenails and trunks to the ground

a. ; therefore, we need to do all we can to protect them.

b. ; therefore, scientists knew which vibrations she could feel.

c. , so they believe that elephants form social bonds.

d. ; therefore, they can feel danger coming.

e. , so they are able to hear through vibrations.

f. , so they guessed that elephants communicate through vibrations in the ground.

USING COMPLEMENT CLAUSES AFTER *ABOUT*

Complete each sentence with *why* or *how*.

TIP

Using a noun clause that begins with *about* can help you explain the main idea of a lecture, article, or discussion. For help with complements clauses, go to MyEnglishLab, Zoology, Part 2, Language Skill.

1. The professor's lecture is about .... elephants can "hear" by feeling vibrations.

2. People need to think about .... we can protect more animals.

3. The professor's presentation was about .... we need to study how other animals hear.

4. Can you explain more about .... this is important for humans?

5. This article is not about .... we need to study elephants, but it is about how we can study elephants.

6. My group members are interested in talking about .... we can improve our presentation.

GROUP DISCUSSION
GUIDED RESEARCH

A. Professor O'Connell-Rodwell is using her research on elephants to develop devices for people who have trouble hearing. For centuries, people have used their observations of nature to develop devices that solved problems. Working alone or with a partner, look at the list of devices. What objects or animals from nature could have inspired them? Can you add more to the list?

- airplanes
- boats
- fans / air conditioners

- fins for swimming
- submarines
- wheels

B. Working with a partner, select a device from the list. Using your school's library, or an online search engine, find out as much as you can about what inspired the development. Use these questions to help you with your research:

- Who developed the device?
- When was it developed?
- What animal or object from nature helped develop it?
- What problem does it solve?

C. Prepare your notes. Make notecards with your key ideas that you can discuss during your group discussion.

DISCUSS

A. Work in a small group. One group member will begin the discussion by describing a problem and a nature-inspired device that solved the problem. Once that person has finished, take turns describing other problems and their nature-inspired solutions.

B. As you listen to each group member, be sure to make notes of any questions you have.

C. After the descriptions, use your questions to have a group discussion about the devices. Together, discuss other possible nature-inspired devices that can be created.

◯ Go to MyEnglishLab to complete a collaborative activity.

HISTORY

Four Discoveries

UNIT PROFILE

In this unit, you will watch a lecture on how four different archaeological discoveries changed our attitudes about human history. You will hear how each discovery was made, and how it influenced our view of history.

You will participate in a panel discussion about an archaeological find, and how it has solved a historical mystery.

For more about **HISTORY**, see ❶❷. See also ⟦R⟧ and ⟦W⟧ **HISTORY** ❶❷❸.

EXTENDED LECTURE

BEFORE YOU VIEW

Think about these questions before you view the lecture "Four Discoveries That Changed History." Discuss them with another student.

1. Archaeology is the study of ancient societies. It involves examining the remains of their buildings, tools, and cities. Why is it important to study ancient civilizations?

2. Which of the famous discoveries below do you know about? Have they changed the way we view history?

3. What other discoveries can you add to the list?

Lost City of Machu Picchu, Peru

Tomb of 10,000 Warriors, China

Caves of the Dead Sea Scrolls, the West Bank

Mayan ruins, Guatemala

LECTURE—SECTION 1

Glossary

Paradox: a statement that seems impossible because it contains two opposing ideas that are both true

Dual: having two of something or two parts

Excavate: to dig carefully to find ancient objects

Artifact: an object such as a tool, weapon, etc., that was made in the past and is historically important

Reconstructing: producing a complete description or copy of an event by collecting pieces of information

Amateur: someone who does an activity just for pleasure, without pay

By accident / Accidental: happening without being planned

Deliberately: carefully planned

⬤ Go to MyEnglishLab to view the first section of Dr. Hunt's lecture. Use the organizer to take notes while you listen. Then answer the questions in Check What You've Learned.

```
┌─────────────────────────────────────────────────────────┐
│  Introduction                                             │
│                                                           │
│                            ●                              │
│                            │                              │
└────────────────────────────┼──────────────────────────────┘
                             │
                             │
```

CHECK WHAT YOU'VE LEARNED—SECTION 1

Think about the lecture you have just viewed and refer to your notes. Choose the best answer.

TIP

Identifying the main ideas of a lecture means taking an active role before, while, and after you listen. See History, Part 2, Skill 1, page 181.

1. According to Dr. Hunt's lecture, what is the difference between textual historians and material historians?

   a. Textual historians study texts while material historians study things that are found.

   b. Textual historians study texts while material historians find things.

   c. Textual historians write texts while material historians study things that are found.

   d. Textual historians write texts while material historians find things.

2. According to Dr. Hunt, which statement is true?

   a. People have been studying archaeology for a long time.

   b. Textual historians and material historians look at the past in the same way.

   c. There have been some important discoveries made by everyday people.

   d. Discovering the Romans, Inca, early human species, and Chinese dynasties were the four greatest discoveries in the world's history.

⬤ Go to MyEnglishLab to watch Section 1 again. Check your answers and add details to your notes in the organizer. Then continue to the next section of the lecture.

LECTURE—SECTION 2

Glossary

Explorer: someone who travels through an unknown area to find information about it

Valley: an area of lower land between two lines of mountains or hills

Mountain range: a large group of mountains that are connected to one another

Lost city: a place that was once inhabited by many people, and no longer exists

Mysterious: difficult to explain or understand

Stone: a hard solid substance that come from the ground; a piece of rock

Jungle: a thick tropical forest with many large plants growing very close together

Cliff: a large area of rock or a mountain with a very steep side

Mountain peak and lake in the Andes Mountain range

⬥ Go to MyEnglishLab to view the second section of Dr. Hunt's lecture. Use the next part of the organizer to take notes while you listen. Then answer the questions in Check What You've Learned.

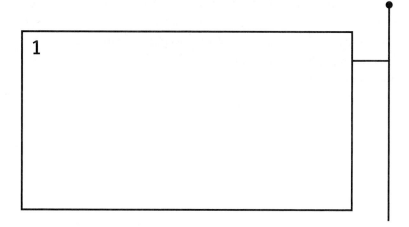

1

CHECK WHAT YOU'VE LEARNED—SECTION 2

Think about the lecture you have just viewed and refer to your notes.
Choose the best answers.

1. Which statements are true?

   a. Hiram Bingham worked on the railroads.
   b. Hiram Bingham explored the Andes Mountains with a group of geologists.
   c. Hiram Bingham had not planned to find the Lost City.
   d. Hiram Bingham found a guide who helped him.
   e. Hiram Bingham found the Lost City of the Inca, Machu Picchu.

2. According to the lecture, why was it so difficult to find Machu Picchu?
   Circle the reasons.

   a. It was hidden.
   b. It was difficult to climb to.
   c. It was in a jungle.
   d. It was buried after the Spanish found the city in 1532.
   e. It was very high in the mountains.

● Go to MyEnglishLab to watch Section 2 again.
Check your answers and add details to your notes
in the organizer. Then continue to the next section
of the lecture.

> **CULTURE NOTE**
>
> The Inca Empire (Kingdom), first appeared at the beginning of the 13th century. It was the largest kingdom in the Americas and had a population of about 12 million. The empire included Ecuador, Peru, Bolivia, Chile, and Argentina. Despite its strong military forces, the last group of Inca were conquered by the Spanish in 1572.

LECTURE—SECTION 3

Glossary

Species: a group of similar animals or plants

Diverse: things or people that are different from one another

Primate: a member of the group of animals that includes humans, apes, and monkeys

Jawbone: the lower bone of your face containing teeth attached to the skull

Omnivore diet: eating both meat and plants

Cranium: the bone in your head that covers your brain

Missing link: an animal which was a stage in the development of humans from apes

Interpret: to explain the meaning of something

AFRICAN PRIMATES

Gorilla

Baboon

Chimpanzee

◐ Go to MyEnglishLab to view the third section of Dr. Hunt's lecture. Use the organizer to take notes while you listen. Then answer the questions in Check What You've Learned.

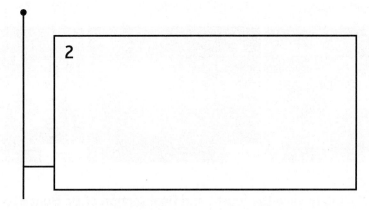

2

CHECK WHAT YOU'VE LEARNED—SECTION 3

Think about the lecture you have just viewed and refer to your notes.
Answer each question.

1. According to Dr. Hunt, Louis Leakey first became interested in studying Charles Darwin because he noticed two things. What two things did he notice?

2. What did the Leakeys discover that changed the course of history?

◐ Go to MyEnglishLab to watch Section 3 again. Check your answers and add details to your notes in the organizer. Then continue to the last section of the lecture.

Skull of an early human

Skull of a modern human

LECTURE—SECTION 4

Glossary

Hole: an empty space in something solid

Pottery: objects such as jars made of baked clay

Enlarged: made something larger

Scribes: people in the past who copied books, letters, and documents

Digging: moving earth to make a hole

Wells: holes in the ground where you can get water

Warrior: a solider or fighter who is brave

Tomb: a stone structure where a dead person is buried

Canyon

Cave

Scrolls

◐ Go to MyEnglishLab to view the fourth and final section of Dr. Hunt's lecture. Use the organizer to take notes while you listen. Then answer the questions in Check What You've Learned.

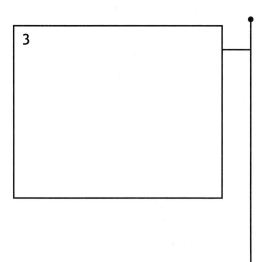

3

4

CHECK WHAT YOU'VE LEARNED—SECTION 4

Think about the lecture you have just viewed and refer to your notes. Choose the best answers.

1. Which statements are true about the discovery in Jordan?

    a. Two boys made the discovery by accident.
    b. The two boys wanted to be archaeologists.
    c. The two boys were looking for pottery.
    d. The two boys found the oldest written Biblical documents.
    e. The boys made this discovery 2,000 years ago.

2. Which statements are NOT true about the discovery in China?

    a. The farmer was looking for the warriors.
    b. The man found over 10,000 dead warriors underground.
    c. Every warrior found looked different.
    d. The discovery was the tomb of the first emperor of China.
    e. This discovery caused changes in China.

⬥ Go to MyEnglishLab to watch Section 4 again. Check your answers and add details to your notes in the organizer. Then complete a script analysis activity.

THINKING CRITICALLY

Look back at your notes and complete the tasks with another student.

1. Compare your notes. Add any details.

2. Take turns summarizing each discovery.

3. As you listen to your partner, complete the organizer.

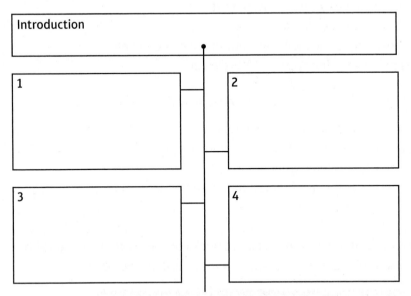

Introduction

1	2

3	4

❶ **Go to MyEnglishLab to complete a critical thinking activity.**

THINKING VISUALLY

A. Work with a partner. Look at the list of archeological discoveries. Which of these discoveries do you know about?

- In 1994, an ancient group of buildings on a hill in Turkey was discovered. This place has one of the oldest buildings in the world, pre-dating the pyramids. It is dated 10,000–80,000 BCE.

- In 1938, a jar was discovered in Baghdad, Iraq. This jar was said to have been used as a battery. It dates back to 250 BCE–224 CE.

- In 2009, in Dorset, United Kingdom, workers found more than 50 Viking warriors buried in the ground, without heads. These warriors date back to 910–1030 CE.

- In 1799, a French solider discovered the Rosetta Stone in the Nile Delta, Egypt. The Rosetta Stone provides a way to understand Egyptian hieroglyphs. It is dated at 196 BCE.

Egyptian hieroglyphs

B. With your partner, put the events on the timeline based on their discovery dates. Box 1 is the earliest discovery.

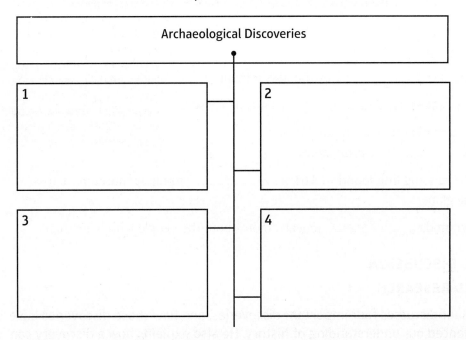

C. Take turns paraphrasing the discoveries on the timeline.

TIP

Paraphrasing involves stating something in your own words, often to simplify the language. See History, Part 2, Skill 2, page 185.

THINKING ABOUT LANGUAGE
UTILIZING THE SIMPLE PAST PASSIVE

Choose the correct verb form.

1. Workers <u>discovered / were discovered</u> Viking warriors.

2. The battery jar <u>found / was found</u> in Iraq.

3. The Rosetta Stone <u>analyzed / was analyzed</u> by archaeologists.

4. The Tomb of 10,000 Warriors <u>found / was found</u> in China.

5. The Inca's lost city <u>built / was built</u> in a jungle on top of a mountain.

6. Two boys accidentally <u>uncovered / were uncovered</u> the Dead Sea Scrolls.

TIP

The simple past passive is used to describe actions or events in the past that focus on the event or action rather than who did the action. To form the past passive, use *was / were* + the past participle. For help with the simple past passive, go to MyEnglishLab, History, Part 1, Language Skill.

CONSTRUCTING THE PRESENT PERFECT PASSIVE

Complete the sentences with the missing verb forms.

1. Archaeologists .... many ancient civilizations.

2. The site .... by the government.

3. The professor .... what archaeology is.

4. Pottery from an ancient civilization .... near my home.

5. The missing link found in Africa .... to many museums across the globe.

6. Pyramids .... to learn more about the people who lived there.

PANEL DISCUSSION

GUIDED RESEARCH

A. Dr. Hunt discusses four important discoveries, and how those discoveries have influenced our understanding of history. He also explains how a discovery can help solve a mystery, like the discovery made by Louis Leakey. Work in a small group. Brainstorm a list of discoveries and what was learned or solved by them.

Discovery	What Was Learned

B. Work with another group and compare your lists. What do you know about each of the discoveries?

C. Together with your group members, choose one discovery that everyone would like to learn more about. When was this discovery made? Who made it? What was learned from this discovery? How has it affected the country where the discovery was made?

D. During a panel discussion, all the group members will present their findings about the discovery. Each group member should choose one of these questions to research:

- What is the discovery? When does it date back to?
- Where was the discovery made?
- Who made the discovery? Was it made by an archaeologist or an amateur?
- What can be learned from this discovery?
- How has this discovery impacted the place or country where it was found?

DISCUSS

A. Work together with your group to develop a panel discussion. Take turns discussing your findings.

B. Practice with your group. Be sure to paraphrase the answers you have found. By using your own words, you will make your findings more interesting and easier for your classmates to understand.

C. Practice presenting your findings to your group, paraphrasing the answers you have found.

D. Listen to each group's panel discussion. As you listen, complete the chart.

Discovery	What was discovered?	Where was the discovery?	Who made the discovery?	What can be learned?

E. After each panel discussion, have a class discussion on the different discoveries. What are their similarities? What are their differences? Be sure to paraphrase what the panelists said.

● Go to MyEnglishLab to complete a collaborative activity.

Our everyday experiences are based on how we interact with nature

CHEMICAL ENGINEERING

The Lake Nyos Disaster

UNIT PROFILE

In this unit, you will watch a lecture on a natural disaster in Africa. You will learn what caused it and how scientists are working to avoid disasters like this in the future.

You will work with a partner to research another natural disaster that caused a large loss of life, or a great deal of environmental damage. You will present your findings to the class.

For more about **CHEMICAL ENGINEERING**, see **1 2**.

See also R and W **CHEMICAL ENGINEERING 1 2 3**.

EXTENDED LECTURE

BEFORE YOU VIEW

Think about these questions before you view the lecture "The Lake Nyos Disaster." Discuss them with another student.

1. What is a natural disaster? Can you think of some examples?

2. Do you think humans have a role in creating a natural disaster? Why or why not?

3. Do you think some natural disasters can be avoided? How?

LECTURE—SECTION 1

Glossary

Tragic: creating a feeling of sadness because of death or suffering

Crater lake: a lake inside a round hole in the ground left from a volcano

Carbon dioxide: CO_2, a heavy colorless gas that is formed by burning fuels or animal and plant matter, and by the act of breathing out—exhaling

Vent: a hole that gases from inside the Earth can escape from

Emitted: sent out gas

Poisonous: containing something that can cause death or serious illness

Asphyxiated: a death caused because the person couldn't breathe

Factor: one of several things that influence or cause a situation

Go to MyEnglishLab to view the first section of Professor Spakowitz's lecture. Use the organizer to take notes while you listen. Then answer the questions in Check What You've Learned.

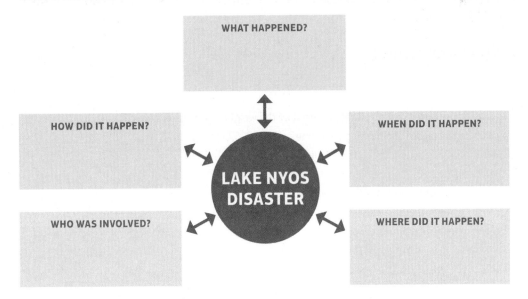

WHAT HAPPENED?

HOW DID IT HAPPEN?

WHEN DID IT HAPPEN?

LAKE NYOS DISASTER

WHO WAS INVOLVED?

WHERE DID IT HAPPEN?

CHECK WHAT YOU'VE LEARNED—SECTION 1

A. Think about the lecture you have just viewed and refer to your notes. Choose the best answers.

TIP

Identifying the parts of presentations and lectures can help your overall understanding. See Chemical Engineering, Part 1, Skill 1, page 91.

1. How does Professor Spakowitz introduce his lecture? Match the questions with their answers.

   .... 1. What happened?
   .... 2. Where did it happen?
   .... 3. When did it happen?
   .... 4. How did it happen?
   .... 5. Who was involved?

   a. August 21, 1986
   b. most of the villagers and their livestock
   c. Poisonous gas was emitted from the lake.
   d. Lake Nyos in Cameroon, Africa
   e. a tragic natural disaster

2. According to Professor Spakowitz, what three main factors that caused the disaster?

   a. the depth of the lake

   b. the day-to-day lives of the people

   c. carbon dioxide in the lake

   d. the environment around the lake

   e. the geographic location of Cameroon

Go to MyEnglishLab to watch Section 1 again. Check your answers and add details to your notes in the organizer. Then continue to the next section of the lecture.

LECTURE—SECTION 2

> ### Glossary
>
> Hydrostatic pressure: the force that is caused by the weight of the water above it pushing down on it
> Build-up: an increase in something over time
> Overwhelming: so strong that it is difficult to deal with
> Gravitational pull: the force of gravity that pulls objects down to the Earth
> Element: a part or feature of a system
> Presence: when something exists in a particular place
> Release: to let a substance flow out

HYDROSTATIC PRESSURE

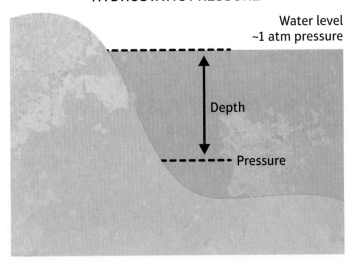

Water level
~1 atm pressure

Depth

Pressure

● Go to MyEnglishLab to view the second section of Professor Spakowitz's lecture. Use the organizer to take notes while you listen. Then answer the questions in Check What You've Learned.

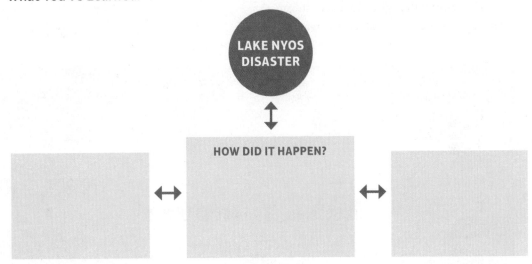

LAKE NYOS
DISASTER

HOW DID IT HAPPEN?

CHECK WHAT YOU'VE LEARNED—SECTION 2

Think about the lecture you have just viewed and refer to your notes.
Choose the best answers.

1. Which statements are true about hydrostatic pressure?

   a. The deeper you go, the more pressure you feel.
   b. Hydrostatic pressure decreases as you go deeper.
   c. The gravitational pull is very strong.
   d. The pressure depends on the speed you swim down.

2. Which statements are NOT true about the presences of carbon dioxide?

   a. Whenever carbon dioxide is present, there is less pressure.

   b. Carbon dioxide is present in soda cans.

   c. Releasing the carbon dioxide causes bubbles.

   d. Carbon dioxide does not affect large bodies of water like it does soda.

⬥ Go to MyEnglishLab to watch Section 2 again. Check your answers and add details to your notes in the organizer. Then continue to the next section of the lecture.

LECTURE—SECTION 3

Glossary

Subtle: not easy to notice or understand

Temperate climate: the weather changes and there are four seasons

Thaw: to turn ice or snow into water

Properties: the qualities or characteristics that a substance has

Density: the relationship between an object's weight and the amount of space it fills

Spontaneous: not planned or organized

Flow: movement through a continuous stream

Circulates: moves around within a system

⬥ Go to MyEnglishLab to view the third section of Professor Spakowitz's lecture. Use the organizer on the next page to take notes while you listen. Then answer the questions in Check What You've Learned.

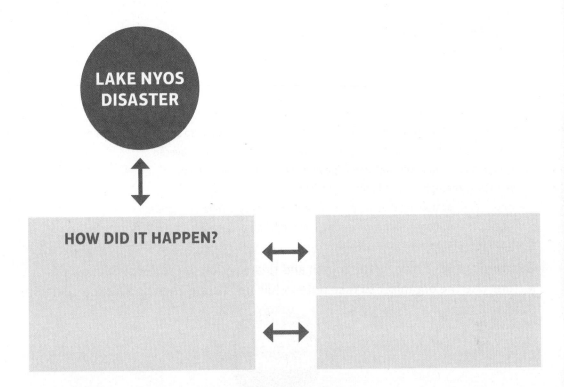

CHECK WHAT YOU'VE LEARNED—SECTION 3

A. Think about the lecture you have just viewed and refer to your notes. Answer each question.

1. What steps does Professor Spakowitz list in the process of lake turnover? Number the steps in the correct order.

   .... Ice gets pushed to the bottom.

   .... Ice disappears.

   .... Temperatures begin to rise.

   .... Fluid on top is forced to the bottom.

   .... Ice begins to break up.

TIP

Understanding the steps in a scientific process is a regular part of science and engineering courses. See Chemical Engineering, Part 2, Skill 1, page 203.

2. Professor Spakowitz mentions that he grew up in Wisconsin in a "temperate climate." In what ways does a temperate climate help create lake turnover?

⬆ Go to MyEnglishLab to watch Section 3 again. Check your answers and add details to your organizer. Then continue to the last section of the lecture.

LECTURE—SECTION 4

Glossary

Stagnate: to stop developing or making progress

Landslide: a sudden fall of a lot of earth or rocks down a hill or cliff

Saturate: to put a lot of something into a particular place, especially so that you could not add any more

Immersed: something put deep into a liquid so that it is completely covered

Tragedy: a very sad event that shocks people because it involves death

Pipe: a tube through which a liquid or gas flows

Phenomenon: something that happens or exists in society, science, or nature

Root cause: the initial or primary reason for something happening

⬤ Go to MyEnglishLab to view the fourth and final section of Professor Spakowitz's lecture. Use the organizer to take notes while you listen. Then answer the questions.

WHY WAS IT IMPORTANT?

CHECK WHAT YOU'VE LEARNED—SECTION 4

A. Think about the lecture you have just viewed and refer to your notes. Choose the best answer.

1. According to Professor Spakowitz, which two natural disasters could have caused the lake to be mixed up?

    a. a hurricane and a landslide

    b. a tornado and a landslide

    c. an earthquake and a tornado

    d. an earthquake and a landslide

2. According to Professor Spakowtiz, Lake Nyos is especially tragic because it _____ .

   a. was a disaster that had never happened before

   b. was not a typical natural disaster

   c. could not have been predicted

   d. was a relatively easy problem to fix

◑ Go to MyEnglishLab to watch Section 4 again. Check your answers and add details to your notes in the organizer. Then complete a script analysis activity.

THINKING CRITICALLY

Look back at your notes and answer the questions with another student.

1. What were the three factors that caused the Lake Nyos disaster?

2. Why does the professor use the examples of a soda can, scuba diving, and a frozen lake?

3. What is the key message Professor Spakowitz wants listeners to understand about natural disasters?

◑ Go to MyEnglishLab to complete a critical thinking activity.

THINKING VISUALLY

A. **Work with a partner. Look at the diagram of the lake turnover process that happens in more temperate climates—climates with noticeable seasonal changes. Label each picture in the diagram with the correct season.**

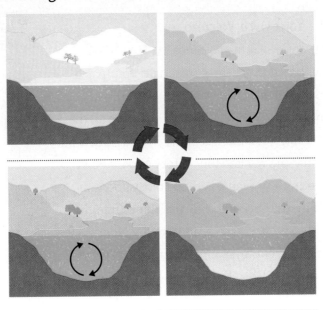

B. **Using the diagram and your notes, take turns describing each step of the lake turnover process.**

THINKING ABOUT LANGUAGE
EXPLAINING ORDER WITH LINKING WORDS

Complete each item with the correct linking word or phrases from the box. More than one correct answer may be possible and not all the time adverbs will be used.

TIP

Linking words that show time order serve an important purpose. They help listeners understand the order of events. For help with explaining order, go to MyEnglishLab, Chemical Engineering, Part 1, Language Skill.

after that	finally	my final point	next
second	the next point	to begin with	toward the end

1. Our lecture today is on natural disasters. .... I will define what a natural disaster is. .... , we will examine different natural disasters. And .... , we will see how humans impact the occurrence of natural disasters.

2. I have three main points to discuss regarding natural disasters. First, they come in many forms. .... is that while we can predict their occurrences, there is little we can do to prevent them. And .... is that while we can't prevent them, we can prepare for them.

SHOWING SEQUENCE WITH TIME ADVERBS

Read the paragraph. Circle the correct adverb.

How to Make Your Own Volcano

Many students enjoy making volcanos. **At first / First / Firstly**, you will need to get these materials: your paper volcano, a small container, vinegar, and liquid dish-washing soap. **When / While / Second**, you have all the materials, you can go outside. **Second, / When / Then** put the container into the volcano top. **After / First, / Next,** the container is in the volcano, add two tablespoons of baking soda. **Finally, / Second, / At the same time**, you can add one tablespoon of dish soap. **Third, / Next, / When** put a small spoonful of vinegar into the container. Finally, stand back and watch the eruption!

TIP

When explaining a process, it is important to use time adverbs to clearly describe each step. For help with showing sequence, go to MyEnglishLab, Chemical Engineering, Part 2, Language Skill.

PAIR PRESENTATION
GUIDED RESEARCH

A. In his lecture Professor Spakowitz explains all the details surrounding the Lake Nyos disaster. Working alone, use your notes to complete the chart.

What was the disaster?	
When did it occur?	
Where did it occur?	
How did it occur?	

B. Working with a partner, compare notes. Then brainstorm other natural disasters. What do you know about each disaster?

Natural Disasters

C. Together, choose one of the disasters from your list to research and present. Use your school's library or an online search engine to find out as much as you can about that disaster. Use the graphic organizer to help you with your research.

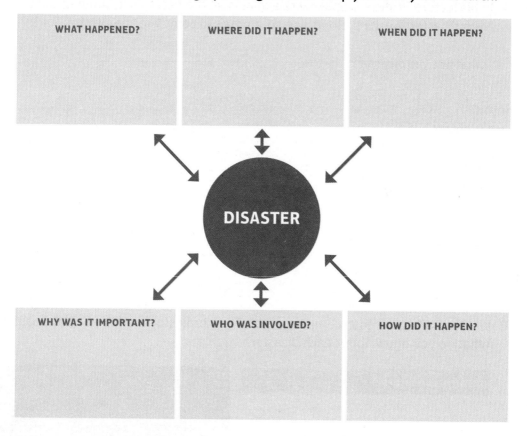

PRESENT

A. With your partner, prepare your presentation. Describe the sequence of events that led to the natural disaster. Be sure to use words and phrases for describing a scientific process. Include visuals in your presentation. Use text, charts, graphs, images, or diagrams.

B. Practice with your partner. Be sure to include time adverbs to make the sequence of the process clear.

C. Listen to each pair's presentation. As you listen, complete the chart.

Disaster	When did it occur?	Where was it?	Who did it affect?	How did it happen?

D. After all of the presentations, have a class discussion on the different disasters. Could any of these disasters have been prevented?

● Go to MyEnglishLab to complete a collaborative activity.

Credits

Cover image: Alamy D075RG = nik wheeler / Alamy Stock Photo; Page viii (top): Popoudina Svetlana/Shutterstock; viii (middle, right): Pearson; ix (middle, left): 501room/Shutterstock; ix (bottom, left): Shane Gross/Shutterstock; xi (middle, right): Pearson; xv (O'Connell-Rodwell): Mark Salomon; Page 1: (multiple uses): Budai Romeo Gabor/Fotolia (gold coins); Nik_Merkulov/Fotolia (green leaf with drops of water); Scisetti Alfio/Fotolia (old letter); Vichly4thai/Fotolia (red molecule/DNA cell); Tobkatrina/123RF (hands holding Earth); orelphoto/Fotolia (honeycomb background); 2: Andrew Pearson/Alamy Stock Photo; 5 (top, left): Wrangel/123RF; 5 (top, right): PaylessImages/123RF; 9: Arco Images GmbH/Alamy Stock Photo; 15: Roee Fung/Shutterstock; 19: John Elk III/Alamy Stock Photo; 22: 3drenderings/Shutterstock; 24: Vladgrin/Shutterstock; 34: Cm studio/Alamy Stock Photo; 48: Victor Shova/Shutterstock; 60: Vladimir Melnik/Shutterstock; 64 (left and right): Bahareh Khalili Naftchali/Shutterstock; 68: PhotoStockIsrael/Alamy Stock Photo; 70: Hung Chung Chih/Shutterstock; 71: Shujaa_777/Shutterstock; 73: Peter Hermes Furian/Shutterstock; 75: Mark Kostich/iStock/Getty Images; 84: Daniela Barreto/Shutterstock; 89: Orlandin/123RF; 90: Popoudina Svetlana/Shutterstock; 94 (left): Topseller/Shutterstock; 94 (right): Bob Gibbons/Alamy Stock Photo; 97: Encyclopaedia Britannica/Universal Images Group North America LLC/Alamy Stock Photo; 100: NASA; 102: Dan Barba/Stock Connection Blue/Alamy Stock Photo; 105: Shane Gross/Shutterstock; 112: Benjamin Albiach Galan/Shutterstock; 115: Roberto Biasini/123RF; 122 (top): Arun Roisri/123RF; 122 (bottom): Pakhnyushchyy/123RF; 134: Alphaspiritl/123RF; 134 (within chapter opener: woman on right): Stockyimages/123RF; 156: Mitchell Krog/Shutterstock; 168 (left): Alenavlad/Shutterstock; 168 (right): Salih Kuelcue/123RF; 170: Flaperval/123RF; 180: Shi Jinshou/123RF; 182: Pavel Rusak/123RF; 186: SeanPavonePhoto/Shutterstock; 190: Jjspring/123RF; 202: Brett Allen/Shutterstock; 209: Designua/Shutterstock; 210: Designua/Shutterstock; 221 (bottom): Designua/Shutterstock; 221 (top, left): Vaclav Volrab/123RF; 221 (top, right): FCG/Shutterstock; 224 (bottom, left): 1xpert/123RF; 224 (bottom, right): Ben Goode/123RF; 224 (top, light): Brad Perks Lightscapes/Alamy Stock Photo; 224 (top, right): Opel2b/Shutterstock; 226: Leonello calvetti/Shutterstock; 227 (left): Awe Inspiring Images/Shutterstock; 227 (middle): Jason Benz Bennee/Shutterstock; 227 (right): Ueuaphoto/123RF; 228: Para/Shutterstock; 230 (left): Torsten Lorenz/Shutterstock; 230 (middle): Dancestrokes/Shutterstock; 230 (right): Ecostock/Shutterstock; 232: Esteban De Armas/Shutterstock; 237: HL Studios/Pearson Education Ltd; 238: LDprod/Shutterstock; 244: Fotoluminate LLC/Shutterstock; 248: Johan Swanepoel/123RF; 253 (left): Panuruangjan/123RF; 253 (right): Aflo Co. Ltd./Alamy Stock Photo; 256: Lefteris Papaulakis/123RF; 257 (top, left): Amy Nichole Harris/Shutterstock; 257 (top, right): Shi Jinshou/123RF; 257 (bottom, left): SeanPavonePhoto/Shutterstock; 257 (bottom, right): Dr. Alan Lipkin/Shutterstock; 259: Pichugin Dmitry/Shutterstock; 261 (top, left): Aaron Amat/Shutterstock; 261 (top, middle): Eric Isselee/Shutterstock; 261 (top, right): Eric Isselee/Shutterstock; 261 (bottom, left): Wlad74/123RF; 261 (bottom, right): Mega Pixel/Shutterstock; 262 (left): Anton Foltin/Shutterstock; 262 (middle): Andreiuc88/123RF; 262 (right): Froe_mic/Shutterstock; 263: Hung Chung Chih/Shutterstock; 264: Pavel K/Shutterstock; 268: Your Design/Shutterstock; 277: Evgeni Gitlits/Shutterstock; 279: Caitlin Mirra/Shutterstock.